DOWN IN TENNESSEE.

DOWN

IN TENNESSEE,

AND

BACK BY WAY OF RICHMOND:

BY

EDMUND KIRKE,

AUTHOR OF "AMONG THE PINES," "MY SOUTHERN FRIENDS," ETC.

NEW YORK:

CARLETON, PUBLISHER, 413 *BROADWAY.*

M.DCCC.LXIV.

M'CREA & MILLER, STEREOTYPERS. C. A. ALVORD, PRINTER.

TO

SIDNEY HOWARD GAY,

THESE SKETCHES

ARE DEDICATED

WITH THE TRUE AND EARNEST REGARD

OF

HIS FRIEND,

THE AUTHOR.

CONTENTS.

CHAPTER I.

PAGE

At Louisville.......... 9

CHAPTER II.

On the Road.......... 23

CHAPTER III.

Guerillas.......... 35

CHAPTER IV.

The Union Scout.......... 45

CHAPTER V.

The Nashville Prison.......... 59

CHAPTER VI.

The Army Chaplain.......... 70

CHAPTER VII.

The Captain's Story.......... 83

CHAPTER VIII.

The Poor White Man.......... 104

CHAPTER IX.

The Old Negro's Story.......... 122

CHAPTER X.

The Regimental Hospital.......... 134

CHAPTER XI.

The Man who "don't Surrender Much.".......... 139

CHAPTER XII.

PAGE

Bible Smith.......... 144

CHAPTER XIII.

Bible's Story.......... 158

CHAPTER XIV.

Bible's Scouting Adventures.......... 169

CHAPTER XV.

The "Poor Whites".......... 182

CHAPTER XVI.

A Day with Rosecrans.......... 196

CHAPTER XVII.

Views of Southern Men.......... 219

CHAPTER XVIII.

A Projected Insurrection.......... 229

CHAPTER XIX.

Colonel James F. Jaquess.......... 233

CHAPTER XX.

Why I went to Richmond.......... 248

CHAPTER XXI.

On the Way to Richmond.......... 252

CHAPTER XXII.

In Richmond.......... 265

DOWN IN TENNESSEE.

CHAPTER I.

AT LOUISVILLE.

A DESIRE to study the undercurrents of popular sentiment at the South, and to meet some of "my Southern friends," whom the fortunes of war had made our prisoners within sight of their homes, led me, early in May, 1863, to visit the Southwest. While there I came in contact with many intelligent men, of all shades of political opinion; and from them gathered much that is illustrative of the real state of Southern feeling, and of the real purposes of the leaders of the Rebellion. In the hope that what I saw and heard may not be without interest to those who have not had the opportunity of personal observation, I propose to give in the following chapters some sketches of the men I met, and the scenes I witnessed, during a month's sojourn in a section which is being upheaved by the passions and desolated by the fires of our civil war.

Arriving at Louisville I at once sought out Colonel Mundy, the gentlemanly commandant of that post, to ascertain the whereabouts of my captive friends. He could give me no definite information, but presumed they were at Nashville. "However," he said, "prisoners are not kept there long. They are sent to Vicksburg for exchange as quickly as possible. If you desire to see them, you had better push on immediately."

This put me in a dilemma. The railroad below Bowling Green was infested with guerillas, and on several recent occasions, they had assailed the trains, and robbed and maltreated passengers. The cars were insufficiently guarded, and travelling was therefore attended with considerable personal hazard. In these circumstances I had gladly listened to the suggestion of Parson Brownlow—whom I had met at Cincinnati—to lie over at Louisville and accompany him and Governor Johnson to Nashville. They would be attended by a guard strong enough to beat off any roving band that ventured to attack the train; but would, perhaps, not start for a week. In the mean time, my Secession friends might be sent to "parts unknown." Therefore, if I waited, I was likely to miss one of the main objects of my journey, and if I went forward I ran the risk of getting a bullet under my waistcoat, or such an "inside view" of Rebeldom as might not be agreeable. Either horn of the dilemma seemed objectionable. While uncertain which one to choose, the small clock in the office of the Louisville Hotel sounded twice, and I walked up to the dining-room.

On my right at the table sat a tall, squarely built man, wearing the uniform of a lieutenant-colonel of infantry. He had a broad, open, resolute face—ridged and sun-browned, and a stiff, military air, but there was something about him that seemed to invite conversation, and after a while I said to him:

"You are travelling, Sir?"

"Yes, Sir, I am returning to my regiment at Triune."

"Is it entirely safe going down the Nashville road?

"Not entirely so. When I came up, a week ago Monday,

we were fired into by a band of forty-eight, but we beat them off."

"What were the circumstances?"

"It occurred just this side of Franklin. We heard there of a party being in the vicinity, and took on board a squad of thirty men. We had gone on about three miles, when the engineer discovered the track was torn up, where a wood lines the road, and at once reversed the engine. The guerillas were posted behind the trees, and as the train halted, poured a volley into us, and, yelling like devils, made a rush for the cars. I got this in readiness"—taking from his belt a large army repeater, and tapping it rather affectionately—"the moment I heard the train slacking-up, and when the leader came within fifteen feet of the platform I fired through the window and killed him. My second shot brought the next devil to his knees, and made the rest halt for an instant. In that instant the soldiers in the forward car, who had waited to cap their muskets, gave them a volley, and they skedaddled, leaving four dead and three wounded on the ground. We had on board three paymasters with over four hundred thousand dollars in money, and the fellows might have made a rich haul."

"And they would have done so but for your prompt shots giving the soldiers time to fire. You saved the train!"

"No, Sir," replied the Colonel, pleasantly, as if not displeased with my compliment, "the *General* saved it."

"How so? Was Rosecrans on board?"

"No; but a little while ago he ordered all officers to wear side-arms when off duty. But for that my pistol would have been in my valise; for it's a nuisance to carry ten pounds of iron all the while dangling at your side. The General foresaw just such emergencies. He thinks of every thing, Sir. I reckon he never sleeps."

"I suppose he *is* a vigilant officer."

"Yes, Sir; I was all through the Mexican war, and have seen something of generals. Rosecrans is the ablest one I ever knew."

"He certainly is successful."

"Always; never was defeated, and never will be. He planned and won McClellan's battles in Western Virginia; did the same for Grant in Mississippi, and at Stone River—why, Sir, when we were thoroughly whipped, and every man in the army knew it, he, singly, regained the battle. There is not another man living who could have done it."

This was said with an enthusiasm that provoked a smile; but I quietly remarked: "I am glad to hear such an account of him. I intend to visit him, but am undecided whether to go down at once, or to wait till the Governor arrives, and take advantage of his escort."

"It will be safer to go at once. The Governor will stay here a day or two, and as this place is full of rebels, every guerilla in Tennessee will know when he starts. If they can muster strong enough they'll surely attack him. I go down by the next train, and will be glad to have your company."

"Thank you. Your revolver has acquitted itself so well, that I am disposed to trust it. I'll go with you, Sir;" and rising, we left the table together.

The cars were not to start till the following morning, and the afternoon being on our hands, we seated ourselves in the smoking room, and resumed the conversation. I soon gleaned something of the Colonel's history. He had started in life with only a clear head and a strong pair of hands, but was then the owner of a well-stocked farm of three hundred and twenty acres, and in affluent circumstances. His experience in Mexico had given him a military education, and on the breaking out of the war, Governor Morton tendered him a colonel's commission. Having a young family growing up about him, and being past the age when love of adventure lures men into danger, he declined it. But when the new regiments were called for, and it seemed doubtful that his county would furnish her quota, he volunteered, to set, as he said, "the boys an example." His regiment, the 82d Indiana, at once filled up, and he was appointed its lieutenant-colonel. He had been in many small engagements, and at Stone River was in command of the six hundred skirmishers who, at the close of the last day's fight, in the darkness of midnight, advanced two miles, and for three hours "felt" a hostile force of five thousand. So long as the West sends such men to the war, the friends of the Union may be of good heart, for they cannot be beaten.

After a time the conversation turned upon politics, and my new acquaintance said to me: "A large majority of Rosecrans's men went into the war friendly to slavery; but not one of them would now consent to any peace that did not destroy it root and branch. Nine months ago I left home a Breckinridge Democrat, and now, sir, I'm as black an Abolitionist as Wendell Phillips."

"And what, pray, turned you about so suddenly?"

"Seeing slavery *as it is.* One little incident convinced me that a negro is a man—just as much of one as I am—and therefore not fit to be a slave. It occurred at Triune, where I am now stationed. Just outside of our lines lives a planter who professes strong Union sentiments. He used to mix freely with our officers, keep open house for them, and was, apparently, a whole-souled, hospitable fellow. He owned a good many negroes, and among them a quiet, respectaful old darky of about sixty, who supplied my mess with eggs and poultry. Not long ago our pickets, stationed about one hundred yards from this planter's house, were fired upon several times from the woods near by. It was done regularly twice a week, and on each occasion occurred about two o'clock in the morning. At last one of our boys was hit, and, being in command of the pickets, I set about investigating the matter. There was nothing to point suspicion at the planter, except the fact of his being a slaveholder, but *that* convinced me he had a hand in it. I never knew one of them, however strong his professions of loyalty, who was not at heart a rebel.

"I sent for the old darky, to question him, and, learning of it, the planter came to my quarters, and insisted that he had a right to hear what his negro said. I was satisfied I couldn't get the truth out of the slave in the master's presence, but I consented to go on with the examination. I put some leading questions to the old man, and in a quiet, straightforward way he told me that an officer of Bragg's army had been in the habit of visiting the mansion every few nights for several weeks. He said he came about midnight, left his horse and orderly concealed in the woods, and went up to the mistress's room as soon as he entered the house. There the master would join him, and remain with him generally for an hour or two. And he added, with perfect coolness: 'D'rec'ly af'er de cap'n wud leab, Sar, I'd allers yere de shootin' 'mong de trees. I reckoned dat wus bery quar, till finarly, one day, I yered Massa a tellin'

Missus dat de Cap'n war bound to wing *one* ob dem Yankees anyhow.' I asked him why the officer went there, and the old fellow, scratching his wool, and assuming a very stupid look, said:

"'I doesn't knows, Cunnel. It allers 'peared bery quar ter me dat he shud come, but I reckons de Secesh wants ter larn whot's gwine on in de camps. Massa, heseff, wus allers bery curous 'bout dat, Sar, an' he sot me, ober an' ober agin, ter fine out—tole me I muss keep my yeres wide open wheneber I toted you de truck; but, you allers hab your moufh shet so bery close, Cunnel, dat I neber could fine out a ting—not a ting, Sar.'"

Here the Colonel burst into a fit of laughter. As soon as he could readjust the muscles of his mouth to the English dialect, he continued:

"Through the whole of this, the planter threatened him, and he finally stormed, and raved at him like a madman, but the old Christian went on as quiet as a Quaker meeting, only once in a while answering his master, with—'You knows it'm de Lord's trufh, massa. I karn't say nuffin else, massa; I'se bery sorry, massa—'pears like I'd die fur you, massa, 'case I toted you when you's a chile, an I'se allers lubed you; but I karn't say nuffin else—de Lord woant leff me say nuffin else, massa. No, He woant!'

"The darky knew we might march at any moment, and that, when we did, there were ninety-nine chances in a hundred of his being whipped to death by his master, or by some of the neighbors, if his master wasn't left to do it; and yet he was as cool as I am. Martin Luther, when he went into Worms, expecting to meet the devil himself, didn't show the moral courage of that old negro. He convinced me that the black is altogether too much of a MAN to be a slave."

"And what did you do with the master?"

"Nothing. Our Brigadier, who had been a frequent guest at his house, thought it not exactly the thing to hang a white man on a 'nigger's' testimony, and so let him off. If I had had my way, he would have hung higher than Haman."

"And what became of the negro?"

"Not many days after his master was released, he came to my tent one evening, and with a little hesitation, said: 'Cunnel, I don't want ter 'sturb you, but de Lord come ter me lass night, Sar, an' he telled me ter leff you know what's a gwine on.'

"And what is a going on?" I asked.

"'Wall, you see, Cunnel, de debil hab got inter massa; an' he swar he'm gwine ter kill me fur tellin' you 'bout de Secesh cap'n.'

"I assured him I would protect him, and accordingly, in a day or two, I packed him off, with his traps and family, to the Free States. It wasn't exactly according to Tennessee law, and his owner protested warmly against it, but I advised him to prove his loyalty and claim his property of Uncle Sam.

"The old darky lived in a little lōg cabin near his master's house, and the day he was to leave I rode out to see him safely off. His small amount of personal property was stowed away in the ambulance, which was to take him to Nashville; and his wife, a good-looking mulatto (the old fellow himself was blacker than ink) had already mounted the wagon. A pretty quadroon woman of about thirty, who passed as his daughter—though she couldn't have been of his blood—was helping on to the seat one of the most beautiful white children I ever saw. She was well dressed, and had a fair, clear, rosy skin, and an eye as blue as indigo. Supposing she was the master's child, I asked her where she was going. 'Way up Norfh, massa, 'long wid gran'dad,' she answered.

"I was thunderstruck. She was the old woman's grandchild, the planter's own child, and a *slave!* I never till then realized what an accursed thing slavery is."

While sauntering about the hotel during the day, I had noticed a placard which read somewhat as follows:

"Passengers for the Louisville and Nashville road are notified that the wagon will be in readiness to take baggage to the Examiner's Office at four P. M."

As this notice applied to us, I suggested, as the Colonel finished his story, that we should repair to the "Custom House."

We found it on a side street, a dingy room about twenty feet square. It was densely crowded with carpet bags, portmanteaus, packing trunks, and a score of German Israelites, each one of whom was soliciting the immediate attention of the single examining official to the general assortment of dry goods and groceries which his particular trunk contained. Another official was behind the counter affixing to the "passed" packages, a strip of white muslin, and two mammoth daubs of red sealing wax. The office was advertised to close at five o'clock, and it then wanted but ten minutes of that hour. As our luggage could not leave the State without having two of those red seals upon it, each duly stamped U. S., the prospect of its going in the morning seemed decidedly dubious. With a little inward trepidation, I said to the coatless official: "Is there any probability of our turn coming this evening, sir?"

"Are you an 'Israelite indeed?'"

"No, sir, neither in name nor in deed. *I'm* a gentleman at large; my friend here, is a Union officer."

"Ah, Colonel! how are you?" exclaimed the official, looking up and touching his cap to my companion. The Colonel returned his salutation, and in a moment the other was at the bottom of my trunk, taking an inventory of the spare waistcoats, extra socks, and under-garments which it contained. In five minutes the ceremonies were over, and we left the "receipt of customs" devoutly thankful that we were not of the wandering tribes of Israel. The whole scene was decidedly suggestive of a landing among the French or Austrian officials; and it was with difficulty I realized that I was in an inland American town, and merely passing from one State of the Union to another.

As I was seated, after supper, in the porch of the hotel, enjoying a fragrant Havana, and the cool evening breeze, a lean, elongated "native" approached me. He had a thin, haggard face; a tawny red skin; and a mass of coarse black hair, which fell round his neck, like hemp round a mop-handle. His butternut clothes were much the worse for wear, and torn in many places; and the legs of his pantaloons, which made no effort to reach the coarse brogans that encased his feet, disclosed a skin so scratched and furrowed that it seemed to have been gone over with a harrow. I had seen thousands of his class, but there was a look of such intense wildness in his gray eyes, which moved in their sockets with the unsteady glare of a wild beast's, that I involuntarily started and turned toward him. Seeing my movement, he said, in a quiet, civil tone:

"How dy'ge, stranger? Dy'ge b'long yere?"

"No, Sir."

"B'long ter the army?" (I wore a suit of regimental blue, minus shoulder-straps and brass buttons.)

"No, Sir, I'm a peace man."

"Peace man!—Copperhead?" and his eyes glared a little more wildly than before.

"No, Sir, not exactly that, but I let others do the fighting."

"Ye does! Wall, Sir, you uns is a cuss ter the kentry. Ye orter be druv out uv hit. The man thet woant fight *now* haint fit ter live."

"You're right, my friend. Sit down;" and I motioned him to a vacant chair beside me. He continued standing, evidently not inclined to approach nearer to a man of peace principles. Observing this, I added:

"You misunderstand me—I'm a peace man, but I fight in my way—with a pen."

"Oh! thet's hit? Wall, thet'll do, ef ye gwo hit powerful strong."

"And how do you fight?"

"Ary how? The rebs 'll tell ye thet."

"But you don't wear the clothes; how is that?"

"Why, me an' twelve right smart uns hes been beatin' the bushes—keepin' the deestrict clar; but they's grow'd ter much fur us."

"Oh! bushwacking."

"Yas, but I hed ter put out. I'se gwine inter the army now—but I muss sell my mars fust. Dy'ge know whot Government 'll pay fur a right smart chunk uv a mar?"

"A hundred and five dollars, I believe, is the regular price."

"Taint 'nuff fur mine. They's powerful good brutes. I must git more'n thet, case my 'ooman 'll hev nothin' else, an' she's sickly like."

"But if you go into the army you can save a part of your pay for her."

"No, I karn't. I'll be shot—I feel hit—I'se made up my mind ter hit." As he said this, he seated himself in the chair I had offered him, and stared at me with a still wilder, crazier look. I saw that some terrible calamity had unsettled his intellect, and I said, in a sympathizing tone:

"You're not well: you're not fit to go into the army now."

"Yas, I is, Sir. I kin fight as hard as ary man *ye* knows. I'se a little gin out jest now, 'case I'se rid nigh onter a hundred an' fifty mile, an' hed ter tote my 'ooman a powerful piece o' the way."

"Where have you come from?"

"Clay county, nigh on ter Manchester. I lived thar. I'se plumb from thar this evenin'."

"And were you driven away?"

"Yes, Sir; druv away—robbed—hous'n burned—every thing burned, an' my ole mother—killed—killed! killed!" He bent down his head while he spoke, and as he repeated the last words they seemed to well nigh strangle him.

"It can't be possible!" I exclaimed; "human beings don't do *such* things!"

"But they haint human bein's—they's fien's—devils from hell—from hell, Sir."

"I know their passions are roused, but I did not know they murdered *women*."

"They does, Sir. I'll tell ye 'bout hit;" and grasping one

arm of my chair, and leaning forward with his unsteady, blazing eye looking into mine, he told me the following story:

"'Bout a mile from whar I b'long thar lived a ole man by the name of Begley—Squire Begley we called him, though he didn't own no slaves. He wus nigh on ter seventy, but wus a right peart ole man, an' Union ter the core—two on his boys—Sam an' John, is in the army now—8th loyal Kaintuck. Wall, 'bout a fortnit gone, on the mornin' uv the fifteenth uv April, three men, dressed in Union cloes, comes ter the ole gentleman's house, an' telled him they wus round raisin' a company ter put down the rebs thet wus poreing inter the county. The ole man wus mighty pleased, an' I reckon he wus unprudent in his talk; fur when they'd drawed him out, they telled him they wus raally Secesh soldiers. Then he ordered 'em ter leave, but they trottled him, an' dragged him off ter the edge uv a branch, 'bout half a mile away, an' thar hung him ter the limb uv a tree. A ole nig thet war passin' 'long the road heerd the ole Squire's cries, as he begged 'em ter hev marcy on his gray hars; an' knowin' I war ter home, he put fur my house, and telled me on it. I axed him ter tote my mars ter the bush, fur I know'd thar wus more on 'em round, an' feared they'd be arter the nags, and then I put off ter save the ole man. I war too late. He war dead, an' the infernal devils hed got nigh back ter his house, meanin' to steal his fillies an' what plunder he hed thet could be toted. I follered' 'em an' so soon as I come in distance, I drapped one on 'em. Then me an' tothers tuk ahind trees, an' blazed away ter one another fur more'n a hour. I winged one, but I got a ball yere," showing an ugly wound in his shoulder. "Arter a while six more on 'em rid up the road an' come at me. I seed it warnt no use, so I put fur the thick timber, an' finarly, seein' they couldn't kotch me, they guv up the chase. I know'd twouldn't do ter gwo home, so I made a long spell round, ahind a hill, an' put for the bushes whar I thort the ole darky'd be with the mars. It hed got ter be nigh onter dark, an' I'd grow'd powerful weak, on 'count uv the blood I'd let, so I sot down an' tried ter stop it. I hedn't sot long 'fore I thort I heerd a 'ooman schreechin', an' lookin' round I seed my own wife. She'd jest lost har baby, an' hedn't been out uv bed fur nigh a month, but she'd come six mile through the brush arter me. She couldn't speak, but she brung me a short piece from ahind the hill, an' show'd me my hous'n an' barn—all I hed in the world—a heap uv black an' ashes! They'd burn'd 'em, Sir, an' druv my sick wife, an' my ole mother, who'd been bedrid for more'n two year, out uv doors!"

He paused for a moment, and then in a slow, broken voice, added: "Thet night she died. Died—thar—in the dark, an' the cold—nothin' under har but the yerth—nothin' over har but the ole gown thet my 'ooman helt up to keep the rain off har face; an' when I kneeled down thar on the ground tèr yere har last words, I swore, Sir, I'd never rest till I'd drunk thar blood—the heart's blood uv every rebel in Kaintuck!

"The next day the darky buried har. I couldn't be thar. They wus huntin' me like a wild beast. For more'n a week me an' my sick wife lay out in the woods; but we're yere now, an' all I ax is ter sell my mars, an' git my 'ooman ter a safe place, an' then I'll guv 'em—whot they's guv'n me!"

From various sources I afterward received confirmation of the native's story; but it needed none; for in the fierce passion which blazed in his eyes, and lit up his haggard face, there was nothing but TRUTH.

CHAPTER II.

ON THE ROAD.

The next morning I started for Nashville. At the railway dépôt I was again reminded that I might be entering the French or Austrian dominions. At every turn my military passport was called for. I offered to pay my fare, and, "Please show your pass, Sir," greeted me from the small opening in the ticket office. I tried to force my way through the crowd which blocked the inner gateway of the station-house, and, "Please show your pass, Sir," arrested my footsteps. I applied for a check to my trunk, and, "Please show your pass, Sir," sounded from the lungs of the luggage department. I attempted to get upon the train, and, "Please show your pass, Sir," was echoed by a slim gentleman in shoulder-straps at the foot of the platform; and, finally, when congratulating myself that at least one-fourth of my perilous passage was accomplished, "Please show your pass, Sir," was smilingly repeated by a young man in military cap and citizen's nether garments, who had halted abreast of me in the aisle of the car. I drew it forth in despair.

"Will this never end?" I exclaimed, in evident ill-nature.

"Oh yes, Sir. We'll not trouble you again—till we reach Nashville. It is annoying, Sir; but absolutely necessary."

The car, when we entered, was already packed with a general

assortment of Kentucky jeans, butternut linseys, regimental blues, regulation buttons, and shoulder straps; but a single, timid-looking woman in the corner, and a small sprinkling of civilians among the soldiery, told plainly that none of our fellow-travellers were leaving home on a pleasure excursion.

Near the forward door were a number of citizens, who, politely displacing some pieces of luggage, invited the Colonel and myself to squeeze ourselves into seats by the side of two fat men in secession gray, who turned out to be planters from Western Tennessee. They were of a party of neighbors, who had been to Louisville together, and were then returning to their homes.

As the train moved off from the station, one of them said to me:

"You're from the North, Sir?"

"Yes, Sir."

"Things are rather disturbed with ye jest now—aren't they? That Vallandigham affair is creating some trouble?"

"Not much, Sir—the best ale will foam; it is only a little froth on the surface."

"It seems to me it's more than froth," said my right-hand neighbor. "I reckon your people are about tired of the war. If the Democrats were in power, they'd stop it."

"How would they stop it?"

"By letting the South go. I'm a Union man, Sir, but I've had enough of the war—I want peace. You people at the North know nothing about it. We're robbed by both sides; we can't stir out of our houses in safety; I never wake in the morning but I fear the day will be my last."

"It is a sad state of things, no doubt; but I fear it will continue till the South submits."

"Then it will last forever," exclaimed another planter, who sat facing me. "The South will never submit, Sir! It will never come back! Every Southern man will die first."

"Allow me to ask if you're not a slaveholder?" said the Colonel, leaning forward, and smilingly addressing the last speaker.

"Yes, Sir; I own some twenty negroes."

"I thought so. I never heard a man with less than that number express such sentiments."

"But I own more, and I'm not of that opinion," said the quiet gentleman beside the Colonel. "I would be glad to see the South back."

"You're not a native, Sir."

"No, Sir; but I've done business here for thirty years. My friend, the Doctor here," pointing to another gentleman, sitting opposite to me, "*is* a native, and a slaveholder, and as rabid on the Union as I am."

"And how many slaves have you, Doctor," asked the Colonel, with another of his pleasant smiles.

"Only two quarters of one, Sir, an old man and a woman, who were playmates of my mother," answered the medical man.

"I thought so," said the Colonel, quietly.

"Come gentlemen," I exclaimed, laughing, "as the Colonel thinks the number of darkies a man owns a sort of political barometer, suppose we take a census at once."

My suggestion was received good-naturedly, and in five minutes I had the statistics. The corpulent planter, who expected each day would be his last, had seventy odd; the Northern born merchant had twenty-seven; the doctor, two, and the others, respectively, one hundred and nine, sixty-two, twenty-four, and twenty-one; the latter number representing the interest the belligerent planter had in the peculiar institution. A half-hour's desultory conversation followed, and during it each one, except my right-hand neighbor, and the "No submission" man, expressed a willingness to sacrifice his chattels to save the Union.

"Ah, Colonel," I exclaimed, as I learned the sentiments of the last of the party, "you are floored—your theory won't stand fire."

"*Perhaps* it won't," he replied, dryly.

More extended observation subsequently convinced me that his views are fully supported by general facts.

As the planter of secession proclivities was rather warmly combating my views on the Emancipation Proclamation, a singularly self-possessed, gentlemanly-looking man, of about fifty, approached us, and leaning against the arm of the opposite seat, accosted me as follows:

"And when the South is subdued, and the war is over, what will you do with four millions of emancipated blacks?"

"Set them at work, and pay them."

"And would you, a white man, consent to live where every second citizen is a black, and your political and social equal?"

"Freedom of itself, Sir, will not make the black my equal. At the North he is not politically or socially on a par with the white, and there he has had fifty years of freedom."

"But your black is inferior to ours. The negro is of a tropical race; he comes to perfection only under a warm sun."

"If that be true, your negroes are fit for freedom, for our blacks are as orderly, industrious, and quietly disposed as any class we have."

The new-comer was about to reply, when the Doctor, turning

to him, said: "Colonel, you consider our whites superior to our blacks; do you not?"

"Certainly I do."

"Then give the blacks freedom; subject them to free competition with the poor whites, and you'll soon be rid of them, for they'll *die out.* The Indian is naturally superior to the negro, but two centuries of contact with the white man—the Indian being *free*—has reduced the race from sixteen millions to two millions. Set the black free, leave him to himself, and his fate will be the same."

"Then slavery keeps the race alive among us?"

"Of course it does; for, while the black labors for us, we feed, and clothe, and *think* for him; and, besides—and this is the principal reason—we are constantly infusing fresh white blood into his veins. That would not be if he were free, for the black does not seek the white, but the white the black."

"You have stated the strongest argument for Slavery that I ever heard. You say it will save the black, and yet, while you admit that freedom would destroy him, you would set him free!"

"I would—to save the whites. The social and political corruption which absolute control of him has bred among us, is destroying us. It has produced the present state of things, and God is using this war—the fruit of our corruption—to purify us. He has written on the wall—any man can read it—"Slavery is doomed!"

"*I* cannot read it, and I do not believe a good and just God ever decrees the destruction of his creatures."

"Has he not destroyed other races? He works by general laws, and one of the plainest of His laws is, that the weak shall give way to the strong, the inferior race to the superior. There is no hardship in this. Every man submits cheerfully to it—the old give up their places to the young—the father dies, and the son succeeds him, and nobody grumbles. We have obstructed the operation of this law on the black race, and now, in tears and blood, we are paying the penalty."

"You bookish men can spin fine theories, but we have to deal with facts, and hard facts at that."

"I have formed my theory on facts, Colonel, hard and black facts, too," replied the Doctor, laughing.

"But you never loved the slaves—never had them love you, as mine love me. When Grant's army was at Memphis I told them they would be free if they went to it, and not one of them left me."

"That only proves, what everybody knows, that you are a kind master; and that your negroes would work cheerfully for you, if they were free."

"Well, there's no use talking to you; you're an incorrigible Abolitionist; but come, Squire," addressing my right hand neighbor, "exchange seats with me. I want to talk with this Northern gentleman, and I can't stand this any longer." The cars were jolting considerably, and his position was not an easy one. The fat planter rose, and the other seated himself beside me. As he did so, I said to him:

"I never discuss slavery, Sir; it's a waste of words."

"I don't wish to discuss it, Sir; I want to ask you the real state of public feeling at the North. Where do you live, Sir?"

This was spoken in a tone which showed he was accustomed to a good deal more deference than is yielded to the ordinary run of planters. I quietly gave my name and residence, and asked him for his.

"George W. H——, of H—— Springs, near Clarksville, Tennessee."

"Your name is familiar to me, Sir; I formerly knew General H——, of South Carolina—he whose son commands the H—— Legion."

"He was a near kinsman of mine. We're all of the old Virginia family."

He then went on to ask me a multitude of questions about the condition of things at the North. I answered frankly, and he listened attentively, but made no comment when I expressed the opinion that the mass of our people would never consent to the re-establishment of slavery.

* * * * * * *

We were entering a beautiful region, where the thick grass was waving in the meadows, the early flowers were blooming by the road sides, and the spring birds were singing in the great old trees; but where the rich, red soil lay unturned by the plough, the stalks of the Autumn corn stood rotting on the ground, and ruin and desolation stared at us from every thing. Broken fences, wasted fields, deserted plantations, dismantled dwellings, and now and then, a burned woods, or a charred chimney, standing a lonely sentinel over a weedy garden, or amid a blackened grove, told that the whirlwind of war had passed that way, and left only ravage and devastation in its path. A ragged woman, looking out from a wretched hovel; a solitary man, lingering around a heap of ashes and crumbling bricks that might once have been his home, or a group of half-clad negro children, gambolling on the porch, or lolling lazily on the lawn of some deserted homestead, that still looked down in faded grandeur on the ruin around it, were the only indications of human existence, and the only remnants of a once peaceful and happy population. It was one of the most lovely regions of the earth, naked, but beautiful even in its nakedness. I called the attention of my new acquaintance to its appearance, and he remarked: "No portion of this wide country has so fine a climate, or so rich and fertile a soil. Before we reached Elizabethtown, we passed through what is called the 'bed of the Ohio'—a white clay region, heavily timbered, but deficient in iron and lime, and devoted mainly to grazing. Now, we are ascending an elevated plateau of *red* clay, rich in every thing except ammonia, and producing, almost spontaneously, enormous crops of wheat, rye, corn, hemp, blue grass, and tobacco. At Bowling Green this plateau is broken by irregular ridges that spring out from the Cumberland Mountains, and sink into the lower lands bordering the Mississippi. They give a more beautiful diversity to the surface, but the character of the soil continues the same, as, indeed, it does over nearly the whole of this State (Kentucky) and Tennessee. Anywhere in this region the subsoil, turned up by the plough, and exposed for a short time to the action of the air, becomes a manure almost as valuable as guano. These two States, Sir, were meant by nature to be the garden of this continent. Adam when he first woke in Eden, did not look on a more beautiful landscape, or a more luxuriant vegetation, than is everywhere spread around you; but now—what has war done! A curse has fallen on these once happy homes—the 'abomination of desolation' sits in these pleasant places."

"But the day will soon come, Sir, when free labor, free schools, and free men will people this region, and make it in reality, the paradise which God designed it should be."

"We cannot foresee the end, Sir, but my heart sickens when I think of what it may be—these old homesteads dismantled, these rich plantations cut into little plats of a half dozen acres, and divided among the negroes, or squatted on by a vulgar herd of Irish and Germans. I hope I may not live to see it, Sir; but let even *that* come rather than disunion and the perpetual war that would follow."

"And are you a Union man, Sir!" I exclaimed in pleased surprise. "I feared from what you said of slavery, that you were not."

"Union, sir! my Unionism has been tried; it has stood the test—every test but death; and I am ready to meet that for it. I believe in slavery; I think it the normal condition of the black race; I know my negroes are happier than they would be in freedom; and—I love them, sir. But I love my children better. I do not want to leave them a heritage of endless war; and therefore, I am willing to abolish slavery, if the Union cannot be saved without it."

"You must have suffered greatly, Sir, living as you do, in a section where the secession element is so strong."

"I have. My plantation has been sacked, my life has been threatened—every relative I have in the world has turned against me. A committee waited on me, just before the June (1861) election, and told me that fifty ropes were ready to hang me if I did not cease my Union talk, and vote the separation ticket. With two of my negroes, armed to the teeth, I went to the polls, and defied them. I voted 'No Separation.' Then they dragged me and Judge Catron before the Military Commission at Nashville. They questioned us, and ordered us to leave the State. The Judge consented, but I charged them with sending us away because they had changed, while we had not, and I told them to their faces that I would not go—that I would die first. One of my near kinsman was on the Commission, and I accused him of being recreant to every principle of our ancestors. He only answered, 'I'll not argue that question with you. We may be wrong, but we're embarked in this thing; our lives are at stake, and self-preservation, which makes a man sacrifice his dearest friend to save himself, impels us to go on. We cannot turn back.' It is that feeling which holds the leaders together. After that, my wife entreated me, and I am ashamed to say it, I was less outspoken. But I was a *marked* man; they annoyed me and plundered me in every way. At one time they quartered a whole regiment upon me. I went out and told them: 'You are my neighbors; I love you, and would not kill you, but I curse you. I curse you for the ruin you are bringing on your country.' God heard me, Sir, and that curse rested on them. Out of the fifteen hundred that went to Richmond, only two hundred were left when Grant took Memphis! The rest had answered the muster-roll in eternity! Then every man felt justified in taking my life. I walked every day arm-in-arm with death. I was waylaid, shot at, my well was poisoned. How I escaped, the Providence that guarded me only knows. When the soldiers left, society became reduced to a state of anarchy—a struggle for self-preservation. Brothers turned against brothers, parents against children, children against parents. No man was safe. Even my friend Shackelford, law partner of Gustavus A. Henry, member of the Confederate Senate, was threatened with death. At the outset he had gone with the current, and his only son had volunteered; but when he saw the ruin which Secession was bringing on his section, he applied to Henry for the young man's release. An order was at once issued for his own arrest, and he only escaped by fleeing the State. No words can picture to you, Sir, the state of things that existed. All that Dante and Milton have told us of hell falls short of what we experienced."

"And through all this you stood true to the Union! I honor you, Sir; from the bottom of my soul, I honor you."

"You need not, for I knew their plans. I knew that all their talk about the extension and perpetuation of slavery is mere sham, to cover their real designs, which are to *subvert republican institutions, and found a bastard monarchy on the ruins of their country!* I loved slavery, Sir. I love it still; but even to save it I could not aid in overthrowing the institutions founded by my fathers. I could not lift my puny arm in opposition to the manifest designs of God, which are that all men shall be *free* and *equal*."

I did not ask him why the blacks had been overlooked in the designs of DEITY; I merely remarked: "And are you satisfied that such are the intentions of the rebel leaders? I know that Spratt, and other Southern theorists, advocate monarchy as the only government compatible with slavery; but I have not supposed your practical statesmen had adopted such views."

"They have. Those ideas are the main-spring of the Rebellion. But for them it would never have been undertaken. I *know* it. The whole scheme was opened to me. If it had not been I should have gone with the current. I could not otherwise have stemmed it. The English and French governments know it, and that is the reason the rebels have so much sympathy from them. They have kept the design carefully out of sight; only the ringleaders have been in the secret, for they knew that if the masses discovered it before they had them bound hand and foot by military despotism, the whole jig was up."

He paused, for just then the engine-whistle sounded shrilly through the trees, the train broke up, every man in the car sprang to his feet, and a dozen voices cried out:

"The guerillas are on us!"

"Are you armed, Sir?" said my new acquaintance to me, as coolly as if we were at his dinner-table.

"No, Sir, I am not."

"Take this; it may be useful."

Cocking the revolver, and giving one thought to those I had left at home, I seated myself, and breathlessly awaited the expected assault.

CHAPTER III.

GUERILLAS.

As the train came to a halt, the Doctor, who had been enjoying a quiet nap, opened his eyes, and asked:

"What's to pay?"

"Reckon the Bushwhackers are on us!"

"That can't be, this side of Bowling Green—some one had better reconnoitre," and rising from his seat, he drew from his pocket a pistol about as large as a boy's pop-gun, and strode toward the doorway."

"For God's sake, Doctor, don't go there! Keep inside!" exclaimed half a dozen voices.

Not heeding the warnings, the medical gentleman stepped upon the platform, saying, "Where's the guard? Well, these fellows are never where they should be."

The single soldier who had been stationed before the door, had suddenly disappeared. Naturally objecting to standing as a target for fifty rebel rifles, he had retreated into the forward car. The Doctor, then glancing cautiously around, and apparently seeing nothing to satisfy his curiosity, made a sudden spring for a huge tree which grew a short distance from the track. He alighted within a few feet of it, and by the movement secured two breastworks; the tree in his front and the car in his rear.

"He jumps like a wild cat," exclaimed the Colonel, "but look at our neighbors here! Ha! ha!"

Turning about, I beheld nearly all of the citizens crouched on the floor, beneath the windows, and not a few of the officers with arms (and legs) *couchant.*

"I say, Squire," said the Colonel, laughing, "'The wicked flee when no man pursueth.' The devils would have been on us before now if they were coming."

"The wise man foreseeth the evil and hideth himself—the fool holdeth up his head and getteth hit," responded the Squire, with a ludicrous effort at merriment.

"That isn't in my version. But, Doctor, what's the detention?" to the latter, who that moment re-entered.

"Two or three rails displaced—that's all. Some scoundrel meant to throw us off the track."

I breathed more freely; for, if the truth must be told, my respiratory apparatus had not performed its usual functions during the preceding occurrences. My whole being had been absorbed in two senses—sight and hearing. With my eyes ranging intently around, and my ears strained to catch the lightest outside sound, I had made those organs do the work of at least five days in those five minutes. Even a brave man—and bravery is not essential to one of my profession—is shaken when confronting an unseen danger; and how the Colonel and the Doctor maintained such perfect coolness I could not imagine. I said as much to them, when, at the end of a half-hour, we resumed our seats, and the train got again under way.

"Courage," replied the Colonel, "like almost every thing else, is a thing of habit. A man who has for two years daily expected every bush would give him a bullet, gets indifferent to danger; but, after all, I had rather have death come at me face to face, than spring on me suddenly from behind a rail fence."

"It is barbarous—this guerilla system," I remarked, again dovetailing my legs within the Doctor's.

"It's more than that—it's hellish," he replied; "Jeff. Davis should be hung for inaugurating it."

"If you imagine," said the Colonel, "all the thieves and cut-throats of New York let loose upon the city, with unlimited license to kill, burn, and destroy, you will have a faint idea of what it is. The lowest dregs of society, our gamblers, horse-thieves, and criminals, make up these bands. Now and then a respectable man, too cowardly to go into the regular army, joins them; but he soon becomes as bad as the rest. They submit to no restraint, but range the country, plundering and murdering friend and foe. If a worthless fellow has a grudge against a neighbor, he joins them, denounces his enemy as a Union man, and stealing on him at night, either shoots him down before his wife and children, or burns his house over his head. They spare neither sex nor age. Lone women are outraged, old men are murdered by them. I paid them eleven thousand five hundred dollars for my own life only last fall. Wherever they go terror reigns; and more than one-half of this State and Tennessee is under their control. In fact, their raids extend even within the Union lines. Mounted on swift horses, they make a sudden dash on a picket-station, or a railway train, and are ten miles away before pursuit can be commenced."

"And the King Devil among them is a Yankee," said the Doctor, smiling.

"Is that true?"

"Yes—but don't be offended. I know you export your

meanest specimens; and that our people have some traits worse than yours. The North loves gold—the South loves power; and the love of power is infinitely worse than the love of gold. One absorbs a man in self, but makes him orderly, quiet, and law-abiding; the other renders him restless, turbulent, and impatient of control—ready to overturn every thing, human and divine, that stands in the way of his personal ambition. It led Satan to rebel in Heaven, and it made our leaders rise against the best Government on earth; and, Sir, we cannot end this war until we serve them as the Lord served the devil—send them to h—l!"

This was said with a warmth that, in one of the Doctor's cool temperament, surprised me; but I merely remarked:

"You would go too far. Strip them of their negroes—their power is in them—and they will be harmless. Reduced to earning their bread by the sweat of their brows, they'll find no time to plot revolutions."

"You are mistaken. Our people are ignorant, and accustomed to being led by them. Seeing them impoverished, they'll pity them, and be just as much under their control as now. We must weed the whole race out of the South. I wouldn't hang them—they are too many for that; but I'd expatriate every one of them. Until that is done, there'll be no lasting peace."

"Well, it strikes me we'll have to catch the birds before we cage them."

"And going on as we are going now we'll never catch them," remarked the Colonel; "I sometimes think God has struck our rulers with judicial blindness to punish the nation for its sins. Why, Sir, I have half a dozen negro boys who could manage things better than they are managed at Washington. Half-way measures—always acting a little too late—scattering our forces over the whole continent, when we should concentrate them against vital points, is ruining us; and if it goes on, will make the South independent."

"I can see where the Administration has blundered; but it is easier to see mistakes than to suggest remedies. How would *you* suppress the Rebellion?"

"By calling out a million of men; and coming down on the South like an avalanche. That would end the war in ninety days. Now, with six hundred thousand on the outside of a circle, we are trying to whip four hundred thousand on the inside. It can never be done. The rebels can so quickly re-enforce any threatened point, that they will always be numerically superior where a battle is to be fought. It takes nearly half our present force to keep up our communications. Rosecrans here—our best General—has, perhaps, seventy-five thousand men, but thirty thousand are required to protect his lines of two hundred and fifty miles, and he is kept idle because he cannot bring into the field as many men as Bragg."

"And do you think the rebels have four hundred thousand?"

"Every man of them; and they can bring out another one hundred thousand, besides two hundred thousand negroes."

"And dare they arm the negroes?"

"They do it now. The first company raised in Memphis was of blacks. When they are driven to the wall, they'll put a musket into the hands of every negro within their lines, and *make* him fight. My own opinion is that the slave is to end this war. Each side will use him. He'll be put in the front ranks, and the result will be the present generation will be exterminated. Thus, though not in the Doctor's way, may be brought about the fate he predicts for the blacks."

"God speed the day!" exclaimed the Doctor. "You see I'm an Abolitionist, Sir, but not one of the Yankee stripe."

"I perceive you're not a negro worshipper; but, Colonel, after the North has crushed out this immense force, how can it bring the Southern people into a cordial reunion with it?"

"They'll come into it of themselves. Nine-tenths of the rank and file of the rebel army would gladly lay down their arms, and go peacefully back to their homes to-day. They have been misled and forced into this thing; their hearts are not, and never have been, in it. Only the leaders are irreconcilably in earnest. The Rebellion is merely a shell. We have but to crack it, to find it hollow. The Southern people have had false ideas of the Yankees—the war has made them know them better and like them better. Our masses had seen none but the sneaking, cowardly, money-loving kind. One of my own brothers-in-law is of that sort. He got a hundred and fifty negroes by my sister, and the first thing he did was to whip one of them to death—an old house-servant, who had carried his wife in his arms when she was a child. He is now a rabid Secessionist, as are all of his class."

"And who is this King Devil of the guerillas, as the Doctor calls him?"

"His name is Woodward. He was a schoolmaster at Hopkinsville, Thurston County, Kentucky. He knew all the thieves and rascals in the district, and at the breaking out of the war raised a regiment of fifteen hundred among them and offered it to Mr. Davis. Davis refused it, because the men were not enlisted for three years. Then Woodward divided his force into squads of from twenty to two hundred, and overran the State. There are five or six thousand of these devils now, in this State and Tennessee, and some of their atrocities are past belief."

"I have heard something of them," I replied. "Parson Brownlow introduced me, at Cincinnati, to a number of East Tennessee refugees, who had suffered every thing but death at the hands of these men. One of them, a farmer by the name of Palmer, from near Pikeville, in Bledsoe County, was attacked by a party in his own house in the daytime. He killed two of them, but was shot in four places, and left for dead. His wife, who attempted to shield him, was also wounded; but after incredible hardship got her husband to Lexington, and from there to Cincinnati, where the Parson secured him a place as conductor on the street cars. When I came through he was about to volunteer under Burnside, being determined to have vengeance for what he had suffered. Another one was Knights, a noted scout, who has served under Rosecrans, and is now with Burnside. His adventures would make a history as interesting and strange as any romance. He has crossed the mountains as guide to Union men, escaping to join our army, seventy-two times! and, though repeatedly shot, has been taken but once. Then he escaped in a most wonderful way.

"How was it?" asked the Doctor.

"He was captured by a small party while crossing Walden's Ridge. They at first decided to hang him on the spot, but finally, to obtain the reward offered for his capture, concluded to deliver him to the Confederate authorities at Knoxville. He was at once tried and sentenced to be hanged. While he was in jail awaiting execution, his daughter was admitted to see him. He pretended to be unable to sit up, in consequence of a wound received when he was taken, and of course the daughter had to bend down to hear what he said. In these circumstances he managed, though a sentinel stood directly over him, to whisper: 'Under your skirt—a coil!—to-morrow!' She procured a 'coil,' as he termed it, hid it under her clothes, and the next day went again to the jail. The sentinel refused to admit her, but the officer, softened by her entreaties to see her father for the last time—he was to be hanged the next day—finally granted her an interview of five minutes. The soldier stood by all the while, as before, but while frantically embracing her father, she managed to convey the priceless rope under the bed-clothes. The night happened to be dark and stormy, the sentinels kept under shelter, and before morning, Knights, with three others, let himself down from the third story and escaped. He is past sixty, but as hale and vigorous as any young man you ever knew."

"I'll never speak against women's hoops again," exclaimed the Doctor, "for once they've done the country service."

"The East Tennesseeans have suffered terribly," said the Colonel, "but the barbarities practised on them have been committed all over this section. Wherever the guerillas have gone, they have left a trail of burning houses, and butchered men and women. Some of them are such monsters of crime that one is tempted to believe the Devil has become incarnate in long hair, slouched hat, and butternut trowsers. Over here in Clinton County, one named Champ Ferguson was recently living, who, I suppose, has committed more murders than any man in the Union. Before the war he was a gambler, thief, and counterfeiter, and naturally joined the Rebellion. He organized a small band, and for more than a year committed unheard of atrocities unchecked. Reuben B. Wood, an aged citizen of Clinton County, had greatly befriended him. Ferguson rode up to Wood's house one day in September, 1861, called him out, and coolly told him he was going to kill him. 'Oh, no! Champ, you'll not do that! I never done you any harm!' exclaimed the old man.

" 'But you toted the d—d Lincoln flag at Camp Dick Robinson.'

" 'Why, Champ,' said Wood, 'I almost raised you. I held you on my knee when you was a child.'

" 'You're a d—d Lincolnite,' said the monster, and shot him dead.

" On another occasion he had a Union man by the name of Spangler lashed to a tree, and beaten to death. In April, 1862, he and his band came upon a party of neighbors collected at a log raising in Fentress County. He shot a number of them as they were attempting to escape, and took the rest prisoners. Then he bade his men hold each prisoner by the arms, and deliberately ripped open their bowels with a knife! A man by the name of Fragge had incurred his enmity. He was confined to his bed, dangerously sick, his little child lying beside him, and his wife sitting near. Ferguson entered the room and told him he had come to kill him. Fragge pleaded for life; his wife entreated the ruffian to spare her husband, but he raised his pistol and gave him a severe wound. Fragge again entreated for life, but Ferguson again raised his pistol, and while the sick man clasped his frightened child to his breast, shot him dead! The wife supposing both husband and child killed, ran frantically from the house. Then Ferguson stole the dead man's clothes, and the blanket that covered his bed!"

"Tell me no more! You have said enough to convince me that all the passions of hell are 'let loose in this war.'"

"They are. Men have become fiends. They thirst for blood. They gloat over their victims. The last drop of human feeling has gone out of them. Death and ruin follow them everywhere. They have made this lovely country a HELL!"

We soon afterward arrived at Memphis Junction, and bidding me a kindly "good-by," and urging me to visit them if my time allowed, the Colonel and his companions left the car and took the train which was in waiting for Clarksville.

CHAPTER IV.

THE UNION SCOUT.

THE States of Kentucky and Tennessee have been made one vast battle-ground by this war. Every county and every township has been the scene of some fierce struggle, or the theatre of some bloody drama, whose memory will live for generations. Grass-grown cross-roads, where rude guide-posts point ways no traveller ever went; sleepy hamlets, unknown to the census-taker and the tax-gatherer, where the spelling-book and the mail-bag never were seen; lonely log meeting-houses, where some ignorant pastor doled out to a scanty crowd of more ignorant "white trash" weekly potions of "wholesome admonition," and—the country newspaper; have become world-famous. Distant lands have heard of them; distant times will speak of them, and romance and poetry will couple their names with heroic deeds, and make them holy places in our nation's history.

At every station on the Nashville road the traveller sees indications of the fierceness of this struggle, and evidences of a valor worthy of the most heroic ages. At Mumfordsville, on a little mound overlooking the Green River, is a low earthwork encircled by a shallow ditch, and enclosing less than an acre of ground. There Colonel Wilder and a small band of raw Indianians arrested the northward march of Bragg's army for forty hours!

"It is the whole of Bragg's force! It is madness to resist! We must surrender!" exclaimed one of Wilder's lieutenants.

"I know we must surrender. But we'll do it *when they make us*," replied the brave commander.

Five thousand rebel muskets belched fire upon them during six hours, but crouching behind those mud walls that handful of brave men sent back a storm of hail that mowed down the advancing ranks as the scythe mows down the summer grass.

"Surrender at once, or we'll give no quarter," was borne to them by the flag of truce.

"We ask none," was the sole reply, and the work of death went on.

Twelve thousand men, in ranks six deep, their bayonets gleaming in the sun, then enveloped that little hill, and again and again, within eighty feet of that frail breastwork, poured in their deadly volleys, but at each discharge clear and loud rang out the words: "Aim low, boys. Let every shot tell!" and broken and decimated the assailants fell back to their quarters.

At sunrise of the third day another flag approached. "You are brave men. We would spare your lives. We have posted cannon at every angle. We can level your intrenchments in half an hour!"

"I do not believe it; convince me of it, and I'll surrender."

They led him out. He saw the guns, and surrendered.

"If he had held out another half hour I should not be here to tell you of it," said the modest young corporal who told me the story.

Into a stagnant pool at the left of the fort three hundred and fifty mangled rebels were thrown at nightfall. Seven hundred now lie buried in the woods hard by. How great a graveyard for so small a town!

But I cannot particularize all that I saw, where at every bridge was a stockade, and on every hill a battle-field.

Here and there broken cars and charred rolling-gear strewn along the track showed that the guerillas had been recently at work. At Bowling Green, in the bed of the Big Barren—a little stream which flows near the town—were the fragments of a train that, with its freight of mules, had been burned on the bridge only three weeks before, and at the station next south of Gallatin, was a similar wreck; but, closing my eyes on these relics of an almost savage warfare, and these uncomfortable reminders of personal danger, I perched my legs on the seat just vacated by the Abolition philosopher, and soon fell asleep.

I was dreaming of home, and of certain flaxen-haired juveniles who are accustomed to call me "Mister Papa," when a heavy hand was laid on my shoulder, and a gruff voice said:

"Doan't want ter 'sturb yer, stranger, but thar haint nary nother sittin'-place in the whole kear."

I drew in my extremities, and he seated himself before me. He was a spare, muscular man of about forty, a little above the medium height, with thick sandy hair and beard, and a full, clear, gray eye. There was nothing about him to attract particular attention except his clothing, but that was so out of all keeping with the place and the occasion, that I opened my eyes to their fullest extent, and scanned him from head to foot. He wore the gray uniform of a Secession officer, and in the breast of his coat, right over his heart, was a round hole, scorched at the edges, and darkly stained with blood! Over his shoulder was slung a large army revolver, and at his side, in a leathern sheath, hung a weapon that seemed a sort of cross between a bowie-knife and a butcher's cleaver. On his head, surmounted by a black plume, was a moose-colored, slouched hat, and falling from beneath it, and tied under his chin, was a white cotton handkerchief stiffly saturated with blood! Nine motley-clad natives, all heavily armed, had entered with him and taken the vacant seats around me, and at first view I was inclined to believe that in my sleep the train had gone over to the enemy and left me in the hands of the Philistines. I was, however, quickly reassured, for, looking about I discovered the Union Guard and my fellow-travellers all in their previous places, and as unconcerned as if no unusual thing had happened. Still, it seemed singular that no officer had the new comer in charge; and more singular that any one in the uniform he wore should be allowed to carry arms so freely about him. After a while, having gleaned all the knowledge of him that my eyes could obtain, I said in a pleasant tone:

"Well, my friend, you appear to take things rather coolly."

"Oh, yes, Sir! I orter. I've been mighty hard put, but I reckon I'm good fur a nother pull now."

"Where are you from?"

"Fentress County, nigh onter Jimtown (Jamestown). I'm scoutin' it fur Burnside—runnin' boys inter camp; but these fellers wanted ter jine Cunnel Brownlow—the old parson's son—down ter Triune. We put plumb fur Nashville, but hed ter turn norard, case the brush down thar ar thick with rebs. They'd like ter a hed us."

"Oh, then you wear that uniform as a disguise on scouting expeditions?"

"No, Sir; I never hed sech a rig on afore. I allers shows the true flag, an' thar haint no risk, case, ye see, the whole deestrict down thar ar Union folks, an' ary one on 'em would house'n *me* ef all Buckner's army wus at my heels. But this time they run me powerful close, an' I hed ter show the secesh rags."

As he said this he looked down on his clean, unworn suit of coarse gray, with ineffable contempt.

"And how could you manage to live with such a hole there?" I asked, pointing to the bullet rent in his coat.

"Oh! I warn't inside uv 'em jest then, though I warrant me he war a likely feller thet war. I ortent ter a done hit—but I hed ter. This war he;" and taking from his side pocket a small miniature, he handed it to me.

It was a plain circlet of gold, attached to a piece of blue ribbon. One side of the rim was slightly clipped, as if it had been grazed by the passing ball, and the upper portion of the ivory was darkly stained with blood; but enough of it was unobscured to show me the features of a young man, with dark, flowing hair, and a full, frank, manly face. With a feeling akin to horror I was handing the picture back to the scout, when in low, stammering tones he said to me:—

"'Tother side, Sir! Luk at 'tother side."

I turned it over, and saw the portrait of a young woman, scarcely more than seventeen. She had a clear, transparent skin, regular, oval features, full, swimming, black eyes, and, what must have been dark, wavy brown hair, but changed then to a deep auburn by the red stains that tinged the upper part of the picture. With intense loathing, I turned almost fiercely on the scout, and exclaimed: "And you killed that man?"

"Yes, Sir, God forguv me—I done hit. But I couldn't holp hit. He hed me down—he'd cut me thar," turning up his sleeve, and displaying a deep wound on his arm; "an' thar!" removing the bandage, and showing a long gash back of his ear. "His arm wus riz ter strike agin—in another minhit he'd hev cluv my brain. I seed hit, Sir, an' I fired! God forguv me—I fired! I wouldn't a done hit ef I'd a knowd thet," and he looked down on the face of the sweet young girl, and the moisture came into his eyes: "I'd hev shot 'im somewhar but yere—somewhar but *yere!*" and laying his hand over the rent in his coat, he groaned as if he felt the wound. With that blood-stained miniature in my hand, and listening to the broken words of that ignorant scout, I realized the horrible barbarity of war.

After a pause of some minutes he resumed the conversation.

"They killed one on our boys, Sir?"

"Did they! How was it?"

"Wal Sir, ye see they b'long round the Big Fork in Scott County; and bein's I war down thar, an' they know'd I war a runnin' recruits over the mountins ter Burnside, they telled me they wanted me ter holp 'em git 'long with the young Cunnel. They'd ruther a notion ter him—an' he *ar* a feller thet haint growd everywhar—'sides all the folks down thar swar by the old Parson."

"Well, they ought to, for he's a trump," I remarked good-humoredly, to set the native more at his ease.

"Ye kin bet high on thet; he haint nothin' else," he replied, leaning forward and regarding me with a pleased, kindly expression. "Every un down my way used ter take his paper; thet an' the Bible war all they ever seed, an' they reckoned one war 'bout so good as 'tother. Wall, the boys thort I could git 'em through—an' bein's it made no odds to me *whar* they jined, so long as they *did* jine, I 'greed ter du hit. We put out ten days, yisterday—twelve on 'em, an' me—an' struck plumb fur Nashville. We lay close daytimes, 'case, though every hous'n ar Union, the kentry is swarmin' with Buckner's men, an' we know'd they'd let slide on us jest so soon as they could draw a bead. We got 'long right smart till we fotched the Roaring River, nigh onter Livingston. We'd 'quired, an' hedn't heerd uv ary rebs bein' round; so, foolhardy like, thet evenin' we tuk ter the road 'fore hit war clar dark. We hedn't gone more'n a mile till we come slap onter 'bout eighty Secesh calvary. We skedaddled fur the timber, powerful sudden; but they war over the fence an' on us, 'fore we got well under cover. 'Bout thirty on 'em slid thar nags, an' come at us in the brush. I seed twarn't no use runnin'; so I yelled out: 'Stand yer ground, boys, an' sell yer lives jest so high as ye kin!' Wall, we went at hit ter close quarters—hand ter hand, an' fut ter fut—an' ye'd better b'lieve thar war some tall fightin' thar fur 'bout ten minhits. Our boys fit like fien's—thet little chunk uv a feller thar," pointing to a slim, pale-faced youth, not more than seventeen, "laid out three on 'em. I'd done up two myself, when the Capt'n come onter me—but, I've telled ye 'bout him;" and drawing a long breath, he put the miniature back in his pocket. After a short pause he continued:—

"When they seed the Capt'n war done for, they fell back a piece—them as war left on 'em—ter the edge uv the timber, an' hollered fur 'tothers ter come on. Thet guv us time ter load up—we'd fit arter the fust fire wuth knives—an' we blazed inter 'em. Jest as we done hit, I heer'd some more calvary comin' up the road, an' I war jest tellin' the boys we'd hev ter make tracks, when the new fellers sprung the fence, an' come plumb at the Secesh on a dead run. Thar warn't only thirty on 'em, yit the rebs didn't so much as make a stand, but skedaddled as ef Old Rosey himself had been arter 'em."

"And who were the new comers?"

"Some on Tinker Beaty's men. They'd heerd the firin' nigh two mile off, an' come up suspicionin' how things wus."

"But, are there Union bands there? I thought East Tennessee was overrun with rebel troops."

"Wall, hit ar; but thar's a small chance uv Union goorillas in Fentress and Overton county. They hide in the mountins, an' light down on the rebs, now an' then, like death on a sick parson. Thar is places in them deestricts thet a hundred men kin hold agin ten thousand. They know 'em all, case they wus raised thar, an' they know every bridle-path through the woods, so its well nigh unpossible ter kotch 'em. I reckon thar's a hundred on 'em, all mounted, an' bein's as they hain't no tents, nor wagins, nor camp fixin's they git round mighty spry. Thar scouts is allers on the move, an' wharever thar's a showin', they pounce down on the rebs, cuttin' 'em ter pieces. Thet's the how they git powder an' provisions. They never trouble peaceable folk, an' haint no sort o' 'spense ter Guverment; but they does a heap uv damage ter the Secesh."

"Well, they did you a 'powerful' good turn."

"They did thet; but we lost one on our boys. He war only sixteen—brother ter thet feller thar," pointing to a young man sitting opposite. "They hung his father, an' now—they's killed him," and he drew a deep sigh.

"Why did they hang his father?"

"Wall, ye see, they kunscripted him—he war over age, but they don't mind thet—an' he desarted, meanin' ter git ter the Union lines. They kotched him in the woods, an' hung him right up ter a tree."

"Was only one of your men hurt?"

Yes, two on 'em wus wounded too bad ter come wuth us. The calvary toted 'em off ter the mountins, an' I reckon they'll jine 'em when they gits round. But we left elevin uv the rebs dead on the ground."

"Did your men kill so many? The cavalry had a hand in that, I suppose?"

"Yes, they killed two—thet's all. They couldn't git at 'em, they run so. We done the rest."

"You must have fought like tigers. How many were wounded?"

"Nary one; what wan't dead the boys finished."

"You don't mean to say that your men killed the wounded *after the fight?*"

"I reckon they did—some four on 'em."

"My friend, that's nothing but murder. I had hoped the rebels did all of that work."

"Wall, they does—anuff on hit; an' I never could bring my mind ter think it war right or human: but I s'pose thet's case I never hed a father hung, or a sister ravig'd, or a old mother shot down in har bed. Them things, you knows, makes a difference."

"And have any of your men suffered in such ways?"

"In sech ways? Thar haint one on 'em but kin tell you things 'ud turn yer blood ter ice. D'ye see thet feller thar?" pointing to a thin, sallow faced man, two seats in our rear.

"Not two months gone, some twenty rebs come ter his house while he war layin' out in the woods, an' toted his wife—as young an' purty a 'oman as yer own sister—off 'bout a mile, an' thar tuk thar will uv her—all on 'em! She made out ter crawl home, but it killed har. He warn't wuth har when she died, an' hit wus well he warn't, fur he'd hev gone clean crazy ef he hed been. He's mor'n half thet now—crazy fur blood! An' kin ye blame him? Kin ye 'spect a man thet's hed sech things done ter him ter show quarter? 'Taint in natur ter do hit. All these boys hes hed jest sich, an' things like hit; an' they go in ter kill or be kilt. They doan't ax no marcy, an' they doan't show none. Nigh twenty thousand on 'em is in Burnside's an' old Rosey's army, an' ye kin ax *them* if they doan't fight like devils. The iron has entered thar souls, Sir. They feel they's doin' God sarvice—an' they is—when they does fur a secesh. An' when this war ar over—ef it ever ar over—thar'll be sech a reckonin' wuth the rebs uv East Tennessee as creation never know'd on afore. Thar won't be one on 'em left this side uv hell!" This was said with a vehemence that startled me. His eyes actually blazed, and every line on his seamed face quivered with passion. To change the subject, I asked:

"And what did you do after the fight?"

"Not knowin' what moight happen, we swapped cloes with sech uv the rebs as hed gray 'uns, an' put North—plumb fur the mountins. Nigh onter Meigsville we come onter a Union man, who holped us ter cut some timber, an' make a raft—fur we 'lowed the Secesh would track us wuth houns, an' ter throw 'em off the scent we hed ter take ter the water. We got inter Obey's Fork, an' floated down ter the Cumberland; hidin' in the bushes in the day time, an' floatin' at night. We got nigh onter Carthage, an' knowin' the river wan't safe no longer, we left hit an' struck 'cross fur the railroad. Thet kentry ar full uv rebs, but hevin' the Secesh cloes on, we made out ter git 'nuff ter eat till we got yere."

We had crossed the Cumberland, and were then approaching Nashville. Its beautiful suburbs, though covered with the early foliage of spring, wore a most desolate appearance. Magnificent villas were heaps of ruins; splendid plantations and charming gardens were overrun with weeds. How fearfully have their owners expiated the mad crime of Secession! How have they sown the wind and reaped the whirlwind!

At the station-house we ran the gauntlet of another set of military officials. Passes were examined and luggage was looked into, but after a while the Colonel and I squeezed out of the crowd, and into an omnibus. "I go to the 'Commercial,'" he said to me. "I've tried the 'St. Cloud,' and I'm disposed to see if the other is quite so bad."

"Well, I'll go with you. I'm familiar with Southern hotels, and don't expect much."

If I *had* expected much, I should have been disappointed; for truth compels me to say—and I've been somewhat of a traveller and seen strange lodging-places in my time—that the "Commercial Hotel" of Nashville is the filthiest, buggiest house, public or private, I ever passed a night in. In any Northern town it would be indicted as a nuisance, calculated to breed pestilence and bad morals among the people. Biscuit, heavy as lead; steak, tough as leather; coffee, thick as mud; and corn-cake so saturated with smoke that all its original flavor had departed, was its unvarying bill of fare. No, not unvarying, for a small fee to the ebony waiter did procure me some strawberries, and for them I blessed him, and of them I made my supper.

Being fatigued with my journey, I asked, early in the evening, to be shown to a room, and a servant conducted me to a dingy apartment in the rear of the house, where I had full advantage of all the fumes and perfumes of the kitchen. Its dimensions were about eight feet by twelve, and its walls were smeared with soot and tobacco juice. The bare floor, which had never known a mop or a scrubbing-brush, was coated with a layer of soil thick enough to raise a crop of potatoes—but the bed, and the curtains, and the linen! (though, to be exactly truthful—it wasn't linen)—these I must leave to the reader's imagination, for no description would do them justice. Suffice it to say that after an hour's persistent effort, I did effect some improvement in them; and then, "wrapping the drapery of my couch" about me, I lay down, but not to "pleasant dreams;" for at that moment the darkies in the barber's shop below stairs struck up "de banjo an' de bones," and for two mortal hours I was forced to listen to all the Ethiopian songs, written and unwritten, in existence. In sheer desperation I finally rose, took a seat by the window, and to the intense delight of the sable melodists, joined in the refrains. To give the reader an idea of what I had to endure, and of what "public sentiment" among the darkies of Nashville may be supposed to be, I subjoin one of the songs, which I tried to take down in the dark:

"I'll sing you a song to suit de times,
Called bobbin around, around, around;
You'll see dar's reason in de rhymes,
As dey gwo bobbin' around.
Ole Rosey's down in Tennessee,
Bobbin' around, around, around;

An' settin' all de darkies free,
  As he gwo bobbin' around.

"He'm straddled on de big ole gray,
  Bobbin' around, around, around;
An' all Secesh—dey clar de way,
  As he gwo bobbin' around;
Dey yere de Union fife and drum,
  Bobbin' around, around, around;
An' know de judgment-day am come,
  Wen dey am bobbin' around.

"Ole massa see dat ole war hoss,
  Bobbin' around, around, around;
Says he: 'You Pomp—it all am loss,
  Fur Rosey's bobbin' around!'
He use to cut a mighty dash,
  Bobbin' around, around, around,
But den he tuk a brandy-smash,
  An' *did* gwo bobbin' around.

"He bob so bad dat down he fell,
  Bobbin' around, around, around;
An' neber riz dis side ob—well—
  Dis side—a bobbin' around.
He leff dis nig ahind to play,
  Bobbin' around, around, around;
I reckon he'll play it all de day,
  An' den—gwo bobbin' around.

"Come all you darkies jine de song,
  Bobbin' around, around, around,
You all am free—so gwo it strong,
  As you gwo bobbin' around.
De big Secesh no more will be
  Bobbin' around, around, around;
Fur Rosey's down in Tennessee,
  An' *he* am bobbin' around."

It was nearly eleven o'clock when the good-natured darkey who led the minstrels, put his head out of the window, and said to me: "Now, massa, we'll 'clude de ex'cises ob de evenin' by singin' Ole John Brown, wid de variations; and you'm 'spec'-fully 'vited to jine de chorus."

I did "jine de chorus," and therefore the reader is deprived of the "variations," which I might otherwise have committed to paper. However, if he is curious about them I can gratify him with others quite as good, for while I was in Tennessee I assisted at the martyrdom of "Ole John Brown" at least twenty times, and each time it was done with "variations."

Nothing, perhaps, so forcibly illustrates the progress of emancipation sentiment in the army, and among the people of Tennessee, as the wonderful popularity of that song. It is sung by every one, high and low, and everywhere its spirit is felt. Truly John Brown s "soul is a marching on!"

CHAPTER V.

THE NASHVILLE PRISON.

The next day was Sunday. I rose early, and going down to the office found my friend the Colonel already stirring. "Ah," he said, as I bade him "good-morning," "I'm in luck. An orderly has come in with my horse, and an ambulance goes out under an escort this morning. In half an hour I shall be off."

[Triune was distant only eighteen miles, but the road was infested with guerillas, and was unsafe for single travellers.]

"I am glad for that, on your account, but sorry on my own. I had reckoned on your aid in procuring access to my friends at the prison."

"You'll have no difficulty about that. Call on Colonel Martin at the Capitol; tell him who you are, and he'll give you a permit."

After breakfast, with mutual expressions of good-will we parted. I have formed many agreeable acquaintances while travelling, but never one more agreeable than the sturdy Indiana Colonel. He had a frank, glowing, genial nature that attracted me irresistibly to him, just as one is attracted to a warm wood fire on a winter evening. Indeed he is somehow associated in my mind with a generous wood fire—one of the glorious, old-fashioned kind; of oaken logs, piled high on a broad hearth, and giving out oxygen enough to supply a small village.

When he was gone, the landlord said to me, "If you don't know none of the military folk, Sir, you stand a sorry chance of gittin' inter the prison. Ye see, they karn't admit them as they don't know. 'Twouldn't do, nohow."

If that was true, I was in a dilemma. I had provided against such a contingency by taking with me, on leaving home, half a dozen introductory letters to Governor Johnson, but that gentleman was not in Nashville, and might not arrive for a week, therefore they were of no present value.

As I sat down to ponder over "the situation," I suddenly remembered having heard that the son of an old friend was an officer in a Tennessee regiment. "Landlord," I said, addressing the publican—(he told me he was also a Re-publican, but other trustworthy persons assured me that he was a rabid rebel. This I thought accounted for the filthy condition of his establishment). "Landlord," I said, "can you tell me where the —— Tennessee is stationed?"

"Here, Sir; 'bout two miles out—nigh to Fort Negley."

This was agreeable news, and writing a few lines to the young Tennesseean, in which I alluded to my long friendship with his father, and asked him "to come over and help" me. I despatched a messenger at once to the camp. In about an hour the negro returned, but with the unwelcome tidings that "de Cap'n am off, Sar; off scoutin' it, Sar, and dey doan't know *when* he'll be back, but dey reckon he'll come yere, d'recly he come, Sar; d'recly he come, Sar."

The morning was passing away while I was thus casting about for an escort, and at last I determined to do what I should have done at first—set out alone.

As I climbed the steep hill which leads to the Capitol, I was struck with the gloomy aspect of the silent, sombre houses, and the noiseless, deserted streets. It was a bright, summer-like day, and near the hour for morning service; but, with the exception of a solitary soldier, or a smartly-dressed darkey, sauntering idly along, no one was abroad. The white population had mostly fled, and the few that remained welcomed the "Northern intruders" with bolted doors and barred windows. I realized I was walking the streets of a conquered city. Arrived at the Capitol—an imposing pile of white marble, more spacious and beautiful than any similar edifice in the Northern States—I found myself under the walls of a huge fortress, frowning with cannon and encircled with breastworks. Its marble steps were flanked by stockades, and its broad battlements crowned with artillery, which, from its elevated position, commanded the entire town and surrounding suburbs. In the distance, the Casino and Forts Negley and Confiscation looked down from rocky elevations, and beyond them a broad belt of military camps engirdled the captive city. To my unpractised eye the defences seemed, as they no doubt are, impregnable, and with what emotions must they be contemplated by Nashville's tobacco lords, who skulking back from exile in Dixie, stand now and then on those neighboring hills, and look down on the homes their own mad treason has shut them out from forever.

Approaching the sentinel at the principal stairway, I said: "Will you tell me where to find Colonel Martin?"

"An shoore an' I 'will, Sir. Foller the grand hall till ye come forninst the Guv'ner's room—ye'll spy it over the dhoor, thin, say nothin' to nobody, but go straight in, Sir, an' ax fur the Cunnel, an' ye'll have him."

"Thank you. And pray, what brought you here—all the way from auld Ireland."

"Fath, yer honor, an' I come to fight—to fight for the naygur;" and he shrugged his shoulders, as if what he said might not be strictly true.

"You don't mean that."

"Troth, an' I does. I niver loiked the black divils—though them as is here hain't black, fur they's *yaller*—till I come out to fight fur 'em; but I've sort o' takin' to 'em since. An Irishman, ye knows, if he's niver a hapenny in his pocket, has allers a feller feelin' fur a poor divil as is poorer thin he is—an' sorry a bit of any thing in the world has the naygur. He don't own his own children, Sir; not avin the flesh on his bones."

"Your kindred, where I live, are not of your way of thinking."

"An' where may that be, yer honor?"

"In New York."

"Oh, yis, I know; they's all Dimocrats there, an' Fernandy Wud Dimocrats at that—bad luck to thim. If you'd loike to kinvart 'em, Sir, jest send 'em out here. I warrant ye they won't be four an' twenty 'oours in the State till they's Black Republicans—as black as the naygurs themselves. An Irishman's a heart in him, Sir, an', be gorry, he can't see the poor craytures wid his own eyes widout havin' a feller feelin' fur 'em."

"Well, good-by, and good luck to you."

"Good-by, an' good luck to yerself, yer honor;" and he called out as I passed up the stairway, "Go straight on, yer honor, an' say nothin' to nobody; but ax fur the Cunnel, an' ye'll find him, right forninst the Guv'ner's room, ye mind, its over the dhoor."

I found the "Governor's room," in blazing gilt, "over the dhoor," and entered the opposite apartment. I had less difficulty than I had anticipated in procuring access to the prison. The potent "open sesame" were certain names I carried in my pocket, and in less than half an hour I was on my way elate with the expectation of shortly seeing "my Southern friends."

The Nashville Penitentiary was burned at the taking of the city by the Union forces. The building now used as a State Prison is located about a mile outside of the city limits, and is of brick, surrounded by a high wall covering an area of perhaps two acres. It was built, as I learned from a marble slab imbedded in the wall over the doorway, in 1828, and looks substantial enough to last for a dozen centuries. As I approached its broad entrance-way, I saw at my right, in a spacious yard surrounded by a low stone fence, a hundred or more motley-uniformed Confederates, engaged in the favorite out-door occupations of their class, such as "seven-up," "quoits," "pitch and toss," and "chuck-a-luck." A sad-visaged man, dressed in seedy black, was pacing to and fro among them, now and then pausing to gaze abstractedly at the players, and again walking on, his eyes fixed on the distance, as if searching for some sign of "the good time" which every mortal thinks is "coming." To him, poor man, it is a long way off, for he will not go out, he says, until the South is independent. He was the political editor of *The Baptist Standard*, and refusing to take the oath of allegiance, has been confined there seven long months. A few more decently clad persons were in the assemblage, but much the larger portion were the most wretched specimens of "white trash" I had ever seen. In all sorts of habiliments—coatless, hatless, shoeless, with matted hair and dirt-incrusted faces, they seemed recently exhumed from some pig-sty or barn-yard. Love of "our native soil," with them, was evidently a living sentiment.

Passing on, I asked the guard at the doorway to call the keeper. That gentleman soon appeared, and I made known to him my business.

"No persons of those names are here, or have been here, Sir!"

And such is the vanity of human pursuits! I had travelled a thousand miles on a fruitless errand! Vexed and disappointed, I was turning away, when the keeper politely said:

"You look tired; won't you walk in and sit down?"

I followed him into the prison, and after I had rested a while he invited me to look through it. It is in two divisions, one devoted to criminals, the other to prisoners of war. None of the latter are confined in cells, but, during the day, are allowed to range freely over the yard and the several floors of the building. At night they are locked into roomy apartments, where often a dozen, and sometimes twenty, camp down together on straw mattresses spread on the floor. The sleeping accommodations are not much to boast of, but they are, no doubt, far superior to what the prisoners are accustomed to in Dixie. As we were passing over the second floor the keeper said to me:

"In the further room is the Colonel of the first Tennessee cavalry—Colonel Brewer, formerly a lawyer in this place. He was taken at Brentwood, some five weeks ago. He is a very sociable, gentlemanly man, and would be glad to see you. Will you go in?"

"No, thank you, I'll not intrude upon him."

"He'll consider it no intrusion. I'll ask him."

He rapped at the door and a voice called out, "Come in."

"Ah, Colonel, good-morning," said the keeper, stepping into the apartment. "I'm showing this gentleman over the building. He's right from the North, and I knew you'd like to see him."

"Most certainly I should. Ask him in."

As I entered, the prisoner measured me with a rapid glance; then, without rising, held out his hand, saying cordially, "I'm glad to see you, Sir; pray be seated. Mr. Keeper, be so good as to hand a chair."

"No, excuse me, Sir," I replied; "I'll not stay; I'll not intrude on you in your present circumstances."

"My present circumstances are the very reason you should, Sir. I see no one, except the sentinel, from one week to another. I've nothing to look at but these blank walls, and the 'human face divine' has grown wonderfully attractive to me. It's as pleasant as thoughts of home. So pray, sit down. I'll return the favor to the first one of your 'countrymen' who falls into my hands."

Thus entreated, I could not decline. As I took the proffered seat, I glanced around the apartment. It was spacious and well lighted by mullioned windows. Along its sides were ranged half a dozen camp beds; and as many chairs, and two small tables straggled about the floor. Its walls were not over-cleanly, but the floor was nicely sanded, and the whole had a tidy, comfortable appearance. It was evidently reserved for the better class of political prisoners. Its occupant was a man of about thirty-five, and of decidedly prepossessing appearance. He had a fine, intellectual face, and long brown hair, as soft and glossy as a woman's; but a full, dark eye, wide, strong jaws, and a firmly cut mouth, showed him possessed of a manly, determined character. I saw at a glance that he was no common man. He was dressed in the Confederate uniform, and as he lay on the outside of a cot, in a half-recumbent attitude, he every now and then moved uneasily, as if in pain. Seeing this I said:

"Are you wounded?"

"Yes; your boys gave me a pill when they captured me. The ball entered here," opening his shirt, and showing a large scar just below his heart. "The flesh has healed, but the ribs are not yet well knit together. It bothers me some to keep an easy position. But, tell me, what is your name, and where do you live?"

I told him.

"And do you know a gentleman of your name—let me see, what is his first name? ——, I think,"

"I can't say that I know him, though I ought to. I'm the man himself."

"*You* are!" and raising himself on his elbow he shook me again warmly by the hand. "I'm delighted to know you. I've heard Dick —— speak often of you."

"I know him well; we were intimate friends for twenty years."

"So he's told me. We've been all through the war together. He's a prince of a fellow. Davis has just made him a general. But he says you've turned Abolitionist."

"Not exactly that; but I go for putting you rebels down, and I think it can't be done without taking away your slaves."

"But you can't put us down," he replied, good-humoredly; "you'll have to crush our military power before you reach the darkies, and *you* ought to know you can't do that."

"I don't know it. It's a mere question of time and numbers; three against one are sure to conquer in the long run."

"When the three have brains; but, you see, your three haven't."

"I know your generals have thus far shown more ability than ours; but occasions are sure to develop men, though it may take time. How long was it before the English Revolution produced Cromwell, and the French, Napoleon?"

"A long time, I know. But generals are not what you want. You have them now. You have Rosecrans, and Banks, and Grant, and little Phil. Sherridan down there at Murfreesboro. Either of them is a match for any leader we have, and Rosecrans is head and shoulders above any general on this continent. *He* has a great, organizing, military mind. He checkmated Lee so handsomely in Western Virginia that Lee himself isn't ashamed to own it. If *we* had him we'd whip you in ninety days; but you shut him up, without supplies or horses, where he can do nothing, and where our cavalry can walk round him, as a clown walks round the pole at a circus. It is not generals you want. You want brains. You want an Administration."

"But we think we have one," I answered, laughing; "slow, it may be, but sure; and 'as honest as the times allow.'"

"Slow, it's true; but—honest! Talk of its being *honest*, with Stanton in it! a man as corrupt as sin, as venal as a Tombs lawyer! and as ignorant as a darkey. And you trust the management of a great war to him! But, it suits us exactly. It convinces me the Almighty means we shall be free."

"You never will be free. Your Government is a despotism already, and whatever may be said of ours, our liberties are safe with it."

"Liberties! There's an awful amount of cant about that word. Our people are as free as people should be. This idea of universal suffrage—making a small sovereign of every ignorant clodhopper who comes into the country, is played out. We've tried it under the old Government, and had enough of it. Republican institutions are a failure, and you'll be convinced of it before many years."

A two hours' conversation, ranging over these and kindred subjects, ensued between the Colonel and myself, and in the course of it he stated, that it is the purpose of the rebel leaders to found an elective monarchy, and that they had that design at the inception of the Rebellion. "I own no slaves," he said, "and am therefore not personally interested in sustaining the institution. I am fighting for something that I can leave to those after me—a title that can be perpetuated in my family; and I know, whether I live or die, I shall be successful; for, if I am killed, my country will do me justice in my children."

He spoke freely and openly of this. "I am willing," he said, "that all mankind should know it. The time has gone by when it was policy to conceal it from our poorer classes. We have them now where they *must* submit, and with the rest of the world—England, France, Spain, and even Russia, which now so cottons to the North—it will vastly help us."

He expressed the opinion that a rupture is imminent between England and the United States. "England, till now, has covertly played into our hands. She will soon throw off the mask, and do overt acts that will make war inevitable, if the Northern people have a spark of manhood or self-respect left."

If Vicksburg had not fallen—if Lee had not been defeated—if the Copperhead leaders had not been foiled in their attempt to force New York into the Rebellion, what the rebel Colonel predicted might, ere this, have proved true.

CHAPTER VI.

THE ARMY CHAPLAIN.

WALKING slowly back through the open fields, I came, at the distance of a short half mile from the prison, upon the white tents of a regiment of infantry. A few sentinels were pacing to and fro among them, but they were otherwise deserted. Near by, however, under the broad branches of a mammoth maple, the denizens of the canvas city were gathered around a spare, gray-haired, thin-visaged man, dressed in a stiff black stock, a check *neglige* shirt, and blue lower garments, who, in his shirt sleeves, was holding forth on the beauties of Freedom. Attracted by his earnest manner, and his rich, mellow voice, which rang out on the still air like the call of a bugle on the eve of battle, I joined the half-a-thousand martial auditors, who, seated on camp-stools, leaning on muskets, or lolling on the thick green grass which carpeted the ground, were drinking in his words as if they were the notes of an opera singer.

"I am tired and disgusted," he said, "with this endless talk about the everlasting negro. I doubt not he is a man, with very much such blood, and bones, and brains, and soul as we have. I doubt not his destiny is linked with ours—and that in the coming life many, very many of his sooty race will hold the highest seats in the synagogue, and look down on us as we now look down on them. But that is no reason why we should worship him—no reason why we should settle him comfortably in his master's easy chair, and let him idle away his life smoking bad tobacco and drinking mean whiskey, while we are fighting for his freedom. No, boys, give him freedom—every man, whatever his color, is entitled to that—but make him fight for it. Make him do what we have to do—work out our own salvation on hard tack and salt pork, with often not half enough of that. Tell him that John Brown *is* a marching on, but 'marching on' over Tennessee roads, with sore feet and weary legs, and the mud over his boots; and tell him, too, that the black man, if he would be free, must follow where John Brown leads. If he will not do this—give him Hail Columbia, and never let his ugly face be seen among you again.

"And those of you who worship the ebony idol, who in pity for the wrongs of the black forget that our own race has greater wrongs and deeper woes than his, let me tell you what is worthy of your worship—what all good and true men, in all times, have worshipped—what they have fought, and suffered, and died for, with songs on their lips and joy in their hearts—and then, if you persist in shutting your eyes to every thing in heaven and earth but the black man, you are past all hope, and —'may God have mercy on your souls.'

"What I would have you worship is Freedom—*white* Freedom—FREEDOM FOR ALL MEN. Poets have sung of it as a beautiful maiden, glowing as the dawn, radiant as the stars, smiling as the sun when he first looked on the earth. They have said that her throne is the glory of Heaven, her light the hope of the world; that her home is the bosom of God, her resting-place the hearts of men; that she has crowned the earth with beauty, and filled its dwellings with joy; that its fragrant fields waft her incense, and its gorgeous cities speak her praise; that on lowly cots and lofty mansions, on teeming workshops and hallowed temples, her name is written—written in letters that will outlast the marble, and grow in splendor forever. And this is true; but, I have seen her stripped of her glory—a wanderer and a fugitive in the earth. I have seen her fleeing from the haunts of men, and hiding away among the rocks and caves of the wilderness. I have seen her back scarred with lashes, and her limbs quivering with pain; her soul racked with anguish, and her body tortured with fire; I have seen her weeping like Rachel for her children—weeping amid the ruins of all she loved; and, worse than this, I have seen her fainting in her misery and grovelling in her shame, and I have heard her deny the God who made her and the heaven from which she came!

"And all this I have seen *here*—in this land, every inch of whose soil is wet with the blood our fathers shed to make it free!

"And shall this longer be? Shall we shut our eyes and steel our hearts to the woes of the white man, while we weep salt tears over the wrongs of the black? Shall we let this accursed race of men-stealers and women-whippers go free when the slave is liberated? Or, shall we say to them, take your foot from off the neck of the poor white, release *his soul* from its bondage—a bondage more galling than the fetters of the slave—give him the light of heaven and the knowledge of earth, and let his children know there is a God and a life to come. Shall we not say this? Shall we be men if we say less? What one of you will consent that this war shall end till the white man, as well as the black, be Free?"

And then the Chaplain descanted on the condition of the

poor white man and on the system and the men that have made him what he is; and for another half hour I listened to as odd a medley of slang and poetry, highfaluten and quaint eloquence, as ever fell from preacher's lips.

When a hymn was sung and a benediction said, I turned slowly away and resumed my walk towards the city. As I neared the camp I saw the Chaplain, still divested of his coat, approaching me at a brisk pace. As he came opposite, I instinctively touched my hat to him, and, returning the salutation, he said: "A pleasant evening, Sir."

"Very pleasant," I replied. "Let me thank you, Sir, for the very eloquent address I have just listened to."

"Let me thank *you*, Sir, for your flattering opinion of it. Not all, however, who praise my sermons, subscribe to my doctrines."

"I heard nothing to cavil at. You think the white trash more to be pitied than the black slaves, and that the slave-owner must be shorn of his power to give the poor man a chance to rise."

"I do; and that is reason enough for freeing the negro. The slaveholders more than the slave *system*, are the curse of this country; less than a hundred thousand of them have ruled it for fifty years."

"I know it. I gave that idea to the public more than a year ago."

"Did you? In what?"

I told him, and the announcement secured me a cordial grasp of his hand, a hearty "God bless you," and an urgent request to join him at dinner. Being curious to see more of so original a character, I accepted the invitation.

The Chaplain's "lodge" was at the further end of the encampment, and looked down a well-swept, gravelled avenue, which the soldiers had built between the two rows of canvas houses. It was much more spacious than those about it. Its roof was formed of two "shelter-tents," meeting together at the ridge, and its two gables were constructed of triangular pieces of coarse cotton cloth. One end and its two sides were covered with strips of weather-boarding, roughly nailed to short stakes, and showing, by the vestiges of paint which still adhered to them, that they had already done service on some of the dismantled dwellings in the vicinity. Two camp-cots, several amputated chairs, a small, unpainted pine table, two or three travelling trunks, and an old negro—to all appearance old enough to have been with his forefather, Ham, in the Ark—who lay fast asleep in one corner, composed the furniture of the interior.

Tendering me one of the broken-backed chairs, the Preacher touched the negro lightly with his foot, and said to him: "Wake up, Julius. Wake up." As the ancient African turned over and slowly opened his eyes, the Parson continued: "Come, old fellow, order dinner—dinner for three, and then give us a taste of whiskey-punch. D'ye hear?"

"Yas, yas, Massa, I yeres. I'll git 'em quicker no time. W'at a powerful sermon dat wus o'yourn, massa—powerful," replied the black, as, raising himself from the ground, first on one knee, and then on the other, and steadying himself by one of the camp-cots, he painfully clambered to his feet. When he had reached his highest altitude he might have been four feet and ten inches from the enormous brogans which formed his base of operations; but if nature had denied him height, she had, true to her system of "compensation," given him breadth and thickness. He certainly measured four feet around the hips, and across the chest—on his back was a protuberance as large as a bushel basket—some unknown quantity I did not even guess at. With his low stature, his hump-back, his white, frizzled locks, and his short, bandy legs, which bowed in like a cow's horns, he might have been taken for Richard III., risen from Bosworth field, and, in his old age, turned negro preacher.

"Yes, powerful," rejoined the parson, "but mighty little *you* heard of it. You were fast asleep the whole time."

"Well, Massa, but I yeard it. Dis pore ole body wus a sleepin' down dar, but de sperrit soared 'way ter you—it did Massa; it yeard ebery word—ebery word."

"What was the text?"

"I does'nt zactly 'member, Massa Parson," rejoined the black, manipulating his wool in the manner peculiar to his race; "I does'nt *zactly* 'member, but I tinks it wus suffin' loike de Lord am good ter all dat lub Him. *Suffin'* loike dat, Massa."

"No, you old sinner, it wasn't any thing like it—It was: 'Without are dogs and sorcerers, and whosoever loveth and maketh a lie.' And that's where you'll get, old man, if you don't give up your everlasting lying. But come, stir your stumps. Order dinner and get the whiskey."

The old black rolled himself off. When he was out of hearing, I said to the Parson: "You chose your body-servant for his beauty, I suppose."

"No, I didn't. I chose him for his piety. There is more of the spirit of Christ in that old darky than I ever knew in a human being. I'll bet my best sermon against a glass of whiskey that he'll be in heaven a thousand years before any white man living."

"That's great odds," I replied, laughing; "but he *will* lie."

"That isn't his fault. It's one of the effects of Slavery. Slavery has forced him to be a cringing sycophant all his life, and he can't throw off the habit all at once. Habits are like mosses growing to a tree—they must be loosened gently, gradually; if you strip them off violently, you kill the tree."

"But somehow, I've always associated a comely form with a beautiful soul. How can such goodness dwell in such a body as his?"

"It is not the body that expresses the soul—it is the face. Look at his, and tell me if you do not see heaven reflected in it. I have watched it for hours as he has sat there on the ground, his body bent double, his eyes closed, and his chin resting on his knees; and I have fancied that his spirit was really away among the green fields and the pleasant streams that lie on the other side of Jordan. I have no doubt it was."

We were here interrupted by the entrance of a tall young man in a captain's uniform, whom the Parson introduced to me as his messmate. "You see," said he, "in union there is *comfort* as well as strength. The Captain and I have put our tents together, and thus made quite a cosey nest here."

"You have—a *very* cosey one. I think a little experience of this sort of life would so enamor me of it that I should be reluctant to go back to gas and conventionalism."

"It would; I came out here at the prompting of duty—to be a martyr for truth and the Union. But, bless your soul! I've found martyrdom so very pleasant that I'm willing to suffer it every day I live. This sort is pleasanter, with salt pork and cold weather, than the kind John Rogers took with a hot steak (stake) and a roaring fire. Do you know I think man was meant for the savage state!"

"You mean for the green fields, the open air, the breezy woods, and Freedom."

"Yes, you've hit it; you speak like a poet and a philosopher to boot. But, come, try some of this old saint's punch. Let me see—what do you call it, Julius?"

This was addressed to the negro, who had just then entered, bearing a mammoth tray, made of a piece of pine plank, hollowed in the centre, and curiously ornamented at the edges with a variety of grotesque carvings, executed with a jack-knife. On it was a steaming tankard of whiskey-punch, and four (the darky had evidently thought of himself) tin goblets of decidedly plebeian appearance.

Placing them on the small table which he drew up before us, the old negro grinningly replied: "De 'lixer ob de gods, Massa."

"The 'lixer' of the devil?" exclaimed the Captain, laughing: "Why, you old fool, you don't suppose the gods drink whiskey-toddy, do you?"

"Ob course dey does, massa Cap'n: doan't dey hab eberyting whot's good in heaben? an' haint whiskey-toddy, sech as ole Jule make, jess 'bout de best ting you knows on—now, haint it, massa Cap'n?"

"Yes, it is, Jule. And now fill up, old boy—one for yourself—and let us drink to the day when we shall all drink toddy together in heaven."

We all rose and solemnly drained the cups. When they were replaced on the table, the parson remarked:

"There is nothing so unreasonable in Jule's theory as may at first appear. Not that I suppose they drink whiskey-punch in heaven, but the connection between the spirit and the body is so intimate that I can easily conceive of our earthly appetites clinging to us after the soul has thrown off its grosser covering. In that, and in the impossibility of gratifying their depraved longings, much of the torment of bad men in the future life may consist."

Amused at the oddity of the idea, I replied: "Undoubtedly it may, and I'll give you a fact that supports the theory completely. It was given to me by a distinguished gentleman—a Spiritualist. He says that an eminent lawyer—his intimate friend, and an inveterate tobacco chewer—died and came to him about an hour afterwards. They had a long conversation together, and in the course of it he asked the lawyer what his strongest desire was when he first awoke to consciousness in the other life. 'I wanted a chew of tobacco like the devil,' was the lawyer's reply."

At this the Captain broke into a boisterous fit of laughter, in which even the sable saint joined. As soon as he could speak, the officer exclaimed: "He's into you, Parson; you must look out—our friend is a bit of a wag."

"But it'm de trufh, Massa Cap'n," earnestly chimed in the negro, who had seated himself on the ground, and was busily nursing his calves and stroking his knees with his chin. It'm de trufh—haint I *seed* dem dark, bad sperrets, hangin' round doggeries, an' dem low places whar de Secesh hab dar shindies, jess ter git a *smell*—on'y a little *smell* ob dat ar mis'able stuff dey call Knock-em-stiff. An' dat haint no sech stuff as dis, Massa Cap'n; taint no sech stuff as dis, I shores you," and raising his mug, which he had slyly filled again, he drained it to the bottom.

"Shut up, Jule, *you* don't know any thing about such big gentlemen," exclaimed the Captain.

"I don't know nuffin 'bout any *gemmen* whot chaws 'backer," rejoined the darky—who seemed to be a privileged character —"but I knows lots o' cap'ns whot does it, and does it so bad dat I'se afeared dey'll neber git ober it, neber."

"Captain," exclaimed the Parson, laughing heartily, "I've told you Jule is too smart for *you*. But come, old fellow, hurry up that dinner—I'm as hungry as a bear."

The negro slowly picked himself up and waddled out of the tent.

"That darky is no fool," I remarked, when he had gone.

"No, he is as smart as any white man I ever knew. He's of good stock. Though dwarfed and misshapen, he has every mark of good blood about him," replied the Chaplain.

"What do you mean by 'good blood?' he's as black as midnight."

"I mean he has a fine physical organization—as fine as a white man's. The souls of all men, I take it, are essentially alike. Men differ only in organization. On a fine organization the spirit acts more perfectly than on a coarse one. No player can get as good music from a poor piano as from a good one. This accounts for the inequality of mental development we see among men and races of men, and the same difference that exists among the white races, exists among the black. Jule is one of the superior grade."

"I never heard that theory stated before," I replied; "but I have observed that the negro with cucumber-shaped shin, baboon head and face, stooping shoulder and long heel, *is* inferior —greatly so—to the one (however black he may be) of erect and well-formed body, straight shin, and finely developed brain. I have known many of these last that I have thought equal in mental and moral power to the better class of white men."

"*Equal* in mental and *superior* in moral power," said the Parson. "It is useless for us to deny it; the better races of negroes are more receptive of good influences, more familiar with the inmost experiences of faith, and hope, and trust; more suitably organized to be the temples of the Holy Spirit than our own race. They live close to God, are truly His children; their whole souls go out to Him in prayer and worship, and some of them carry a halo always about them, as if they daily saw 'the glory of God, and Jesus standing at His right hand.'"

"Yes, but is not some of this religious exaltation owing to their condition? They cling to Christ because he is their *all* —they have literally nothing else."

"No, I think not. It is the result of organization. Day and Martin will, without doubt, be at a premium on the 'other side of Jordan.' If St. Peter ever lets me in, I reckon it will be because I shall hold on mighty hard to the coat-tail of some old black saint, like Julius here. Eh, Jule?"

"I reckons not, Massa Parson," replied the negro, who had re-entered, and was loading the small table with eatables. "I reckons *you* kin git in fru dat ar gate wid you' own legs and de grace ob God. But ef you can't—ef ole Peter make any 'jection—Jule 'll take you up ahind; you kin git up *dar* (touching the huge hump on his back) an' ride slap inter glory like's ef you wus drivin' you' own six hoss kerridge—you kin, Massa Parson—you may 'pend on dat."

A laugh followed, and in the midst of it we sat down to dinner. It consisted of boiled ham, salt pork, corn bread, buttermilk, and strawberries, and on such fare, seasoned as it was with hunger, exercise, and pleasant conversation, I made a most hearty meal.

"You belabored negro worshippers, in your sermon," I said to the parson after a time; "but it strikes me you're something of one yourself."

"Not a bit of one," he replied; "I can see his good qualities, but I give the negro precious little love or worship; the poor white man has all my sympathy, and he needs it more than the black."

"I know he is lower in intellect and morals than the negro."

"Far lower. The slaveocrats have enslaved his mind as they have the other's body. His degradation is almost past belief. The other day, I was strolling out a little way beyond our lines, and came upon a young woman sitting in the doorway of a mean hovel. She was as beautiful as Eve before she fell—as beautiful as I imagine the angels are who bear parted souls to Heaven. She had long, auburn hair, which fell over her neck like a veil of golden gauze, soft, liquid brown eyes, and features that sculptors chisel for the world to look at. Raphael had a dim vision of such a face, and made it immortal in the Madonna. She sat with her bare legs braced against the door-jamb, and a little higher than her head; and the coarse cottonade gown she wore disclosed the handsomest foot, ankle, and—shall I say it, Captain?" and he paused abruptly, and turned to that gentleman.

"Oh, yes; say it; never mind me," rejoined the Captain, with mock gravity.

"Well then, the handsomest foot, ankle and *knee*, that can be found in Tennessee."

"The Parson's a judge of beauty, Sir," said the Captain. "In women and horses he's a perfect connoisseur. He adores a handsome form, but a pretty leg enraptures him."

"And why shouldn't it? Woman is the most beautiful thing in creation, and a pretty leg is a womanly feature—but we'll not discuss that. As I approached this half-clad beauty she took an old tobacco pipe, blacker than the ace of spades, from her mouth, and said to me: 'Stranger, howdy'ge? Ye haint got no 'backer 'bout ye, hes ye?'

"I pleasantly told her I did not use tobacco, when she put one of her pretty feet to the ground (there was no floor to the cabin), and yelled out: 'Then gwo to——,' the hot place the Captain occasionally alludes to—'we haint no use for no sich old saints as ye is, round yere!' I travelled off at double-quick, I assure you, but I cursed in my heart the men and the system that had reduced so lovely a specimen of my race and blood to such degradation."

"But they are not all so degraded," said the Captain. "When I was a prisoner last fall, I saw a good deal of them, and one of them aided me to escape. He fought like a hero at Stone River, and is now by far the best man in my company."

"Come, Captain; tell our friend your adventures with Tom in Secessia," said the Parson.

The Captain assented, and his story will be found in the next chapter.

CHAPTER VII.

THE CAPTAIN'S STORY.

"It is not much of a story," said the captain, drawing his chair away from the table and lighting a huge cigar; "and, besides, I haven't the parson's handy way of dressing up a common incident so as to make it fit for good society; but such as it is, it is true."

"But, Captain, as it's Sunday," said the preacher, smiling, "suppose you leave out some of your favorite ornamental phrases; truth unadorned, you know, is adorned the most."

"Yes; but if you strip it stark naked you shock modest people. Why, Sir, if I used as many oaths in my talk as the parson does in his sermons, I should expect the earth to open and swallow me, as in ancient times it did that old secessionist, Korah."

"Come, come, you'll make your story like the parsonage my folks in Illinois built for me—all porch and front-door. Get into it, and be brief; for life is short—and I want Mr. —— to hear some of Jule's psalm-singing before he goes."

The captain handed me a cigar, took a long whiff from his own, and without noticing the preacher's remark, began his story:

"It was after the great foot-race between Bragg and Buell, when old 'Slow-coach' won the stakes—two States and—a court-martial; and we soldiers immortalized ourselves by using our legs instead of our muskets. I was stationed at Gallatin in defence of the railway, and, being short of fodder, took a squad of a dozen men one day, and went out on a foraging expedition. I had sent six or seven wagon loads back to camp, and, with the remaining wagons, was scouring the district around Hartsville, when, just after we had set our pickets for the night, about two hundred of Forrest's cavalry came suddenly on us, and surrounded and made us prisoners before we had even time to run. A small party took us in charge, and striking a course due east, made for the Knoxville Railroad. Nothing worth mention occurred during the first two days. At the close of the second we reached a small village called Crossville—consisting of two houses, a barn, and a nigger shanty—just in the edge of Bledsoe County, and halted for the night. We took supper at the house of a well-to-do planter, of the name of Boylan, who gave us a good meal, and was very courteous to the Confederate officer, but, in my presence, cursed and swore at the Union, and the 'Linkum hirelin's,' hard enough to have shocked—the parson. The lieutenant, who was a social fellow and a gentleman, pressed me to share his bed at the house, but I declined, asserting—not very mildly—that I wouldn't sleep under the roof of such an old reprobate as the planter. The Rebel officer appreciated my feeling, and lending me an extra blanket—for the night was cold—consented to my camping out with my men—which meant sleeping in a corn-field, on the ploughed ground, with the sky for a bedquilt. The boys had made a rousing fire of pine-knots, and were eating their suppers near it when I joined them. Spreading a blanket on the ground, and seating myself before the roaring blaze, I lit my last cigar, and fell to studying 'Ayer's

Cherry Pectoral Almanac,' a copy of which delightful work had somehow lodged in the pocket of my overcoat. I was pondering its astrological predictions, when a long, loose-jointed native came up to me, and said:

"Wall, stranger, yer takin' it powerful cool, bein's yer in a purty clus fix."

"Not a very *close* fix," I answered; "there's lots of room round here."

"Yas, lots uv it; but ye hain't the run o' the ground—though I 'spect ye would run ef ye hed the chance."

"I *reckon* I would."

"Whot's thet yer readin' thar?"

"An almanac."

"Almynac! Whot's thet?"

"A book that tells all about the weather; when it will rain and when it won't. A man that carries one doesn't need an umbrella."

"An' do it tell when it wull be fa'r fur shootin' snipe an' kotchin eels?"

"Oh yes, it tells all that, and when husbands may 'look out for squalls.' If you've a wife you ought to have one."

"I hain't morrid. Number one ar' bout so much as I kin find in vittles. But thet mus' be a monstrus nice book; ef I could spell, I'd spill a quart o' humin grease ter git one."

"'T would be worth that; but here, I'll give you this. You can learn to 'spell' it somehow."

"With a look of stupid surprise he took the almanac, but in a moment handed it back, saying, 'I doan't mean ter 'pose on ye, stranger, beca'se yer kotched in the tedders (tethers). I hain't no sech sort o' man, no how."

"You'll not impose on me; you're welcome to it. Make your preacher learn you how to read it."

"Lord bless ye, the parson doan't know how no more'n I does. Ye see we hain't no schules round yere; an' ef we hed, pore men karn't pay no fifty dollar a yar ter guv thar childerings larnin'. Dad an' I, 'fore them dinged Fed'rate rags got so thick in the kentry, nuver seed five dollar' from un' yar eend ter 'tother. But, I say, wouldn't *ye* larn me?"

"Yes, I'd be glad to; but I go off in the morning."

"But, 'spose we gwoed off tergedder," and he sunk his voice to a whisper; "ter night—fru the bush—up thar—plumb ter Nashville."

I looked steadily at him. There was truth in his face, and in a low tone I asked: "To the death?"

"Ter the death, stranger," and he gave me his hand; "I'll draw a jug uv knock-em-stiff on the soger, an' ye kin mosey off 'fore the moon ar up. The boss 'll holp us."

"Who is the 'boss?'"

"The old man thar," pointing to the house.

"Why, he's a red-hot Rebel."

"Ha! ha! He do come the Rebel powerful strong, but thet's put on. He'd guv the dingnation consarn a doze of collermy an' jollerp thet would clean out thar hull innards, ef he could; but he durn't do it open. He's afeard o' pullin' hemp, an' kingdom come. Now, ef whot's said 'bout the kingdom ar true, I'd a durned sight ruther take my chance thar, nur yere; fur, *yere* ye see, a pore man haint no sort o' showin'; put *thar* he'll hev a right smart chance uv gittin' to be somebody."

"No doubt he will. All the promises of the Bible are to the poor man." (That wasn't original; I had it from the parson.)

He then went to the planter's house, and returned in a short time with a gallon jug of whiskey. Coming directly to me, he said in a loud tone; " I say, Leftenant " (I wore only one bar on my shoulder-straps then), " take a swig ter warm yer innards."

As I poured out the liquor, he whispered:

"The old un' say ye mus' put plumb fur the branch; it'r 'bout half a mile frum yere—measured with a coonskin, an' the tail throw'd in. Foller it up 'bout as fur—the water's low, an' ye mus' gwo inter it, case they moight git the dogs onter yer trail—an' ye'll come to a dade tree whot bends over the run. It's holler, an' ye kin git inter it an stay thar agin I come, as snug as a bar in a snow-bank. I'll prime the guard with knock-em-stiff—ye be along—an' when I shouts ' Glory, glory,' twice, as ef the raal camp-meetin' power war on me, ye put fur the bushes on yer han's an' feet, like a wurrum; an' when ye gits thar, pike off like lightnin' chasin' a whirlygust" (hurricane).

"I understand; but be cool and steady."

"Cool? I'll be cooler nur Parson Plewit when death jerked him; an' they say he war so cool he fruz the whole grave-yard so tight they hed ter thaw it out with light'ood."

Our camp was guarded by about a dozen sentinels, who relieved each other every six hours. The one whose station was nearest the bushes that lined the northern side of the corn-field, had built a fire of pine-knots, and every now and then halted before it as he walked to and fro on his round. My way of escape lay through those bushes, and to enable me to reach them unobserved my new friend would have to engage this sentry at the fire long enough to " prime" him so " tight" that he would be oblivious to my movements. This seemed no ordinary undertaking, for, aside from the difficulty of luring him from his duty on the beat, the sentinel was a tough, raw-boned Kentuckian, who looked whiskey-proof, and capable of "totein' a peck of licker." But no time could be lost. It was already nine o'clock, and guard would be relieved at twelve; so the native set himself at once about his spiritual labors.

Approaching the fellow, jug in hand, he asked him to drink, and in an incredibly short time had so worked on his affection for knock-em-stiff, that the Kentuckian was seated cosily hobnobbing with him on a log before the fire. A greasy pack of cards was soon brought out, and they went into euchre, seven-up, and high-low-jack, every now and then relieving the card-playing with a horn, and one of the toughest yarns that mortal man ever listened to. For a long time it seemed doubtful which would conquer in this keen encounter of wits, for though Long Tom—that is the name he goes by—is an incorrigible wag, and "immense" at telling a story, the Kentuckian was no green hand at the business. They each seemed to own a patent for lying, and to be running their inventive machines with no regard to probability, credibility, or possibility. At last, when Tom had told of killing a "sarpunt" whose body was as large round as a "whiskey-kag," and stretched across a bridge thirty feet wide, with "ten foot lappin' onter the road," the Kentuckian shook his head, and rather sadly exclaimed: "Jewhitiker! Thet war the most oncommonest, rantankerous snake I uver yered on. I guv it up."

"Ye mought as well," said Tom, with infinite composure, "fur he *war* a most outdacious sarpunt."

But all this time little progress had been made in getting the sentinel boozy. Mug after mug of clear "blue ruin" had gone down his throat (and Tom's shirt-collar), with no more apparent effect on him than if his stomach had been of cast-iron. At last twelve o'clock came, and with it the relief-guard. When I saw him—another tough, raw-boned Kentuckian—approach, hope fled, and a heavier feeling came, at my heart than was ever there before. I had caught a glimpse of liberty, and captivity seemed the drearier for it. However, hiding my disappointment, I turned to go to where the boys were sleeping, when Tom shouted out:

"Mr. Leftenant, doan't ye be a moseyin' off, we'se the hull night afore us. The world warn't made in one day; it tuck six. I'll git some more licker, an' make ye *as snug as a bar in a snow-bank*, yit."

Giving the last of its contents to the new-comer, he then took the jug under his arm and "moseyed off" to the house, while the relieved sentry again quietly seated himself on the log. The latter evidently meant to levy on the fresh supply of "sperrets," and I saw with consternation that my undaunted friend would have to perform the almost impossible exploit of "flooring" two "double-lined," "fire-proof," Kentucky "whiskey-swillers" at once.

Tom soon reappeared with the jug and three extra mugs—the previous drinking had been done from one—and filling them to the brim, said, looking very hard at me: "Now, let me guv ye a toast. Yere's ter Jeff. Davis, an' may he live so long as the Lord'll let him."

"I can't drink to that," I said, setting down my mug.

"No more'n ye karn't, Leftenant! I nuver thort o' thet, so no 'fence. But, bein's the toast's out, 'spose *ye* drink ter the next."

I took his meaning at once. He had drugged the liquor.

The cards were again brought out, but what "knock-em-stiff" could not do, laudanum soon began to accomplish. The new-comer was the first to show its effects. He played somewhat wildly for a time, then, swaying unsteadily on the log, rolled heavily off to the ground. The other kept his seat a while longer, but when Tom, plying him with a second "swig," swung his mug around his head and cried, "Glory! glory!" he followed his "departed friend," and sunk into a sleep that "knows no waking" for a half dozen hours.

Giving me a strong grasp of the hand, the native pointed to the bushes. Wrapping the blankets about me (the lieutenant's, I confiscated), and taking a last look at the boys—it came awful hard to leave them—I lowered myself on my hands and knees, and crawled to the fence. I reached it without detection, and soon arrived at the branch, up which I waded, as directed by the native.

The moon was just rising when I came upon the hollow tree, and I had no difficulty in finding its opening. Its interior was fully eight feet in diameter, the trunk being a mere shell, and was covered with a thick flooring of decayed wood. On this I spread one of the blankets, and wrapping myself in the other, lay down to rest. The excitement of the escape, and the long ride of the previous day, had so fatigued me that I soon sank into a deep slumber. How long I slept I do not know, but when I awoke the day was "about an hour by sun," and a small army of men and dogs were howling outside of my retreat, as if a legion of infernal devils had been let loose about me.

"I tell you he has waded either up or down the run," said a voice I recognized at once as that of the Rebel lieutenant; "the dogs don't track him over there. He must have hid somewhere near the stream."

"Lord bless ye, Leftenant, them dogs hain't wuth a tetocious d—n. They nuver nosed nuthin more'n thar dinners. A man as wus pikein fur the Union lines, 'ud run streter nur a scared wolf. I'd plank salvation agin a jack-knife thet his legs is a dancin' a hurricane up thar, on Jim Potter's deadnin' (clearing) beyont the mounting, at this pertic'lur minnet."

I held my breath in torture. I have heard a thousand bullets whistling about me without feeling the agony of suspense I endured during the next five minutes. Soon, however, the voices died away, and before many hours I heard the faint baying of the hounds miles off upon the "mounting." Tom had saved me!

When the danger was over I lay down, and, overcome with the excitement, again fell asleep. It was dark when my shoulder was touched lightly, and Tom whispered in my ear: "It ar time ter be a moseyin' off, Leftenant. H—ll mought be tall lodgin's ef the fire war out, but it ar too hot fur us jest now."

I rose, and partaking of a hearty meal and fortifying myself with a liberal glass of brandy—the planter had furnished us with a gallon jug of genuine "Otard,"—sallied from my place of concealment. We struck directly for a wood, half a mile distant, and worked our toilsome way over rocks and through underbrush and laurel bushes all the night. In the morning we lay down by the side of a fallen tree and went to sleep. Tom had brought provisions enough to last for two or three days, by which time he hoped we should be clear of the neighborhood in which he was known, and where the danger of detection was greatest. Travelling by the woods, however, was slow, and if we kept to them, our supplies would be exhausted before we reached the safer district of country. That night, therefore, we took to the high road. We walked till the sun rose without meeting any one, and then "camped out" in the bushes. For two more days and nights we did the same, and then had arrived within twenty miles of Nashville. Our provisions having then given out, Tom, in the small hours of the morning, made a descent on a planter's smoke-house and supplied our larder with two enormous hams. As he threw them into the thicket where I lay, he said to me:

"Won't them infernal nigs kotch it fur stealin' these critters. It'll sarve 'em right; they orten't ter b'long ter no such durned hide-bound secesh."

"How do you know he is a secessionist?"

"By the taste o' the bacon. Ye nuver know'd no sech hog's-flesh as thet ter be curn by a honest Union man. Why, it'r strong 'nuff ter knock ye down, an' tough—it'r tougher nur the yarns dad used ter tell us boys uv cold nights, in the old shanty on the dead'nin'."

In the impatience of his hunger he had cut a slice from one of the hams with his jack-knife, and eaten it raw on his way to "camp." A fire would have betrayed us, so I drew out my knife, and followed his example. The meat *was* rather rancid and very tough, but I never before tasted any thing half so palatable. Hunger is a wonderful condiment. It has made me think a sirloin of mule superior to the finest steak ever broiled.

We lay close through the following day, but the next evening, before the sun was well down—we were within twenty miles of *freedom*, and impatient to get to it—carrying the hams under our arms, we resumed our journey. We took to the highroad, but had not proceeded a mile before we met six men coming briskly towards us. One was dressed as a Confederate sergeant, and had a gun on his shoulder; the others wore the ordinary homespun of the district, and, having no arms, seemed fresh recruits. Avoiding them was out of the question, so, cocking our pistols in our pockets (Tom had confiscated the revolvers of the two sentinels while they lay senseless on the ground), we went boldly forward. They eyed my uniform very closely, but merely saying, "Good evenin'," passed us quietly. They had not gone two hundred yards, however, before I heard the report of a musket, and felt a sharp, burning sensation in my right side, near the shoulder. The infernal sergeant had shot me! His ball entered at my back, and, making a half circle, lodged on my breast-bone.

Tom turned like an aroused panther, and sprang down the road after them, firing his revolver as he ran. He overtook one, and brained him with his pistol-stock, but the rest escaped. In the mean time I was bleeding profusely. I took out my handkerchief and attempted to staunch the blood, but could not. I sat down on a stone by the road-side, and tried to look death in the face, but somehow death wouldn't be looked in the face. I was bleeding at a rate that in a few hours would drain every drop of blood from my body, but I could not realize that I was to die—then—there—only twenty miles from FREEDOM!

Tom, returning in a few minutes, said to me:

"Them fellers wull raise the deestrict, Leftenant, an' all Secesh wull be arter us in no time. We mus' take ter the woods, and feed on hope an' tough ham till the whirlygust ar over."

"Tom," I said, "I'm badly hurt; too badly, I fear, to go any further. You take care of yourself. You can escape; leave me here; they'll take me prisoner, but it will be my best chance to get at a doctor."

"Hurt! Blisters and blamenation, so ye is!" he exclaimed, tearing open my coat, and examining the wound. "Quick, Leftenant! guv me yer wiper—I hain't nary one, I allers does thet bizness the nat'ral way. We must stop thet ter onst—ter onst."

Taking my handkerchief, he saturated it with the brandy, and bound it tightly about my side. Then, squatting on his hands and knees, he said: "Git up thar, back uppermos', and lay flat as a fritter. It'll holp the bleedin'."

I submitted myself quietly to him, and in a moment he was coursing over the open ground which lay between the road and the thick belting of woods we had recently left, with a gait as firm and easy, and almost as fast, as that of my mare Bess. As he went along, he every now and then broke out with some exclamation like the following: "Whot d—n tetocious villuns ter hit a man in the back. D—n 'um! They wus borned in tophet, an' they'll git thar agin, yit. I'll holp 'em on the way. I wull! Leave ye, Leftenant? Ye doan't 'spose Tom's a secesh? a dinged, rottin-souled, blue-blasted, son uv a Rebel, does ye? No! He's wuth ye, Leftenant—ter the death—TER THE DEATH. Didn't he say it, an' d'ye uver know' Tom ter guv his word an' broke it." Then, as he paused to draw breath, he added: "Yer more'n a y'arlin' baby, but nuver ye fear; I hain't gin out; I kin outrun creation yit, an' guv it two mile the start."

And I think he could have done so, for in an incredibly short time he set me down at our camping-ground of the previous night. Gathering some dried leaves for a mattress, and covering me with a blanket, he looked again at my wound. The bleeding had sensibly diminished, and, when more brandy had been applied, and I had rested a while in a horizontal position, it ceased altogether. When he was satisfied I was out of immediate danger, he said to me:

"I leff thet ar bacon an' the 'tother blankets 'side the road, an' I mus' git 'em, Leftenant, or we's gone up. I couldn't gwo it twice ter one smoke-house—the old coon'll be watchin' on it ter night."

"But wait till it's fully dark. It won't be safe to go now."

"Safe now as uver; an' 'sides, I'se afeard o' the dogs. Ef the varmunts shud nose them traps, we might as wull say our pray'rs ter onst. An' bein's thar hain't more'n 'un chance in a thousan' uv thar not hev'n done it, s'pose ye be gittin' a pray'r a'ready, Leftenant—a right smart long 'un, thet'll do for both on us, fur I's 'mazin pore at thet sort o' bizness."

"But, Tom, if we're in such danger—go; secure your own safety while there's time. You can do no more for me; so—go, at once."

"Gwo, Leftenant? Tom nuver flinched, or showed his back ter a friend. Ef the thing ar up with us, we'll see it out tergedder, loike men. I hain't no way purticler 'bout gwine ter kingdom-come jest yit, bein's I'd loike ter guv them ar rantankerous rebels a leetle h—ll fust, but—ef my time ar come; ef the Lord's callin' fur me, as the parsons say—why, I'm a'ready; an' I know He wont ax me in ter the rare door, fur, though I'se pore, an' ign'rant, an' no sort o' 'count ter nary one in all creation, He knows I nuver hed no showin'—thet's I'se done the best I could."

As he said this his voice was as low and soft as a woman's, with an inexpressible sadness in it which brought the tears to my eyes. I grasped his two hands, as I replied:

"God bless you, my *friend!* You're the noblest man I

ever knew. If I die, my last breath shall be a prayer for you."

He made no reply, but, turning away, dashed off through the bushes.

His voice choking with emotion, the captain paused at this point in his narrative, and the parson remarked:

"He is a noble fellow, Mr. ——, and I don't wonder at the captain's attachment to him; but Tom's affection for the captain is something not often seen in this work-day world. I believe no mortal ever felt such devotion for another as he feels for him."

"Oh yas, dey hab, Massa Parson; *I*'se seed it;" exclaimed the old black, who had resumed his seat on the ground; "My young massa, he got morrid, an' de fuss munfh he feel like he'd eat his wife up; but de second munfh—he wish ter de Lord he hed."

"Speak when you're spoken to, Jule;" said the parson, restraining his inclination to laugh, and trying to look stern.

"And give me a mug of whiskey toddy, you old joker," added the captain, laughing heartily.

"Dar hain't anudder drap, Massa Cap'n," replied the negro, with a demure face. "You's drunk ebery drap, ebery bressed drap, Massa Cap'n."

"I have had but two mugs, you old toper. You have drunk it yourself. How much have you had?"

"Not more'n six, Massa Cap'n; an' dat hain't nuffin ob sech stuff as dis; you knows dat, Massa Cap'n."

"No, not for *you*: but get some more at once. This black Christian," he added, turning to me, "can stand liquor enough to float a ship."

"But he's not to blame for the habit," I said, laughing. "It's 'one of the results of slavery,' eh, Parson?"

"I reckon it is," replied the preacher, joining in the general merriment; "but Jule never gets drunk. However, his habit is a little expensive to us, as the rapacious sutlers make us pay five dollars a bottle for decent whiskey. But, Captain, go on with your story, or you'll not get through to-night."

"The next hour," resumed the captain, "was the longest I ever knew; but it came to an end at last, and Tom reappeared with the blankets and bacon. A party of a dozen men, evidently in pursuit of us, were passing down the road, when, on his hands and knees he reached it; but they did not perceive him, and having no dogs, did not detect our 'camp equipage.'

"Again dressing my wound, and wrapping the remaining blankets about me—for the air grew very chilly as the night wore on—my companion sat down on the fallen log, in the lee of which I was lying, and appeared to fall asleep. My wound had grown very painful, and I was tossing uneasily about, unable to rest, when, at the end of several hours, he raised his head, and said to me:

"Leftenant, I luck'd round a leetle when I went fur the traps, an' thar hain't no house'n nigher'n three mile, 'cept thet durned secesher's thet I stole the bacon frum. Ye'll die ef ye doan't git under kiver. What shill we do?"

"*Pray*, Tom; I know the Lord will lead us out of this, if we ask Him aright."

"Then, 'spose ye tries yer hand at it, Leftenant; ye's more larnin', an' yer a better man nur me."

"Learning is not needed in asking of God. He sees the faintest wish of the heart, and he grants it to his children."

("Preaching is not my profession," said the captain, parenthetically; "but, near as I then was to death, I felt very solemn, and I've no doubt I could have beaten the parson at his own trade, and given him—as Tom would say—two in the game.")

"Wall, ef wishin' ar prayin', Leftenant," replied Tom, "I'se bin a prayin' this whole blessed night—uver sence I seed ye'd got a hole inter ye thet moight let the life out. But the Lord doan't yere me—I doan't see no way out o' this but gwine ter thet durned hide-bound secesher's, an' thet 'ud nuver do, nohow."

"But you don't know that he is a secessionist."

"Yas I does. I'd swar ter it on the bacon;" and, heaving a deep sigh, he went to musing again.

The night, though I thought it would never end, at last wore away, and the sun came in through the trees. It had been up about two hours, and was warming even my cold bed under the laurel leaves, when a voice directly over me suddenly exclaimed: "Wh—wh—whot'm—you—doin' down dar?"

It was a tall, stalwart negro man, who had come upon us from the side to which Tom's back was turned. The latter was in a gentle doze, and did not hear his approach, but the moment the black spoke he sprang to his feet, and, seizing him by the collar, cried out: "Ye black thundercloud! whot does ye want yere?"

The negro made no reply, but, drawing back, aimed a heavy blow at the native's face. Tom caught it on his arm, and stepping aside, and making no effort to return it, said with amazing coolness:

"Come, none o' thet, ur I'll lay ye out without ben'fit o' clargy. We's friends ter all sech black devils like ye; so sot down yere an' tell us who ye is. Sot ye down," he added, as the black showed a disposition to disregard his injunction: "Sot ye down! or I'll lamm ye till yer whiter nur Squire Robins' old mar, an' she war so white ye couldn't see har by daylight, fur the fact wus—she war dead."

The negro sat down. "Thet's a sensible feller," said Tom, "Now, whar d'ye b'long?"

"Ter Squar Gibbon, ober dar," replied the black, pointing sulkily in the direction of the planter's.

"An' didn't ye lose two hams frum the smoke-house las' night? an' didn't the squar guv it ter ye nigs' loike blazes this mornin' fur a stealin' on 'em?"

"Yas, he done dat, Massa."

"Sarved ye right. It'll larn ye better'n ter steal agin. Hain't yer massa a durned old secesh?"

"He am dat, Massa, nuffin' else nur dat," replied the negro, grinning.

"Didn't I tell ye, Leftenant?" cried Tom, in a triumphant tone, giving one of the hams a contemptuous kick, "Didn't I tell ye I know'd it by the taste o' the bacon?"

The darky looked at the hams; and a sudden light seemed to break upon him, for he shouted out, "Yah! yah! an' did *you* stole de bacon, Massa? Did *you* done dat, Massa? Yah! yah!"

"No, we didn't *stole* it; white men doan't steal; only ye cussed nigs does thet. We *kornfiscated* it."

The black looked at us as if he didn't know the exact difference between stealing and confiscating; but he said nothing. Tom rested his head on his hand for a moment; then, looking up, said to the negro:

"I say, thundergust, which'll ye take—death or yer freedom?"

"I doan't 'zactly understand, Massa," replied the black, with more coolness than he could have been expected to exhibit under Tom's eye, which startled even me with its fierceness.

"I mean thet we is Union men, 'scapin ter the lines; an' thet we'll take ye 'long, an' guv ye yer freedom, ef ye'll holp us; an' *kill ye, if ye woan't.* Thet's all."

"I'll holp you, Massa. Ef you'm Union I'd do ut widout ony freedom, but, ob course, Massa, I'd rudder hab dat."

"Uv course ye w'ud; ony fool w'ud. Whot der ye think, Leftenant? Kin we trust the nig?"

"I think so; I like his face," I replied.

"So does I. But, my black booty, ye jest 'count on it, ef ye come the varmunt over us ye'll kotch fryin' pans over a slow fire: ye wull. Wull ye 'member thet?"

"Oh, yas, Massa. But neber you f'ar, Massa, I'll be true. Shore, Massa."

"I'll trust ye," said Tom, at once proceeding to talk affairs over with the darky. We ascertained from him that the district was filled with Union men, who would gladly aid us, but they all lived at too great a distance to be safely reached in my wounded condition. A poor white man, however, who could be trusted, had a small "dead'nin'" about a mile away, and to him we determined to apply. The negro set off at once for his house—which stood on a narrow wagon track running through the woods—and in about an hour returned with the native.

He was an odd-looking specimen of humanity, with a lean, gaunt frame, round, stooping shoulders, short, crooked figure; long, bony arms, and knees that seemed to love each other. His eyes were small and restless; his nose long, thin, and hooked at the end; and his ears large enough to have been intended for a quadruped renowned for braying. He wore a pair of pants made of butternut linsey, a coat and shirt of the same material, and an old broad-brimmed slouched hat, turned up in front, and falling over his shoulders like the cape of a Mackintosh.

He at once consented to receive me into his house, and to keep me until my wound was sufficiently healed to allow of my again setting out for Nashville. "I'se mighty pore fixins, stranger," he said; "but whot I hes ar' yourn, ter komand."

My wound had become greatly inflamed, so that the least motion gave me excruciating pain, and attempting to rise, I found myself too weak to stand. Perceiving this, Tom and the negro, making a seat of their arms, took me up and carried me to the native's. His cabin was of the meanest sort, and, for effectual concealment, my bed was made in one corner of its half-floored attic; but his kindness, and that of his tidy, tender-hearted wife, with Tom's never-ceasing attention, made those mean lodgings as pleasant as quarters under a much more pretentious roof.

As soon as I could bear the pain, Tom extracted the ball with his jack-knife; but my strength returned slowly. It was ten days before I could sit up. Then I gave Tom his first lessons in the alphabet, putting Ayer's Almanac to a much better use than it was ever put to before.

At the end of a fortnight we held a general consultation over affairs, and decided, as it might be weeks before I was able to travel, that Tom should attempt to make his way to Nashville, with letters to my colonel. They would probably induce him to send a party of cavalry to my rescue.

Tom reached Nashville safely, and just after dark one evening, about a week afterward, I was gladdened by the sound of his voice entering the cabin. In a moment more his good-looking face, lit up by the blaze of the roaring light-wood fire on the hearth below stairs, shone out at the top of the rickety ladder which led to my lodging place. "I'se done it, Leftenant," he cried. "They's over ter Squire Gibbon's, kornfiscatin' Jake an' a fass hoss an' kerridge. They'll be yere in a jiffin, so ye be up an' ready."

I soon dressed myself, and mounting Tom's back, descended to terra-firma. In half an hour I heard the clatter of horses' hoofs, and turning to my kind friends, said: "I have been a prisoner, you know, and therefore have no money about me; but I shall not forget you—you shall not go unrewarded."

"Nuver tork in thet how, Cunnel," replied the native. (He persisted in calling me colonel, though he knew my rank.) "Yer guvin' yer life ter the kentry, an' it war a rantankerous shame ef we couldn't guv ye whot leetle ye's hed."

I said no more, but grasping him by the hand, and kissing his wife—she was a young and pretty woman—I walked to the door and took a seat by the side of Jake, the colored man, in the "kornfiscated" buggy. A "kornfiscated" horse, ready saddled, stood beside it. Tom mounted him and we rode off to Freedom. We reached Nashville before daybreak, and—that is the end of my story."

"Give the captain some punch, Jule," said the parson; "he must be dry after spinning so long a yarn."

As the captain took the toddy I said to him: "And you say Tom is a member of your company now?"

"Yes, he enlisted with me as soon as I recovered from my

wound. At Stone River he fought like a hero, and when they promoted me, they gave *him* a shoulder-strap."

"Then, he's an officer now."

"Second Lieutenant in my company. His tent isn't half a dozen rods from here."

"Indeed, I should very much like to know him. He is a character."

"And a wag of the first water," said the parson; "if you talk with him, and don't keep your wits about you, he'll 'sell' you, sure."

"I'll look out for that. Pray let me see him."

The Captain went out, and in a few moments returned with the "native." My interview with him, and some of the yarns he spun, are narrated in the next chapter.

CHAPTER VIII.

THE POOR WHITE MAN.

THERE are two classes of poor southern whites, of marked and decidedly opposite characteristics. The type of the one is of low stature, with abbreviated body, elongated arms and legs, dull heavy eyes, coarse carroty hair, saffron-hued skin, and a small head, shaped like a cocoa-nut. The type of the other is tall, and well formed, with a gaunt, loose-jointed frame, a rough dark skin, wiry black hair, keen restless eyes, and an artless, confiding manner, which, with a certain air of self-possession, indicates that he knows little of the world, but feels fully able to cope with what little he does know. The first is physically and intellectually a "bad job," and it might sensibly be questioned why he was created, for he appears incapable of either mental or moral culture; but the other possesses all the "raw material" of manhood—and manhood, too, of the noblest type. Education, discipline, social advantages, and political freedom are needed to bring out his nature, but when it is brought out he shows himself a Man. The first class, who are few in number, and fast melting away before the advance of a stronger race, and a more robust civilization, are found principally on the Sand-hills of North Carolina, and in the mountain regions of Lower Virginia and Upper Georgia. There, a little above "the brutes that perish," and a "long way lower down dan de darkies," they build their pole cabins, and glean a sorry subsistence from hunting, fishing, and a few sterile acres. The other class, who are counted by millions, and are scattered from the Potomac to the Rio Grande, are the bone and sinew of the South, the prop of Slavery, and the hope and expectation of Freedom, for on them, more than on immense armies or garrisoned cities, will depend the safety and perpetuity of the Union. An unprincipled aristocracy has robbed them of knowledge, and moulded them to its own base uses, but whenever truth has reached them they have shown an unselfish devotion to it, and to the Union, which we time-servers and money-lovers of the North know nothing of. In East Tennessee, where Parson Brownlow has been their great apostle, and *The Knoxville Whig* their Bible and spelling-book, they have exhibited a heroic patriotism which the world—I say this with a very small smattering of history—has seldom witnessed. The deeds they have done, the sacrifices they have made, the sufferings they have endured for a Government which has closed its eyes to their sorrows, and its ears to their complaints, will be read of and wondered at, when this generation has passed away. Their story is not yet told, but when it is told, many a cheek will mantle with shame—as mine has—to hear of what these poor, unlettered men, women, and children have done and suffered for their country, while we have been growing fat on its necessities, and looking idly on, as it seemed tottering to its ruin.

From this latter class sprang Patrick Henry, Thomas Jefferson, Andrew Jackson, Henry Clay, John C. Calhoun, Andrew Johnson, Parson Brownlow, President Lincoln, and—Long Tom, whom "the captain" told the reader something about in my last chapter.

The "native" gentleman entered the tent with a quick, energetic step, and bowing respectfully to the parson, and giving me a grasp of the hand and a cordial "How dy'ge, stranger?" turned suddenly on the old negro, with:

"Wall, old thundergust, how's ye?"

"I'se well 'nuff," replied the black, giving his shoulder a petulant shrug.

"Go to the colonel's, Jule, and borrow a chair for the lieutenant," said the captain.

The negro glanced inquiringly at the parson, but seeing no answering look in his face, turned his head away, and, again shrugging his shoulders, replied:

"Leff him gwo hisseff; Jule 'tends on gemmen: he doan't 'tend on no poo' white trash—he doan't."

"Thet's yer Christun sperret, ye black hyppercrit," rejoined the native, laughing, and at the same time drawing the captain's traveling trunk from the corner, and seating himself upon it. "One of these days I'll show ye how we white Christuns guvs good fur evil, fur I'll tend on *ye*—I'll *bury* ye! an I woan't pile more'n six inches o' sile on yer bones, so ye'll hev a right easy time gittin up ter the resumrection."

As the "native" took his seat I glanced at his appearance. He seemed somewhere between twenty-five and thirty, and was about six feet three inches high, with well-formed limbs, finely developed frame, clear, dark eyes, and a broad, full forehead. His face was open, frank, and manly, and there played about it a mingled expression of kindness and sadness, which was strangely blended with a latent mirth, that seemed ready to break out on the slightest provocation.

As he seated himself he turned to me, and in an abrupt, energetic tone, said:

"Wall, stranger, the capt'n sez ye'd loike ter luck at me; so, I's yere. I's six foot three, without leathers, weigh a hun'red an' eighty, kin whip twice my heft in Secesh, bars, or rattlesnakes, an' uvry inch on me ar yourn ter komand, ef ye gwoes in, body an' boots, fur the Union; an' the capt'n reckons ye does, though he sez ye gwoes it the talkin', an' not the fightin' way: an' I ruther 'spect ye Yankees 'ud gin'rally 'bout as lief talk as fight."

"I had much rather," I replied, laughing; "but I reckon *you* might do a little talking, if you tried."

"My old muther allers said I hed suthin' uv a tongue. She use ter 'clare ter gracious it war hung in the middle, an' hed a way uv gwine at both eends; an' yet somehow, it nuver done me no good. But whar dy'ge b'long, stranger?"

"In New York."

"Oh, yas, I's hearn uv thet place. Up thar Nurth, clus ter the Nurth Pole, hain't it?"

"Not very close to the Pole, but in that direction."

"An' hes ye uver seed the Nurth Pole?"

"No, I never saw it, but I believe there is such a thing,"

"An' whar mought it be?"

"It 'mought' be here, but it is'nt;" I replied, smiling "Boston is the 'hub of the universe'—I reckon it's there."

"It mus' be a rantankerous Pole. How big d'ye 'spose it ar'? Big as thet ar maple?" pointing to the tree under which the parson had preached his sermon, and which was visible from the doorway of the tent.

"Larger than ten of that placed one on the other, and spliced at top and bottom."

"Jerusalamm! but it ar a pole! D'ye know I's made out whot the yerth has sech a thing fur?"

"No, why is it?"

"Fur steerin'! I's bin orr the Big Drink (Mississippi) an' seed how they does it. But, Parson, it upsots whot ye sez 'bout the yerth bein' round."

"Indeed!" exclaimed the chaplain, laughing; "and if the earth isn't round, how is it shaped?"

"Loike a steambut, ter be shore," replied the native, with a gravity so well assumed that, for a time, it deceived even the parson; "hain't ye seed them ar big poles 'at the fore' as they call it, uv the buts on the Big Drink; an' how them fellers at the wheel plumbs thar coorse by 'em. Now, ef the yerth hev' un' o' them, doan't it nat'rally foller thet it's shaped loike a steambut? An' I *knows* it ar', 'case I's bin whar I c'ud luck slap down over the side, right onter the most relarmin', purpindiclar presurpiss ye uver seed, even in yer dreams."

Amid the general laugh which followed, I asked:

"And how did you get a sight at that 'relarmin', presurpiss'?"

"I'd tell ye, but it'r a mighty long story."

"Never mind its length, Tom," said the chaplain, "tell it."

"Wall, ye sees," said Tom, taking a 'swig' at the toddy, and coolly lighting one of the captain's cigars; "I war a' livin' long uv dad, over thar in Bladsoe, whar I war raised; an' un' mornin' dad sez ter me, sez he, 'Tom, hitch up the two-yar-old he'ffer, an' fotch a load o' light-'ood frum the mounting.' Now, dad hed a small dead'nin' up thar thet we wus a clarin' uv timber; so I hitched up the cow-brute, an' piked fur the mounting. I'd wuckd till 'bout a hour by sun, an' hed got the cart chock heapin' with pine knots an' timber, when I sot down onter it ter eat up whot war left uv my dinner—fur I know'd ef

I tuck it hum, an' dad seed it, my supper'd be brevurated jest so much. Wall, I war jest a swollerin' down the last mossel, when, thinkin' it war 'bout time ter be a hitchin' up the heffer, I luk'd round, an' whot d'ye 'spose I seed? Two on the most oncommonest, riproarin' big cart-wheel snakes ye uver hearn on in all yer borned days, an' they pikin' stret fur me!"

"And what is a cart-wheel snake?" I asked.

"Why, it ar a sarpunt 'bout twelve foot long, thet hes a way uv kotchin' its tail in its mouth—leavin' a small eend out fur a snapper; an' crackin' on it, when it travils, jest loike we cracks a whip—an then roalin' itself over the ground loike it war a cart-wheel. Wall, I seed them ar two outdacious varmunts a comin' onter me, an' I sez ter myself: 'Tom, you hain't got no fambly —an' thet's 'mazin' lucky fur the fambly—but as a lone critter, as yer Arnt Sal use ter say uv herseff, ye'r gone up, sartin'. An' I thort I war, but the Lord know'd better, fur he seed this war wus a cummin', an' he know'd I'd be uv some use in guvin' the Rebels—brimstun. Ye sees, Parson, I's a larnin' ter leave out the tough words."

"Yes, I see," said the chaplain; "you're improving fast in everything but—lying."

"Lyin'," echoed Tom, in an injured tone, "I nuver lied in all my born days—'cept ter Stun River; an' thar I lied fur two all-fired long nights—in the mud up ter my knees. Ye 'scaped thet sin, Parson, 'case ye hed brush fur beddin'."

"And I had you to thank for it. Tom, you *are* a trump—the very Jack of clubs."

"Thank ye, Parson. I sots high on yer 'pinion 'bout uvrything 'cept hoss flesh; but in thet, I does 'sist—agin the capt'n —thet ye doant know a mule from a pile o' light-'ood. But 'bout them snakes. They come stret at me, an' luckin' me squar in the eye fur a minnit, licked thar big jaws with thar forked tongues, as much as ter say: 'Ye'll make a right nice mossel, ye wull,' an' then kiled themselves right tight round the cart-wheels. I didn't 'spicion whot they wus a gwine 'bout, fur, 'lowin' *I'd* make a right smart meal fur 'um, I didn't see whot yerthly use they hed fur the light-'ood. Howsomever, they know'd best, an' in less time nur it takes to tell it, they'd hitched up, an', with the hull apparitus—cart, light-'ood, an' all —war tossin' thar heads, an' crackin' thar whips, an' moseyin' fur sundown streter nur lightin' uver shot from a thunder-cloud. Ye'd better b'lieve they traviled. They piked over the roads, an' through the clarin's, bucklete whit, splittin' the a'r clean in two, an' leavin' a tornado we kotched up with so fur ahind thet I reckon it haint got thar yit."

"But how did they manage the shafts of the cart all this time?" I asked. "I should think they would have caught in the bushes."

"Oh, the snakes knowed too much fur thet; they turned the cart clean round, and toted it hind eend afore."

"They were sensible snakes!"

"Ye nuver said a truer word nur thet, stranger. Wall, as I sot thar, gwine to'ards sundown at thet relarmin' rate, with thet bore-constructor sort uv a team, I jest hed time ter think, an' sez I ter myself: 'Tom, ye haint much larnin', but ye *is* a outdacious, dingnation, nat'ral-borned fool, ef ye karn't outwit two sech flat-noggin sarpunts as these is.' I hedn't more'n got the words out'n my mouth when the new moon riz up 'bove the hoorizon, right afore me, an' not more'n a mile off, with its two horns a stickin' out, as much as ter say: 'Now, Tom—now's yer chance. Jest guv a long leap; git up yere, an' take a tower clar round creation fur nuthin'.' I did'nt need more'n thet hint, so I squatted on my haunches fur a jump, an' when we'd come within a quarter uv a mile uv the moon, I guv a spring, an', d'ye b'lieve it, I landed right squar' on the leetle eend uv one uv the horns. The snakes they run out thar tongues, an' spit fire a leetle, but seein' it warn't no use, they turned squar' round, piked back ter the deadin', and left the cart right whar they found it."

"But I thought you said the snakes had a use for the light wood?" I remarked, with decent gravity.

"Wall, they hed; they kalkerlated on it fur cookin' my carcass; but bein's I'd skedaddled, they toted it back, like honest snakes, as they wus.'

"And then you saw that uncommon 'presurpiss?'" asked the parson.

"Yas," answered Tom. "As the moon sailed 'way frum the yerth, I lucked down; an' Parson, ye'd better b'lieve it, I seed a more abysfuller place than ye uver told on in all yer sarmunts. 'Twar so deep it 'peared ter stretch ter the vury eend uv creation, an' so dark, ye moight hev read fine prent in it by the light o' sech a black thing as Jule's face."

"And how long did you sit there on the horn of the moon?"

"Why, bless ye, stranger, it warn't no horn at all. It war on'y the small eend uv a church steeple, that riz up nineteen mile frum the ground, an' stuck out jest fur anuff fur me ter kotch a hold on as I wus a gwine by."

"Then there are people living in the moon?"

"I reckon thar is, an' the tallest people ye uver heered on. I doan't mean tall in statur'—fur they haint much ter brag on thet way, an' I war a sort o' curiosity 'mong 'em, on 'count uv my hite—but tall uvry other how. They showed me more hosspetality then I uver 'spect ter see agin; toted me round in a rantankerous big kerridge shaped jest loike a coffin; an' treated me ter mint-juleps 'nuff ter flood all creation in the driest spell ye uver know'd on."

"An' Mister Tom," said the old black, who had listened to the "native's" yarn without moving a muscle of his broad face, which seemed made for grinning. "Bein's you's bin dar, will you hab de goodness ter say whot dem ar dark places am dat we sees in de moon?"

"Nigger kentries, Mr. Midnight," replied Tom, promptly. "They doan't let darkies 'sociate with white folks up thar. They hard (herd) 'um all tergether, an' thar's so many on 'em they make the air black as a thunder-cloud, which is the reason why we sees 'um frum yere. An' we'll do the same with ye nigs in this wurle when the war ar over. We'll turn yer hull race inter South Car'lina, an' I reckon ye'll blacken the a'r down thar so loike durnation thet they'll obsarve it 'way off ter the furdrest eend uv the univarse, an' see thar's been a rev'lution down yere thet's altered the very face o' the planet."

The black shrugged his shoulders contemptuously as he replied: "Whot fools ye poo' white folk kin make o' yourselves. Loike as ef Tennessee nigs 'ud 'sociate wid dem white trash an' mean chivarly down dar in Soufh Car'lina. You knows better'n dat—we hain't got so low as dat yit."

"And, Tom," I asked, "how long were you on the moon, and how did you get off?"

"I karn't 'zactly say how long I war thar, case, ye see, thar hain't no clocks on thet planet, nur no Yankees ter make 'um:"

and he looked slyly at me, while the parson broke into a broad laugh, saying:

"You owe him one, Mr. ——."

"I acknowledge the debt," I replied; "but, Tom, can no one but a Yankee make a clock?"

"No 'uns but them kin make 'ooden nutmegs, bass'ood hams, an' clocks thet woant gwo. They makes nuthin' else."

"That may be true, my good fellow; but they make them expressly for the southern market. No other people are green enough to buy them."

"Wall, stranger, I reckon I owes *ye* one now, I nuver know'd nary uther Yankee but onst, an' he war 'bout so smart as ye is, fur he sold dad a clock. Shill I tell ye 'bout it?"

"Yes, but finish the moon story first."

"It hain't a minnet long, an' I kin eend the moon in a jiffen. Ye sees, dad hed nary clock, an' couldn't tell when the sun riz —he hed a great reespect fur the sun, nuver got up afore it in all his life—so, when a peddler come 'long with a whole wagin-load uv clocks, he war dreffül put ter't ter hev one. They wus the eight-day kine, all painted up slick, an' worronted to gwo till the eend uv time. The peddler axed ten dollar fur 'um, an' dad hedn't but three. I hed two thet I'd bin a savin' up, an' dad wanted ter borre 'um, but I wouldn't a lent 'um ter him ter save his soul, fur I know'd he'd nuver pay in nuthin' but promizes, an' fur his age, dad war the most promizin' man ye uver know'd on. Wall, I buttoned up my pocket, and dad eyed the clocks; an' sez he ter the peddler: 'Stranger, I'd loike 'un uv them mightily, but rocks is sca'ce, jest now; I hain't got on'y three dollars in the wurle."

"Hain't ye!" said the peddler; 'wall thet's a all-fired pity;

but bein's ye's a monstrus nice sort o' man, an bein's I allers kind o' took ter sech folks as ye is, ye kin hev a clock fur yer three dollars. But I wouldn't sell 'un ter nary uther man for thet money, nohow.'

"Wall, dad tuck the clock, and the peddler tuck the money and mosey'd off."

"Dad sot druffel high on thet clock. He took on over it fur all the wurle, jest like a chile over a new playthin'. He got up airlier, an' sot up later then I uver know'd him afore, jest ter yere it strike, but arter a few days it stopped strikin', an' nuver struck agin! Dad wus sold—an' sold, too, by a rantankerous Yankee; an' dad allers 'counted (but mind, stranger, I doan't guv this as my 'pinion) thet a Yankee ar a leetle the measliest critter in all creation. Wall, not more'n a month arter thet, as dad an' I wus a wuckin' in the corn patch 'un day, who shud come 'long the road but the Yankee peddler. As soon as dad seed him he sez ter me, sez he: 'Bullets an' blisters, Tom! but thar's thet outdacious Yankee! Now, ef I doan't strike better time on his noggin then his dingnation clocks uver struck in all thar lives, I'll pike stret fur kingdom-come, ef I hes ter gwo afoot." Bilin' with wrath, dad moseyed fur the peddler; but he hedn't more'n got inside 'o hearin', 'fore the Yankee bawled out: 'I say, Mister, ye's got a clock as b'longs ter me. It woan't gwo, an' I want's ter get it, an' guv ye 'un as wull gwo. I hed jest 'un bad one in the lot, an' I'se bin a sarchin' fur it 'mong nigh onter a hun'red folks I'se sold clocks ter, an hain't found it yit, so ye mus' hev tucken it; I knows ye did, case I sees it in yer eye.'

"That mellored dad ter onst, an' ter own the truth, it guv *me* a sort o' good 'pinion uv the Yankee. Wall, dad and he swopped clocks, an' the peddler stayed ter dinner—an' the old man 'udnt take a red fur't, he war so taken with him. As he wus a gwine ter leave, the peddler ope'd the hind eend uv his wagin, an' takin' out a peck measure, heapin' full of whot 'peared the tallest oats thet uver grow'd, he sez ter me, sez he: 'Tom, ye an' yer farder hes bin 'mazin clever ter me, an' I nuver loikes ter be obligated ter no body, so yere's some o' the finest plantin' oats ye uver know'd on; take 'um; they'll grow ye a monstrous tall crop, as big as oak trees.'

"Now ye sees, I hed a four-year-old mar I'd a raised up with my own han's. I sot drefful high on har, an' she got drefful high on oats, an' I'd bin a savin' up them two dollars s'pressly ter buy seed ter make a crap fur her privat' eatin'. So, when I seed them oats o' the peddler's they filled my eye, loike the camel filled the eye of the needle in Scriptur'. He hedn't guv'n me 'nuff ter gwo no distance in plantin', but bein' he war so gen'rous loike, I couldn't ax him ter guv more, so I sez ter him: 'Stranger, wouldn't ye sell a bushel o' them oats?'

"'Wall, Tom,' he sez; 'bein's it's ye, an' ye an' yer farder is sech monstrous clever folk, I doan't know but I'd sell ye the *whole* on 'um, fur the fact ar' they's too hearty loike fur my hoss; ye see the feller's got a sort o' weak stomach, an' can't 'gest 'um. I guess thar's nigh on ter five bushel, an' bein's they hain't uv no use ter me, ye shill have the whole on 'um fur them ar' two dollars o' yourn.' Now, I figger'd on my fingers, an' foun' thet warn't more'n forty cents a bushel; an' oats, sech as war raised in our diggins, an' they warn't no way nigh so nice as them—went fur sixty, so ye kin reckon I tuck 'um, an' ye mought b'lieve it rained big blessin's on thet peddler 'bout the time he druv off. He'd altered my 'pinion o' the Yanks' 'pletely, an' I tole him he orter make hisself intêr a wild munag'ree, an travil the whole southin kentry, jest ter show folk whot the Yankees raaly is; fur I know'd ef he done it they'd swap thar 'pinions jest as I hed, an' thet ye know would do a mighty heap to'ards perpertratin' the Union. Wall, arter he war gone, I tuck the five bushel inter the house, an' kivered 'um up keerful in the cockloft; but, feelin' mighty gen'rous loike, on 'count uv my big bargin', I thor't I'd guv the mar a sort o' Christmus dinner o' the peck measure full. So I put 'um afore her, an' she smelled on 'um ravernous mad fur a minnet, but then she turned up har nose, an' wouldn't luck at 'um agin."

"She found them too hearty loike; I suppose," I said, restraining a strong inclination to laugh.

"I 'spose she did, an' I reckon they *would* hev bin raather hard o' 'gestion, fur they wus SHOE PEGS!"

"Shoe pegs?"

"Yas, shoe pegs! The durnation Yankee hed a scowrn the hull deestrict, an' found no 'un green 'nuff ter buy 'um, but me."

Amid the general laugh which ensued, I asked:

"And how about the clock? how did that turn out?"

"'Twus wuss nur 'tother—it nuver struck onst."

"Well that Yankee was smart," said the captain. "It takes a smart one to get ahead of you, Tom."

"He didn't git ahead uv me," replied Tom, with comic indignation. "I wus three dollars inter him when I got shut o' them oats. Ye sees, I toted 'um ter Pikeville, an' sold 'um fur whot they raaly wus—shoe pegs—an' got five dollars fur the lot. The peddler mought hev done it, ef he could onyhow hev brought his mind to act honest, but he'd ruther cheat fur half price, nur trade fa'r fur full pay. An' thet's the sort o' Yànkee ye's sent 'mong us, Stranger. They's done a heap to'ards guvin us a bad 'pinion on ye, an' brungin' on this war."

"I know they have. I blush to think I was born on the same planet with some of them. But, Tom, about getting down from the moon. How did you do that?"

"Why," replied Tom, with a *sang froid* that was perfectly inimitable, "I jest waited till the moon come round ter the yerth agin, an' when it got 'bout over dad's dead'nin', I let myself drap, an' landed squar in the yam-patch, sound as ye sees me. I moseyed fur home, an' told dad whar I'd bin; an' dad sez ter me, sez he: 'Bully fur ye, Tom; yer a raal chip o' the old block; ye kin travil or spin a yarn nigh up ter yer fader, an' thet 's sayin' a heap.' An' it war sayin' a heap, for dad could lie loike a parson."

After the merriment which followed Tom's stories had subsided, I said to him:

"Speaking of riding round the moon in that 'kerridge' so like a coffin, reminds me of once travelling in a coffin myself."

"An' how wus it, stranger," asked Tom; "d'ye b'lieve ye kin tell a bigger story than thet 'bout the moon?"

"Not a bigger one, but one a little—*truer*."

"Ef ye kin come ony nigher the truth then thet an' not hit it, I'd loike ter hev ye."

"Well, I'll try, but I shall hit it—a thing I reckon you seldom do. It was late in November, twelve years ago. I was coming from Florida with Edward C. Cabell, the Confederate general who is now giving us so much trouble in Arkansas. It had rained very hard all day, and when, at dark, we reached Albany—a little town in South-Western Georgia—we found the

Flint River had risen twenty-five feet. It poured down all that night, and in the morning we learned that the stage, which was to have taken us to Oglethorpe—the terminus of the Savannah Railroad—had not arrived, and that the bridges over all the streams for miles around had been swept away by the freshet. This was unpleasant news to both of us, for Cabell was anxious to be in Washington at the opening of Congress (of which he was a member), and important business demanded my immediate attention in Savannah. Crossing the streams we supposed to be impossible; so we decided to take a horse, buggy, and negro driver, and attempt to head them in the up-country. We would have to ride nearly two hundred miles over rough roads, when it was only fifty to the railroad by the direct route; but that we thought better than waiting a fortnight in so desolate a place as Albany. It would be all of that time before the bridges were repaired, for people in that region are not over 'fast'—in such respects. We started, and riding about six miles, came to a place called Box Ankle—one house, and a cross-road doggery—and the planter there told us that the Kicafoonee, a creek about a mile distant, could be safely swum on the back of a mule, and that he would ferry us over, in that manner for a 'fa'r consideration.' The temptation of swapping two hundred miles for fifty was very great, and we rode down to the stream to reconnoitre. It was fully three hundred yards wide, and the current was running 'like time.' Cabell thought 'the longest way round the shortest way,' to Congress, but I decided to take the direct route and risk the creeks. Agreeing to take charge of my trunk, and to leave it at Savannah, Cabell turned about for the up-country, while I, stripping off my lower garments and tying them to my shoulder, mounted the mule, and breasted the 'swift-flowing waters' of the Kicafoonee. I got safely over, and, walking on about a mile, came upon a planter, who kindly gave me 'a lift' to the Relay Station of the Stage Company. Then I secured a conveyance to the Muckalee, another creek about three miles beyond Starksville. Arriving at the creek, I found it as swollen and furious as the Kicafoonee, and none of the planters in the vicinity willing to risk a mule in an attempt to cross it. I was pondering the adage, 'Make haste slowly,' when the thought of a boat occurred to me.

"'No one yere 'bouts hes one or knows how ter build one,' said the planter to whom I made application.

"'But, your negro boy here can build a coffin;' (he was just driving the last nail into a monstrous large one) 'if he can do that, he can build a boat. I'll show him how.'

"'I doan't b'lieve he kin, Stranger; he nuver went more'n a coffin.'

"'Well, this is mightily like a boat; what will you take for it?'

"'The old 'ooman orter to be buried ter-day—the fact ar she's bin 'bove ground too long a'ready—but ef ye want it right bad, I reckon ye kin have it fur five dollars.' (It was worth about fifty cents.)

"'How deep is the stream?'

"''Bout ten foot, ter the deepest.'

"'Well, give me some tar and a long pole, and the money is yours.'

"Calking the coffin with tar and some strips of old bagging, and nailing a cleat across its middle for a seat, I divested myself of my clothing, to be able to swim more freely in case of 'shipwreck,' and 'launched my bark' on the Muckalee. I got on 'swimmingly' till I reached the middle of the creek; then, the current caught the coffin, and carried it at least two miles down the run to where a jutting bank had made a strong eddy in the stream. Floating into this whirlpool, the coffin began sailing round and round, and kept on sailing round and round for a full hour, despite the united efforts of the pole and myself to extricate it. Night was coming on, and staying there after dark was a thing not to be thought of. I was not more than a hundred feet from shore, so I resolved to attempt swimming to it. Strapping my clothes to my shoulder with my suspenders, as I had done when I swam the mule, I lowered myself into the stream, and at the end of half-an-hour, after desperate effort, and once or twice giving myself up for lost, I reached the land."

"An' whot come on the coffin?" asked Tom.

"I don't know. It may be there yet."

"I reckon it ar," he replied, dryly.

"Then you don't believe the story."

"Wall, Stranger, I kin gwo it all 'cept the swimmin'. But the man as 'tempts ter swim one o' them runs when they's up, ar uther a rantankerous fool or a —Yankee, an' some reckon one 'bout the same as t'other."

"Well, Tom, I knew when I was whirling about in that coffin that I wus a rantankerous fool and a Yankee to boot. However, the story is true."

"And how did Cabell get through?" inquired the parson.

"After various other mishaps, I reached Oglethorpe at the end of seven days, and found Cabell quietly picking his teeth on the porch of the hotel. He had been there just long enough to eat his dinner; so, you see, 'the longest way round *is* the shortest way to Congress,' after all."

"'Ludin' ter freshets, stranger," said Tom, "'minds me uv 'un we hed onst in Bladsoe, whar"——

But the other stories that Tom told, while they might further illustrate the broad native humor of the South, and that spirit of exaggeration which is so important an element in it, and in the Southern character, will keep till the war is over, when you and I, reader, may not feel that we are wasting on idle tales, time and thought that should be given to our country.

CHAPTER IX.

THE OLD NEGRO'S STORY.

My pen lingers lovingly over those four companions, around that little pine table, in that quiet camp by the Cumberland. Each is a "character" and a "representative man" in his way and I long to fill out the sketch I have outlined, and to picture, "as large as life and twice as natural," the brave young captain, the type, as he is, of the glorious West; the droll, earnest chaplain, divested of his clerical clothes, and his soul broadened from long contact with the free life of the prairics; the uncouth, fun-loving old negro, who, by the parson's reckoning, is bound, in spite of lying, stealing, and whisky-drinking, to be "in Heaven a thousand years before any white man living;" and the rough-hewn, irresistible, and indescribable Tom, with his simple heart, his sturdy sense, his rare truth, and magnificent lying, all of which go to make him the type of the poor white yeomanry of the South—the "mean trash," as the chivalry call them, but no more "trash" than is the oak, which stands strong, rugged, and rough-coated in the forest, waiting to be fashioned into forms of use and beauty.

What a mass of exaggeration he was! How he magnified every thing, even himself! He could "whip twice his heft in Secesh, bars, or rattlesnakes. With the captain on his back, he could "outrun creation and give it two mile the start." Though not given to drinking, he could tote a "barr'l of whisky," and then pace "a bee line on the brink of a presurpiss." Even when he went afoot, he "piked faster than a horse kin trot," and when he rode, he out-traveled two tornadoes hitched to a jockey-wagon and driven by a darky in livery. He "'lowed" he was ignorant, but he know'd a log from seven dollars and a quarter, and if he seldom thought, when he did think, he went "plumb down lowerin'" the bottom of things, and up to where imagination grows dizzy, and has to steady herself with a gin cocktail. He didn't believe he was "borned fur the stump," but when he got through the "National Speaker"—which the captain had lent him—he know'd he could talk the legs off the parson, though he had hard *him* spout chain-lightning in the breaks of a thunder-storm. He reckoned Heaven was a pretty comfortable sort of a place, but not quite up to some parts of "Bladsoe" County; but "Bladsoe" itself wouldn't be fit for white men to live in if the Union was split to flinders. And if thet happins, stranger, who'll ye git ter make anuther Decel'-ration uv Independence? Only two livin' men kin do it —me an' Gin'ral Jackson, an' the Gin'ral's dead, an' me—why I hain't got right well inter the writin' bizness yit."

"Split the Union," I echoed, "never fear that, Tom; you can't split a rotten log."

"No more'n ye can't, Stranger," replied Tom, "an' 'tween ye small-soulded, lucre-luvin' Yankees, an' them blue-blasted, nigger-tradin' Secesh, the kentry *ar* got ter be, 'bout as rottin as sin."

What a picture he would make, drawn with a skilful hand, at full length—"six foot three, without leathers!" Some day my pen may attempt him, but now—I must go on with my yarn.

On the following morning I rose early to set out for Murfreesboro. Arriving at the railway station, I deposited my trunk in the baggage car, and was quietly proceeding to take a seat among the passengers, when a civil young man, in a half-military costume, arrested my steps at the foot of the platform, with: "Please show your pass, Sir."

I remembered having heard that summons before, and, at once, drew from my pocket a sheet of foolscap ornamented with General Burnside's autograph.

"This will not do, Sir. We have strict orders to pass no one down without a permit from head-quarters."

"General Burnside told me this would pass me anywhere in the United States."

"But you are not in the United States, Sir. Tennessee has joined New Jersey, and gone out of the Union."

"Well, what shall I do?"

"Go to General Morgan's headquarters, and ask them to telegraph to Murfreesboro. You'll get a reply in an hour."

This would detain me at Nashville another day, but there was no help for it, so, reshipping my trunk, I rode back to the hotel. After an hour spent in parleying with General Morgan's aide, another hour in waiting for a reply to the telegram, and still another hour in again dancing attendance on the same aid—a consequential young gentleman, who will probably be a Brigadier by the time his beard begins to grow (Government has made at least a baker's dozen of the same sort), I placed the "open-sesame" document in my pocket, and went my way, inwardly resolving never again to set foot in Tennessee till the passport system is abolished.

The day was on my hands, and, having nowhere else to go, I turned my steps toward the tent of the Illinois chaplain. Passing the Governor's house on my way—a large, square, dingy brick building, opposite the Capitol—I left my letters at the door, and walked on to the open fields beyond the town. A half a mile away I came upon the city cemetery, a beautiful spot, with growing grass, and waving trees, and unnumbered flowers growing over low mounds, and in one corner, half a thousand new-made graves with little white headboards, whose simple inscriptions told that the soldiers of the Union were sleeping beneath them.

One of these graves was open, and an old negro was filling it with earth—singing as he worked. Seating myself on the low paling, I listened to his song. These are so e of the words:

"Say, darkies, hab you seed de Massa
Wid de mufftash on his face,
Gwo long de road some time dis mornin',
Like he gwine ter leab de place?
He toted 'way a hoss and saddle,
An' forgot ter leab de pay;
So I spec' he'm jined de big skedaddle;
I spec' he'm run away.
De massa run, ha! ha!
De darky stay, ho! ho!
It mus' be now de kingdom comin'
An' de year of Jubilo.

"He leff ahind some likely darkies,
A suffrin' bad wid grief,
Fur dat dar high and mighty massa
Hab turn a mean hoss-tief!
Dey greab as ef dey wus his chillen,
An' I haff suspec' dey ar';
For dey's his nose, his big base fiddle,
An' his reddish wooly ha'r.
De massa run, ha! ha!
De darky stay, ho! ho!
It mus' be now de kingdom comin'
An' de year of Jubilo."

"Lamenting for your master, eh, Uncle?" I said, approaching him. It was wrong in him to turn 'hoss-tief.'"

The old man paused at his work, and turning on me, with a look of wounded pride, said curtly:

"*My* massa hain't no hoss-tief, Sar. He neber done no sech t'ing as dat—neber, Sar!"

"I only took your word for it—that's all," I answered, laughing.

"Oh, dat warn't *my* massa, Sar," he replied, good naturedly; "dat wus some of dem *low* Secesh. My massa run away, Sar, but he'm a gemmen; he leab ebery t'ing ahind, eben ole Joe."

"And did you want to go with him?"

"Oh no, Sar! *I* hain't no secesh; an' I wus fotched up dis away, in Nashville. Massa know'd I didn't want ter leab, an' he reckoned I could shirk fur myseff, somehow, Sar."

"And how do you get on shirking for yourself?" I asked; "you are very old."

He seemed at least seventy. His hair was white and his body greatly bowed, and scarcely more than a skeleton.

"Oh, bery well, Massa, bery well. Union folk bery good ter me, Sar. Eberybody 'pear sort o' kin'er ter ole Joe, eber sence de pore boy wus a killed—eber sence he wus a killed, Sar;" and resting on the handle of his spade he brushed away a great tear that was rolling down his cheek.

"And have you lost a son in the war?"

"Gran'son, Massa, down ter Stun riber; an' he wus a all I hed, Massa—all I hed, ever sence de ole 'ooman die; an' she gwo more'n two year ago—more'n two year ago;" and again his hand found its way to his eyes.

"And was he killed in the battle?"

"No, Sar; dey didn't 'low no brack folks fur sogers den. Dey wouldn't leff him fight, Sar, but dey leff him be shot down in cole blood—in cole blood, Sar!"

"In cold blood! How was it? Tell me."

To screen myself from the rays of the sun I had taken a seat on a low head-stone, in the shade of a small tree. When I asked this question the old negro, laying aside his spade, squatted on the grass near me, and then in broken sentences, and with frequent interruptions, expressive of the intensity of his feelings, he told me about his grandson.

"You sees, Massa, his pore mudder—de on'y chile we eber hed—die when Peter was a bery little t'ing, not no higher'n dat grabestone, so he wus a fotched up 'long ob we ole folks, like as ef he wus our own chile. He wus a great comfurt ter us, Sar, an' eberybody tuck ter him, an' eberybody say whot a likely boy Peter wus—he'd a sole ony time fur a tousand dollar, an' in good backer times (he wuck'd in a backer fact'ry) he'd a brung fifteen hun'red, easy, Sar. Wall, when de Secesh make de big skedaddle, massa gwoed long, an he tuck Peter wid him. Dat a'most broked my ole heart, Sar, 'case he wus all I hed—all I hed, Sar; but it wus de Lord's will, an' 'sides it couldn't be holped, nohow. Wall, Peter kept 'long wid de Secesh nigh onter a y'ar, an' den dey want ter make him gunner ter a bat'ry, but Peter tole 'em he wouldn't fi't de nordern gemmen, dat am friends ter de brack folks, no way—not fur no 'sid'ration, Sar. Den dey gib him a awfu' whippin', an' lock him up in de jail. He got 'way dough, an' af'er mos' credible suffrin', Sar, de got widin de lines. Dat wus 'bout de time dat Gin'ral Rosey wus a gwine ter smite de Phillistuns wid de hip an' t'igh, down dar ter Stun riber. Wall, dey want Peter ter gwo 'long wid de wagins, an' Peter axed me whot he should a do. Now, he wus all I hed, Sar, all I hed ; an' I sot my bery life on dat boy, but I tole him," and here the old man straightened up his bent form, and his shrunken features assumed a look of quiet dignity. "I tole him, sar, dat he hedn't but one life, an' ter gib dat fur his country, an' de brack folks. An' he done it, Sar! He done it. An' ef dey'd on'y gib'n him a musket, Sar!" (Here, swaying his body to and fro, he burst into a paroxysm of grief,) "on'y gib'n him a musket, Sar, an' leff him fit de Secesh—but, ter die so, Sar—ter die so ; it wus too hard—it clean broke ole Joe's heart, Sar."

"And how *did* he die, Uncle ?" I asked when he became somewhat composed.

"I'll a tell you, Sar. It wus dis a way. Peter, he gwo off wid de wagins, an' I gwo off wid him, 'case, ye sees, I couldn't be ob no use yere, an' dar wus no tellin' but I mought do *suffin* down dar; sides, I couldn't bar ter be 'way frum Peter, fur suffin yere, Sar (laying his hand on his heart), telled me dat trubble wus a comin'. Wall, on de day ob de fust battle we wus in de r'ar—'bout firty wagins on us, all wid brack dribers, an' a white leftenan'—an' a planter libin' 'bout dar rid up an' telled de leftenan' dat McCook wus a druv ter nowhar, an' dat he'd jess a seed Wheeler's calvary—'bout free t'ousand on um—headin' norf, an' he reckoned dey wus a gwine ter come down on Cunnel Innis up ter Laverne. He say some one orter gwo up an' leff de cunnel know, but *he* couldn't a gwo, case he went fur Secesh, an' ebery one round dar know'd him. De leftenan' he say I'd hab ter gwo, case der wus no one dat could be speered but me —ye sees, Peter an' me driv de same wagin, an' hed de same wages; but de leftenan', he sot high on me, an' he gib me my rations, so I tort I could gib my cloes ter de country. We hedn't none but de wagin hosses, but de planter, he say we wus welcome ter his'n; so I got on ter him, an' rid off ter tell Cunnel Innis. (De Lord's hand wus in dat, Sar. Sometimes He cut down de young saplin's an' leab de ole trees a' growin'.) I telled Cunnel Innis whot de planter say, an' de cunnel, dough he hedn't more'n 'bout free hun'red men, 'peared bery glad ter yere it—he'm de gemmen, Sar, dat 'doan't surrender much.' Wall, de cunnel he treat me jess like I wus a white man, an' make me tarry dar ober night. Airly de nex' mornin' I gwoes back ter whar de wagins wus, an' dey wusn't dar, but dar, all around, de ground wus a cobered wid brack men—shotted down—dead!"

Here the old negro paused for a moment. His lips moved silently, but he shed no tears. I said nothing, and he soon resumed his story.

"I luck'd all 'bout, an' I couldn't fine no sign ob Peter; but arter a while I gwoed down de pike, an' dar, right in de middle ob de road, wus some 'un in Peter's cloes, wid his head so nigh blowed off dat I couldn't a tell who he wus. I couldn't b'lieve it wus Peter, but I kneeled down aside ob him an' prayed, an' den I feel in his pocket, an' fine de Bible I hed gib'n ter Peter. It wus him! I shot my eyes, an' groaned. When I open'd 'um agin de sky was brack—it warn't more'n ten in de mornin'—and de yerth wus brack, an' dar warn't no sun, nur no moon, nur no stars in de heabens, an' de Lord hisself 'peared ter hab leff de univarse. I sot dar, an' sot dar, an' sot dar, right in de road, how long I'll neber know, an' at lass de hoss —I'd a leff him gwo a browsin' in de woods—come up ter me, an' puttin' his head down ter mine, cried an' whinner'd jess loike he know'd de great trubble dat was on me. Dat sort o'

6*

brung me ter myseff, an' tinkin' de pore critter wonted some water, I riz up, an' drawin' Peter under a tree, I leff him dar, fur I'd nuffin' ter bury him wid; an' 'sides, I tort ef he wus above ground de Lord—ef der wus any Lord leff—couldn't holp seein' him, an' so He'd be a sort o' 'libin witness' agin dem as hed murdered him."

"And who murdered him?" I asked.

"De Wheeler calvary dat we'd bin a warned agin. Dey come onter de train right arter I gwoed 'way, tuck de wagins, an' shot down de dribers in cole blood, 'case dey wus brack. De leftenan', he sot high on Peter, an' when he seed whot dey wus a doin', he tole de Secesh major he'd gib a t'ousand dollar fur Peter's life. But de major, he say he warn't no nigger-trader an' den he put his 'volver right squar agin Peter's head, an' blow his brains all ober de leftenan'. De leftenan' wus a 'changed arterwuds, an' telled me all 'bout how it wus."

"Wall I toted de hoss off ter de run 'bout a mile back, but he wouldn't a drink—'peared loike he knowed whot wus a comin' on him, an' didn't keer 'bout nuffin' more on dis yerth. I'd a yered de cannon a firin' off on de battle-field all de mornin', an' I wanted ter git out ob trubble—I knows dat wus wrong, Sar, but I couldn't holp it—so I turn de hoss roun' an' gwoes off ter de battle —dey didn't call it no battle dat day, but dey kep' a firin' de big guns all de time. I hadn't rid more'n free mile 'fore a shot hit de pore hoss on de shoulder, right afore me, an' kill him ter onst. At fust I tort I wus dead, too, fur I was frowed a long way, but I warn't hurted at all. Wall, de hoss die, an' I couldn't do nuffin for him, so I gits up an' gwoes on nigher ter de battle. I walk on, an' walk on, an' at lass I come ter de place whar dey fit so two days arterwuds—dey call it 'Hell's-half-acre'—it'm clus ter whar de pike runs inter de railroad. Dey say dar warn't no battle a gwine on den, but de balls wus a flyin' round dar ticker dan bank bills in 'backer times. It 'peared jess de place, so I sot down dar, 'long side de road, an' waited fur de shot dat shud send me ter Peter. Ye sees, he wus all I hed, all I hed, Sar, an' I feel den like I could n't lib wid out him, fur it wus dark wid me, an' dar 'peared no Lord in de heabens."

"Wall, I sot dar, an' sot dar, an' sot dar, an' de sogers march 'long, an' de calvary rid by, an' de sun gwo down, an' de night come on, an' de storm riz up, an' wetted me fru an' fru ter de bery skin, an' I neber feel it 'case no shot come and send me ter Peter. At lass—it wus jess sun up de next mornin'—a whole lot of cavlary, nigh a hun'red, come tunderin' down de road, an' when dey gits ober agin me, somebody cry 'Halt!' an' dey all stop chock still, like dey'd bin a shot, all ter onst. Den a gemman say ter me in a bery kine voice—so saff an' sweet, Sar, as ony music you eber yered:

"Uncle, what am you doin' dar?"

"I look up an' seed who he was—I'd a seed him afore, Sar, an' I know'd him ter onst—nobody eber seed him an' forgot him. Wall, I look up, an' tole him, all cryin' an' moanin' as I was:

"Dey's killed Peter, Gin'ral—shot him down wid de wagins, in cole blood, an' I's yere 'case I wants ter die, Gin'ral, 'case I wants some ob de shot ter fotch me out ob trubble."

"What general was it?" I asked.

"What gin'ral wus it, Sar!" echoed the old negro. "What oder gin'ral dan Gin'ral Rosey, would hab done sich a t'ing as dat, Sar? stop dar, right in de road, wid all him big officers, jess ter say a kine word ter a pore ole darky, as he seed wus in trubble?"

"Well, what did he say to you?"

"He tole me 'bout Peter, Sar, an' he tork ob him jess like he know'd him; but he didn't, 'case he couldn't a know'd a pore brack boy like Peter wus, nohow. He tole me dat I musn't grebe fur Peter, 'case he wus better off dan ef he wus a drivin' de wagins; dat it wus a glorious t'ing ter die fur yer country; dat Peter 'd a done it, jess so much as if he'd a died wid a musket in his hand; dat Gin'ral Washington, nur none ob de great men, eber done more'n Peter done, fur he'd a gib'n all he hed—his life—fur freedom. An' he say dat dem as done dat wus bery precious in de sight ob de Lord; dat He treasured 'um up, up dar," and the old man pointed upward; "an' called 'um His jewels, an' kep' 'um in His eyesight fur eber an' eber. Dat wus whot de gin'ral say, Sar; but it warn't so much *whot* he say, as de *way* he say it, dat tuck de load off my heart, an' brung de light inter my eyes agin. I karn't tell you how he say it, Sar, but it 'peared ter me like he'd a bin a ole brack man onst hisseff, an' know'd all de trubble dey feels when dey hain't nuffin in all de worle, an' hab loss dat. Wall, den he say, 'Tompey,* send two men ter gwo 'long wid dis pore brack man an' bury Peter,' an den he say, 'Good-bye, Uncle,' an' rid off. 'Bout a hour arter dat I yere de cannon begin, an' he wus right amung 'um, but nary shot hit him, Sar, an' nary shot neber will hit him, fur I prays fur him all de time, day an' night, an' de Lord hab promise ter yere de prayer ob dem as tries ter be His chillen."

"Den de light come ter me agin, Sar, and I seed de Lord wus

* Charles R. Thompson, of Bath, Me., then an Aide of General Rosecrans, now Colonel of the First Tennessee (colored) Regiment. A young man of twenty-three, who entered the army as a private. One of "the bravest of the brave."

in de heabens, arter all; an' dough Peter's gone, an' de ole 'ooman's gone, an' I'se bery ole, an' hain't got nuffin in all de worle, de light an' love ob de Lord hab bin all 'round me eber sence de gin'ral spoke so kine ter me down dar on de battle-ground. He'm one ob de Lord's chillen, Sar; one ob His bery best chillen; His chosen chile, Sar, dat am a gwine ter fotch dis people out ob de land ob Egypt, an' out ob de house ob bondage. He will, Sar, fur de Lord am wid him."

CHAPTER X.

THE REGIMENTAL HOSPITAL.

Leaving the old negro at work in the grave-yard, I resumed my way to the tent of the Illinois chaplain. The sun was just sinking behind the trees which skirt the western environs of Nashville when I entered its low doorway.

"Yere'm de Nordern gemman," exclaimed the sooty representative of the great Roman, as I made my appearance. "I's telled ye, Massa Parson, de Yankees can't do eberyting. Dey can't git fru de red tape dey hab round yere."

Giving no heed to the negro's remark, the chaplain, who was drawing on his coat as if to go out, welcomed me cordially, and invited me to accompany him to the hospital of the regiment. "One of my boys is dying," he said—"a Tennessee boy, wounded at Stone River. He has lingered till now, but now is going."

Walking rapidly across the open fields, we entered, at the end of a short half-hour, a dingy warehouse in the very heart of the city. About fifty low cots were ranged along the two sides of a narrow, cheerless apartment on the ground floor of this building, and on one of them the wounded soldier was lying. His face was pallid, his eyes were fixed, a cold, clammy sweat was on his forehead—he was dying. Sitting at his feet was a lad of sixteen; and kneeling at his side, her hand in his, was a middle-aged woman, with worn garments, and a thin, sorrow-marked face.

"You are too late! He is almost gone," said the colonel of the regiment, as we paused before the group.

The chaplain made no reply, but slowly uncovered his head, for the dying man was speaking.

"Mother," he said, "good-by. And you, Tom, good-by. Be of good heart, mother. GOD will take care of you, and save —save the——." A low sound then rattled in his throat, and he passed away, with the name of his country on his lips.

The mother bent down and closed the eyelids of her dead son; and then, kissing again and again his pale face, turned to go away. As she did so, the chaplain, taking her hand in his, said to her:

"The LORD gave: the LORD hath taken away."

Looking up to him with tranquil face and tearless eyes, the woman answered:

"'Blessed be the name of the Lord.' They have murdered my husband, Mr. Chapl'in, my oldest boy, and now John, too, is gone." Then, laying her hand on the shoulder of her living son, she turned to the colonel, and while her voice trembled a very little, she added: "He's all I've got now, Mr. Cunnel—give him John's place in the rigiment."

A tear rolled down the colonel's weather-beaten cheek, and he turned his face away, but said nothing. There was a convulsive twitching about the chaplain's firm-set mouth, as *he* said:

"The Spartan mother gave only *two* sons to her country: would you give *three?*"

"I'd give all—all I've got, Mr. Chapl'in," was the low answer.

And this was a "poor white" woman! Her words should be heard all over the land. They should go down in history, and make her name—RACHEL SOMERS—immortal.

Passing on to the farther end of the room, the chaplain said to a delicate young girl who was attending the sick:

"Lucy, are you willing to show your wounds to this gentleman?"

The young girl blushed, but modestly undoing her dress, showed me the upper part of her back. Deep ridges, striped with red, blue, and white, completely covered it! The slave-driver's whip, with a hundred lashes, had printed our country's colors on her fair skin, because she had refused to betray the hiding-place of her father!

"I could tell you of hundreds of these people," said the chaplain, as he put his arm within mine, and walked with me towards the hotel, "who have been driven to the woods, hunted with blood-hounds, beaten with stripes, hung to trees, tossed on the points of bayonets, torn asunder with horses, quartered alive, and burned at slow fires, rather than deny their country or betray its friends. The world has seldom seen such patriotism as theirs. There is a grandeur about it which lifts these poor people into heroes, and will make their story the brightest page in the annals of this country."

The room appropriated to me at the hotel being unfit for the reception of any animal higher in the scale of creation than "four-footed beasts or creeping things," I invited the chaplain, after supper, to a seat on a dilapidated chair in the long, low, smoky apartment which occupies the ground floor of the "Commercial Building," and is dignified with the name of office.

The chaplain was whiffing slowly away at his cigar, and recounting to me, in his peculiar style, some of his campaign experiences in Dixie—during which he had wielded the sword of Gideon as well as the weapons of the Lord—when the red-faced landlord, with his hat in his hand, and a smirk on his face, approached us, followed by a tall, spare, gentlemanly appearing man, whom he introduced as follows:

"Mr. ——, this is Secretary East—*our* Secretary—Edward H. East, Esq. You've heered uv him."

I rose and replied that I had heard of Mr. East, and was very happy to meet him. Returning my greeting, the secretary said:

"I regret that I was not at home when you left your letters this morning. I am acting in the Governor's absence, and shall be glad to serve you in any way."

Thanking him, and saying I had already fallen into good hands, I asked the landlord to oblige me with a seat for my visitor. That worthy, who accommodates guests with bed, board, and broken-backed chairs, at the rate of four dollars per diem, looked helplessly around for a moment, and then replied:

"I don't b'lieve thar's ary other cheer in the hull room."

"Never mind, never mind," said the secretary, laughing, and drawing a low travelling trunk from a pile in the corner, "this will do."

The second official of the great State of Tennessee seated himself upon the trunk, and we fell into a long conversation on the condition of the country. In the course of it I said to him:

"You are a Southern man, sir; tell me, do the Rebel leaders really mean to establish a monarchy?"

"Undoubtedly they do," he replied. "They have had that purpose from the beginning. Their main object in bringing on the war was to get the Southern people into the clutches of a military despotism, so that they might disfranchise them, and thus prevent their ever overturning slavery. If you will come up to the State-House to-morrow, I will show you volumes of correspondence to prove this."

"But why was it necessary to disfranchise the people? They have followed the lead of the slave-lords blindly. The most of them think slavery promotes their interests."

"That is true, but Northern ideas were working down among them. In Maryland, Kentucky, Missouri, and Western Virginia, they had spread wonderfully. Those States would have been free long ago if the masses had not thought emancipation would make the blacks the political and social equals of the whites. As soon as they came to be disabused of that notion, they would have voted slavery out of existence; and when they had done that, the people in the Cotton States would have asked the reason why, and then slavery on this continent would have received its everlasting death-blow. Slavery cannot any longer live in the Union. The South can save it only by separation and a despotism."

After some further conversation we separated, and early the next morning I set out for Murfreesboro.

CHAPTER XI.

THE MAN WHO "DON'T SURRENDER MUCH."

THE country below Nashville presented the same desolate appearance as that through which I had already passed. At Lavergne, a whole town lay in ashes. On the direct line of communication with Murfreesboro, it had been the scene of frequent conflicts between the Rebel and the Union forces, and, one after another, its peaceful habitations had fallen before the flames. Its inhabitants had all fled, and two or three smoke-begrimed cabins were all that remained of the once thriving and happy village.

"I was in the front room of that small house yonder," said Captain Firman, of General Wheeler's staff, to me a few weeks later, as we halted at this station, while he was on his way, a prisoner of war, to the penitentiary at Nashville, "when a shell from one of your batteries entered just beneath the window—you can see the hole from here—and exploded directly at the feet of Wheeler and myself. A lady sat at the piano. The piano was shivered into a thousand fragments, and the lady thrown to the farther end of the room, but not one of us was hurt. The general and I made a hasty exit by the rear door, but our companion, in her fright, ran out at the front. As she came under that old tree standing by the corner of the house, another shell burst over her head, and its fragments fell all around her, but, strange to say, she again escaped uninjured."

A little elevation at the right of the railway was the scene of one of the most heroic exploits of the war. There Colonel Innis —warned by the old negro I have introduced to the reader—with a little band of three hundred and eighty-nine Michigan men, without artillery or other defence than a hastily thrown up barricade of camp-wagons and underbrush, beat off Wheeler's whole force of three thousand horse and two field-pieces.

"Colonel Innis," said General Rosecrans to him on the eve of the battle of Stone River, "will you hold Lavergne?"

"I'll try, general."

"I ask if you will *do* it!" exclaimed the laconic general.

"I WILL," quietly responded the colonel, and he kept his word.

Just as the New Year's sun was sending its first greeting to the little band that crouched there behind the wagons, the head of the Rebel column emerged from the woods which skirt the southern side of the town, and Captain Firman, riding forward to the flimsy breast-work, cried out:

"General Wheeler demands an instant and unconditional surrender."

"Give General Wheeler my compliments, and tell him we don't surrender much," came back to him from behind the brush-heaps.

Mounting then his Kentucky roan, the heroic colonel rode slowly around the rude intrenchment. "Boys," he said, "they are three thousand—have you said your prayers?"

"We are ready, Colonel. Let them come on!" answered the brave Michigan men.

And they did come on!

"Six times we swept down on them," said Captain Firman to me, "and six times I rode up with a flag, and summoned them to surrender; but each time Innis sent back the message, varied, now and then, with an adjective, 'We don't surrender much.' He sat his horse during the first charges, as if on dress parade; but at the third fire I saw him go down. I thought we had winged him, but when we charged again, there he sat as cool as if the thermometer had been at zero. One of our men took deliberate aim, and again he went down; but when I rode up the fifth time and shouted, 'We'll not summon you again—surrender at once!' it was Innis who yelled out, 'Pray don't, for *we don't surrender much.*' At the seventh charge I was wounded, and the general sent another officer with the summons. Your people halted him a few hundred yards from the breast-work, and an officer, in a cavalryman's overcoat, came out to meet him. ['They had killed my two horses,' said Colonel Innis to me afterwards, 'and I was afraid they would singe my uniform—the fire was *rather* hot—so I covered it.']

"'What is your rank, sir?' demanded the Union officer.

"'Major, sir.'

"'Go back, and tell General Wheeler that he insults me by sending one of your rank to treat with one of mine. Tell him, too, I have not come here to surrender. I shall fire on the next flag.'

"It was Innis, and by that ruse he made us believe he had received re-enforcements. Thinking it was so, we drew off, and the next day Innis sent Wheeler word by a prisoner, that he had whipped us with three hundred and eighty-nine men!"

About a fortnight after my arrival at Murfreesboro, as I sat one morning reading a newspaper in the "Aides' Room" at head-quarters, a tall, erect, sinewy-built, noble-featured man, with dark flowing hair, a long, elastic stride, and a monstrous steel-hilted sword dangling at his heels, and clanking heavily on the floor at his every step, stalked into the room, and, giving me a casual glance, entered General Garfield's apartment. In a moment he returned, and, striding directly up to me, said:

"Sir, are you the man who wrote 'Among the Pines?'"

There was something in his quick, abrupt voice and decided, energetic manner, that made me uncertain of his intentions: so, rising from my seat, and drawing myself up to my full height, I replied, in a half-defiant tone:

"I am, sir: at your service."

"I want to take you by the hand, sir. God bless you!" was the hearty response.

Considerably relieved, I said, as I accepted his greeting:

"And *you* are ——?"

"Colonel Innis—Innis of the Michigan Engineers."

"Oh! You are the man, who '*don't surrender much!*'"

"Not much—that is, I never did."

Saying I would like to know him better, I asked him to be seated. He sat down, and fought the battle over again. When he had concluded, I said:

"I met an old negro at Nashville, who told me he rode up from Murfreesboro and warned you of Wheeler's coming. He said you made him stay over night, and treated him like a white man."

"I tried to, for he saved me from a surprise. Wheeler captured all of my pickets before sunrise, and without the old darkey's warning, I mightn't have been half ready. There is nothing Wheeler would like so well as to take me. We have had several fights, and after each one I have sent him word how many men it took to whip him."

In a western city, a few weeks ago, I met the colonel again. Laying my hand on his shoulder, I accosted him with—

"And you've not surrendered yet!"

"Not yet," he replied, turning round and taking my hand; "but I've had another brush with Wheeler. Just after Chicamauga he came upon me with nearly five thousand men. I beat him off, and then sent him word I had whipped him with one-half of my regiment."

The West has sent many brave men to the war, but none braver than INNIS.

CHAPTER XII.

BIBLE SMITH.

As I alighted from the cars at Murfreesboro, the inevitable official again confronted me.

"Can I get a conveyance to Head-quarters?" I asked him.

"Yes, there's an omnibus here. But the General's not in town. He's at the front."

"And where can I find lodgings for a few days?"

"Don't know. There's not a hotel or lodging-house in the place."

A town of forty thousand people with not a single inn! Surely this was the miracle of the nineteenth century.

After a short search I found the omnibus—a cast-off Northern coach, with a Yankee Jehu.

"My friend," I said to him, "will you take me where I can sleep to-night?"

"Yes: I'll take you to jail. It's the only house here that takes in strangers."

I was about asking him to drive me to Head-quarters, in the hope that my letters, even in the General's absence, might secure me a night's lodging, when a heavy hand was laid on my shoulder, and a strangely familiar voice—a face we may forget, but a voice that has once given us pleasure, lingers in the memory forever—accosted me, as follows:

"I know'd it wus ye. I know'd ye the minnit I sot eyes on ye."

Turning on the speaker, I saw a spare, squarely-built, loose-jointed man, above six feet high, with a strongly marked face, a long, grizzly beard, and silvery black hair hanging loosely over his shoulders like a woman's. He wore an officer's undress coat, and the boots of the cavalry service, but the rest of his costume was of the common "butternut" homespun. Taking his extended hand, and trying hard to recall his features, I said to him:

"I know your voice, but your face I don't remember."

"Doan't remember me! me, Bible—Bible Smith! Why I'd a know'd *ye* ef yer face hed been blacker'n yer Whig principles."

We had not met in many years, but the name brought him to my remembrance. Again grasping his hand, and shaking it, this time, with a right good will, I exclaimed:

"I'm delighted to see you, Bible; and to see you *here*—true to the old flag."

"Ye mought hev know'd thet. I know'd *ye* war right, ef ye war a Whig. But ye wants ter git under kiver. I knows a old 'ooman yere—she's secesh way up ter the yeres, an' her fixins hain't nothin' loike whot ye gits in York, but I reckon ef I ax her, she'll take ye in."

"Any place will do till the General returns—I have letters to him."

The omnibus man went in quest of my trunk, and in a short time, accompanied by my new-found friend, I was on my way to the house of the Secession lady. Before going thither I will make the reader somewhat acquainted with my companion, in the hope that what I shall say of him may lead the public to think better of the whole edition of Southern "Bibles," who, though badly "bound," and sadly deficient in the way of "lettering" and "embellishment," have about as much homely truth and genuine worth as the more gilded things found in higher latitudes.

Late in November, 1850, as I was journeying on horseback from Tuscaloosa, Alabama, to Louisville, Kentucky, I was overtaken by a storm, just at night-fall, and forced to ask shelter at a small farm-house near the little town of Richmond, in Bedford County, Tennessee. The house stood in a small clearing, a short distance from the highway, and was one story high, of hewn logs nicely chinked and whitewashed, with a projecting roof, a broad, open piazza, and an enormous brick chimney-stack protruding at either gable. As I rode up to it, the farmer came out to meet me. He was dressed in homespun, and had a wiry, athletic frame, a dark, sun-browned complexion, an open, manly face, and a frank, cordial manner that won my confidence in a moment. With thirteen years less of life and a century less of hardship, he was the same man who met me at the Murfreesboro railway station. He bade me "good evenin'" as I approached him, and returning his salutation, I asked him for shelter for myself and horse.

"Sartin, Stranger," he replied; "I nuver turned away one o' God's images yit, ef they wus a Yankee—an' some o' them is dreffул pore likenesses, ye mought bet a pile on thet."

"Why do you think I am a Yankee?" I asked, smiling.

"I sees it all over ye. But, come, alight; ye's welcome ter all I hes, an' ef ye kin spin a yarn, or tell a lie, ony bigger'n I kin, I'll 'low a Yankee ar smarter'n a Tennesseean—an' I nuver know'd one as war yit."

Dismounting, I requested him to give my horse some oats, remarking that I made free with him, because I expected to pay for what I had.

"Pay!" he exclaimed; "Nuver ye tork uv pay, Stranger, 'tween two sich men as ye an' me is, or ye'll make me fight another duel. It's agin my principles, but I fit one onst, an' it mought be *ye* wouldn't loike ter hev me fit another."

"Not with me, I assure you. I'd take free quarters with you for a month rather than fight a duel."

"Yer a sensible man; fur I shud, fur shore, sarve ye jest as I done Clingman—thet famous North Car'lina chap. P'raps ye nuver yered how I fit him?"

"No, I never did," I replied.

"Wall, I'll tell ye on it. But yere, Jake" (to a stout, cheerful negro, who just then appeared at the corner of the house), "Yere, Jake, tuck the gen'leman's nag, rub him down, an' guv him some oats, an' mind, doan't ye guv no parson's measure wuth the oats."

"Nuver you f'ar, Massa. Jake'll gub it ter 'im chock-heapin'—loike you gub's eberyting, Massa," rejoined the negro, bounding nimbly into the saddle, and riding off to the barnyard.

The farmer then turned and led the way into the house. At the door of the sitting-room we were met by his wife—a comely, dark-eyed woman of about thirty, neatly clad in a calico gown, with shoes and stockings (a rarity in that region) on her feet, and a spotless lace cap perching cosily on the back of her head.

"Sally," said my host, as we entered the room, "yere'r a stranger, so, tuck him in; guv him fritters an' apple-jack fur supper, fur he'm a Yankee, an' thar's no tellin' but ye mought save the kentry ef ye made him fall in love wuth ye."

The good woman laughed, gave me a cordial greeting, asked me to a seat by the fire, and went about preparing supper. As I seated myself with her husband, by the broad hearth-stone, I glanced around the apartment. It occupied one-half of the building, and had a most cosey and comfortable appearance. On the floor was a tidy rag carpet, and the plastered walls were covered with a modest paper, and ornamented with a half dozen neatly-framed engravings. A gilded looking-glass, festooned with sprigs of evergreen, hung between the front windows, and opposite to it stood a huge piece of mahogany, half a side-board, half a bureau, which in its day had graced some statelier mansion. A dozen rustic arm-chairs, covered with untanned deerskin, a small stand in the corner, piled high with such books as the Bible, The "Pilgrim's Progress," and "Doddridge's Expositor," and a large pine table, on which my hostess was arranging the tea-things, completed the furniture of the room. A little boy of five and a little girl of seven were helping the good wife set the tea-table, and through an open door at the rear, I saw an older child, with her mother's dark-brown hair and her father's expressive features, busily frying the fritters over the kitchen fire.

After asking me where I "come from," where I "mought be a moseyin' ter," and other similar questions, my host said:

"So, ye nuver yered how I fit Clingman—thet big Whig chap over thar ter North Car'lina?"

"No," I replied, "I never did, but I would like to, for I know Clingman, and am a Whig myself."

"Ye is! Wall, I'd nuver a thort it ter luck at ye; an' it do 'pear sort o' quar ter me thet ony *white* man kin go agin free schools, free speech, free thort, and free a'r fur all o' God's critters, but *ye* does, ef ye's a Whig, or I hain't read the dictionary!"

"What dictionary have you read that in?" I asked.

"Wall, ter tell ye the truth, Stranger—an' thet, though it'r gittin' out o' fashion, ar what we orter do—*I* nuver read it in nary one: Sally, ye sees, do all the readin' uv the fambly. But, I allers reckoned them wus whig principles."

"And what are democratic principles?"

"Jest the contrary. Thet's whot dimmocrat means. Whig ar only another name fur big; an' it means big-bugs, fur all o' them goes thet way. But they karn't hev my vote, nohow. I goes fur the Decleration uv Independence—life, liberty, an' the pursoot uv whot ye loikes. I'se got it—hangin' up thar agin the wall. The man as writ thet war some punkins."

"Yes, he was, and it's a good thing to have in the house. But, tell me about your duel with Clingman."

"Wall, ye sees, it war jest afore the last 'lection, when ye put in ole Zack fur President. The Whigs they had a big barbacue down ter Richmond, an' Clingman an' a hull lot uv 'em went inter speechifying ter kill. Wall, in the coorse uv Clingman's speech he said thet Cass, our canderdate, wus a nigger-trader down thar ter Newbern way, an' wus in jail fur passin' counterfit money, an' ef we 'lected him, we'd hev ter bail him out ter 'naugerate him. Now, I couldn't stand thet, no how, so I right up in meetin', an' telled Clingman he lied loike blazes. Wall, he stopped short ter onst, an' axed me fur my redress."

"*Ad*dress," said his wife, pausing in her work, and looking pleasantly at me.

"Thet's so, Sally," replied the farmer. "I telled ye, Stranger, Sally hes all the larnin' uv the fambly. She's a quality 'ooman—she is! Wall, I guv Clingman my name, an' whar I hung out, an', shore 'nuff, jest arter dark, a feller rid up yere wuth a challunge, all writ out in Clingman's own hand—an' ye knows he's a right smart scholard, an' a durned clever feller ter boot, ef he ar a Whig. I couldn't read the thing—I hain't got no furder nur prent yit—so I guv it ter Sally. Sally she screeched out when she seed whot it war 'bout, but I telled har ter stand up, an' die loike a man, an' so—she sot down, an' 'cepted the challunge. Now, ye knows, the challunged 'un allers hes the chise o' weapons, so I said I'd hev swords, mounted."

"Then you are familiar with sword practice?" I remarked.

"Furmilye wuth it! I nuver seed more'n one sword, in all my borned days, an' thet war so durned rusty a ox-team couldn't dror it. It hung over dad's front door when I war a young 'un. Dad said he fit wuth it ter Cowpens, but I know'd he didn't, 'case he couldn't ha' been more'n two y'ar old at thet writin', an' he allers hed a awful way o' lyin'.

"Wall, I said swords, mounted, at sun-up the next mornin', over agin my r'ar pinery. Now, I hes a dreffnl smart ox-brute thet I'se a raised up fur my privat' ridin'—ye knows, we uses them critters jest as ye does hosses. The brute he doan't loike a spur, an' when ye puts one inter 'im, he'll pitch, head-foremose, inter the fust thing he comes ter, be it man or beast. Wall, in the mornin' I tuck out the cow-horn (ye'd think Gabriel war a soundin' the last trump when I blows it), cut a right smart stick fur a sword, put it inter a yaller bag thet lucked loike a scabbard, got out the ox-brute, tied a red rag ter his horns, put on him my wife's best kiverlet—Sally hed it agin we got morried; it hes more colors nur Joseph's coat, but red an' yaller dominates. Wall, I put on the kiverlet fur a saddle, an' moseyed off ter the dueling ground.

"Clingman, he war thar, wuth two seconds, a doctor, an' a hull 'pothecary store uv cuttin' instruments, all waitin' an' ready ter make mince-meat uv my carcass. Soon as he seed how I war 'coutcred, he up an' 'jected ter fightin', but I counted out the terms uv the duel—swords, mounted—an' I telled him ef he didn't stand, an' fight loike a man, I'd post him all over the State o' North Car'lina fur a coward. Wall, finarly he 'cluded ter do it. So, we tuck our stands, the seconds they guv the word, Clingman he put spurs inter his hoss, an' I put spurs inter mine, an', Stranger, ye'd better b'lieve when my ox moseyed down onter his mar, wuth horn a blowin', an' kiverlet a flyin', the mar she piked out quicker'n a whirlygust chasin' a streak o' lightnin', an' she nuver helt up till she got clean inter North Car'lina. I'se allers telled Sally sense thet thet kiverlet ar the flag I means ter live under, ter sleep under, an' ter die under." *

When I had somewhat recovered from the immoderate fit of laughter which expressed my appreciation of the farmer's story, his comely wife said to me:

"Fotch up yer cheer, Stranger. We hain't nothin' 'cept common doin's, but we's 'nuff o' them."

And there was "'nuff o' them." The table was loaded

* Subsequent inquiry satisfied me that Bible's account of this singular duel was substantially true.

down with bacon, venison, wild fowl, hominy, corn-pone, fritters, tea, cider, and apple-jack, all heaped upon it in promiscuous confusion. I had ridden far, and eaten nothing since the morning, but I might have relished the viands had my appetite been much daintier than it was.

A desultory conversation followed till the close of the meal. When it was over, again seating myself with the farmer before the blazing light-wood fire, while his wife and elder daughter went about clearing away the tea-things, I said to him:

"You guessed rightly, my friend. I *am* a Yankee, and I have the Yankee way of asking questions. Now, I want to ask you how you live, what you raise, how many negroes you have—all about yourself, for I've already fallen in love with you and—your wife."

"Fall'n in love wuth *me!* ha! ha!" echoed the farmer. "Stranger, *I* nuver fell in love wuth nary man 'cept Sally, but I fell inter it so deep wuth she thet I'se willin' all creation shud love har jest loike I does—an' they wud, ef they only know'd har so wall as me."

"I have no doubt they would. Does she do all her own housework?"

"Uvery thing—she an' the little gal. She woan't hev no lazy nigger wimmin round. They make more wuck nur they does."

"Do yer wife wuck, Stranger?" asked the lady: "They say wimmin all wucks ter the North."

"Nearly all do—except my wife. *She* don't, because I have none. But I intend to have one. I shall probably wait till your husband breaks his neck, and then pop the question to you."

"Wall, I reckon I'd hev ye, fur I'se sort o' tuck ter ye. 'Pears loike ye Northern gentlemen hain't stuck up, an' doan't 'count tharselfs no better nur wuckin' folk, like the 'ristocracts does round yere."

"The heart, not the wealth or the intellect, Madam, makes the true aristocracy," I replied, gravely.

"Thet's whot our parson sez; an' in heaven, he sez, them as gits the highest hes hearts jest loike little childerin'—thet loves uvery thing, an' uvery body, an' hain't no larnin' at all. Ef thet's so, Bible'll be one on the biggest on 'em, fur he's got nigh ter no larnin'—he kin only jest make out ter spell—an' his heart ar big 'nuff ter holt all o' creation."

"Doan't ye say thet, Sally," said the farmer, looking at his wife with a tender light in his eyes, and a beautiful smile on his rough features: "The LORD moughtn't be uv yer 'pinion."

"Yas, He ar, fur He knows ye jest loike I does."

The farmer made no reply, and a short silence followed. I broke it by saying:

"Come, Bible, answer my questions—tell me all about yourself."

"Thet hain't my name, Stranger, though it'r whot I goes by. Ye sees, my name ar Smith, an' dad chrisund me Jehoshaphat*—ter 'stinguish me frum the t'other Smiths, but, somehow, it got shortened ter Bible, an' it'r been Bible unter this day. Wall, I wuck'd 'long uv dad till I war twenty-one, fur the ole 'un he said he'd a fotched me up when I war a young 'un, an' he war bound ter git his pay out o' me agin I war grow'd, an'—he done it.

* His name according to the army rolls, is WILLIAM J. SMITH.

"Wall, the day I war uv age, dad axed me out ter the barn, an' totein' out a mule-brute as hed been in the fambly uver sense Adam warn't no higher'n lettle Sally, he sez ter me, sez he: 'Thar, Bible, thar's my last wull an' testamunt—tuck it, an' gwo an' seek yer fortun'.' I hadn't nary chise, so, I tuck the mule-brute an' moseyed out ter seek my fortun'. I squatted down right squar onter this dead'nin', hired my nig Jake (I owns him now), an' me, an' Jake, an' the mule-brute went ter wuck loike blazes—all but the mule-brute—he war too tarnal lazy ter wuck; he war so lazy I hed ter git my ox ter holp him dror his last breath. Wall, Jake an' me added acre ter acre, and mule-brute ter mule-brute, as the Scriptur sez, till finarly I got ter be right wall forehanded. Then, one day, I sez ter Jake: 'Jake,' sez I, 'ye's got a wife, an' ye knows whot durmestic furlicity is—ter be shore ye hes ter keep it seven mile away, an' it b'longs ter a durned 'ristocrat, but whot's thet when I guvs ye Saturday arternoons an' Sundays, all ter yerself—now, *I* hain't nary furlicity at all: whot shill I do.'

"'Git a wife, Massa,' sez Jake; 'git a wife, Massa. But dar's mighty fine fish in de sea, Massa, so doan't ye kotch no dolphins whot shows dar colors in de sun but neber comes ter de sufface when it rains. Saddle de mar, Massa, an' gwo out on a 'splorin' expedition; Jake'll luck arter de fixin's while you'm away.' Now, thet nig ar allers right—he's got a head longer'n the moral law—so, I saddled the mar, an' sallied out arter Sally.

"I hed ter scour nigh 'bout all o' creation, an' it tuck me four hull months ter do it, but—I found har. Soon as I sot eyes on har I know'd it war she, an' I telled har so, but she say: Ye must ax Par.' (Sally hes book-breedin', ye sees, so she sez *par* instead o' *dad*, which ar' the nat'ral way.) Wall, I axed 'par'—he's one on yer quality folk, been ter Congress, an' only missed bein' Guv'ner by—not gittin' the nomurnation. I axed him, an' he shuck his head, but I guv him jest a week ter think on it, an' moseyed out ter git ready agin the weddin'. I know'd he'd come round, an' he done it. So I sez ter Sally: 'Sally,' sez I: 'we'll be morried ter-morrer.'

"'Ter-morrer!' screeched Sally, holtin' up har hands, an' openin' har eyes; 'Why I hain't a ready. I hain't no cloes!'

"'Cloes!' sez I; 'nuver mind yer cloes—I doan't morry ye fur them.'

"So Sally she consented, an' I piked out fur a parson. Now, thar warn't none nigher'n over a branch, an' it so happin'd it rained loike blazes thet night, an' toted off all the bridges, so when the parson an' me got down ter the run jest arter noon the next day—we wus ter a been morried at levin'—thar warn't no way o' crossin', but—thar war Sally, on the t'other side uv the run, in har sun-bunnet an' a big umbrell', onpatiently waitin' fur us. Thar warn't no other how, so I sez ter the parson: 'Parson,' sez I: 'say over the Prayer-Book—Sally's got the hull uv it by heart agin this time—we'll be morried ter onst, right yere.' So, the parson he said over the Prayer-Book, Sally she made the 'sponses—all 'bout the 'beyin' an' so on—an' we's been man an' wife uver sense; an' Stranger, I doan't keer whar the t'other 'ooman ar', thar hain't nary one livin' quite up ter Sally."

"An' does ye b'lieve thet story, Stranger?" asked Sally, who, having finished clearing away the tea-things, had, with the older daughter, and the younger children, taken a seat near me in the chimney-corner.

"I can't say that I do. Not altogether," I replied.

"I'm glad on it, fur we wus morried in a house, loike Christun people—we wus."

"Is Jake your only slave?" I asked the farmer after a while.

"Yas, he'r my only 'un, but he's as good as ony two ye uver know'd on. Ye sees, I raises nigh on ter no craps 'cept mule-brutes an' horned critters, an' them, ye knows, browse in the woods, an' doan't make much wuck."

If this chapter were not already too long I would tell the reader more of this farmer's family; how every thing about the house and out-buildings was the model of neatness; how the comely housewife strove, with grace and cheerfulness, to do honor to a stranger guest; how tidily she kept her handsome brood, all clad in homespun of her own weaving, and her own making; how the younger children climbed their father's knee, pulled his beard, and laughed at his stories, as if they had never heard them before; how nimbly the elder daughter sprang to do her mother's bidding, how she fetched the apples from the loft, and the apple-*jack* from the pantry, and, between times, helped to lull the sleepy little ones to sleep, or to keep them, wakeful, out of mischief; how when we parted for the night, Sally read a chapter from the big Bible, and then, all kneeling down, made such a prayer as the GOOD ALL FATHER loves to hear; how when I bade them "good-bye" in the morning, all had to kiss me, from the mother to the youngest; and how Bible, giving me a parting grasp of the hand, said as I mounted to ride away:

"Come out an' settle yere, Stranger; we'll send ye ter Congress—the man as hes cheek enuff ter kiss a man's wife afore his vury face, kin git ony office in this part o' the kentry!"

Of all this and more, I would like to tell, but have I not already said enough to show that true worth and real manliness exist among the "poor whites" of the South? Though ignorant and illiterate, uncouth of speech, and ungainly of manner, have not those who so well observe the obligations of husband and father, mother and wife and daughter, learned some of the higher duties of life?

CHAPTER XIII.

BIBLE'S STORY.

SEATED after dinner on the piazza of the hospitable Southern lady, Bible told me his story.

He had been stripped of all his property, his wife and children had been driven from their home, his house had been burned to the ground, and he himself hunted through the woods like a wild beast, because he had remained true to what he called democratic principles—"free schools, free speech, free thought and free a'r fur all o' GOD's critters."

The world went well with him till the breaking out of the Rebellion. That event found him the owner of fifteen likely negroes, a fine plantation of nine hundred and thirty acres, and a comfortable framed dwelling and out-buildings. His elder daughter had married a young farmer of the district, and his younger—little Sally, whom I remembered as a rosy-cheeked, meek-eyed wee thing of only seven years—had grown up a woman.

In the spring of 1861, when there were no Union troops south of the Ohio, and the secession fever was raging furiously all over his county, he organized one hundred and six of his neighbors into a company of Home Guards, and was elected their captain. They were pledged to resist all attacks on the person or property of any of their number, and met frequently in the woods in the vicinity of their homes. This organization secured Bible safety and free expression of opinion till long after Tennessee went out of the Union. In fact, he felt so secure that, in 1862—a year after the State seceded—under the protection of his band of Home Guards, he inaugurated and carried through a celebration of the fourth of July at Richmond, Tennessee, under the very guns of a rebel regiment then forming in the town.

An act of so much temerity naturally attracted the attention of the Confederate authorities, and not long afterwards he was roused from his bed one morning before day-break, by three hundred armed men, who told him that he was a prisoner, and that all his property was confiscated to the Government. They at once enforced the "confiscation act;" "and this," he said, taking from his wallet a piece of soiled paper, "ar' whot I hed ter 'tribute ter the dingnation consarn. It'r Sally's own handwrite, an' I knows ye loikes har, so, ye kin hev it, fur it'll nuver be uv no manner uv account ter me."

The schedule is now before me, and I copy it *verbatim*: "14 men and wimmin" (Jake eluded the soldiers and escaped to the woods), "1600 barrils corn, 130 sheeps, 700 bushls wheat, 440 barley, 100 rye, 27 mules, 5 cow-brutes, 105 head hogs, 17 horses and mars, and all they cud tote beside."

"Wall, they tied me, hand an' fut," he continued; "an' toted me off ter the Military Commission sittin' ter Chattanooga. I know'd whot thet meant—a short prayer, a long rope, an' a break-down danced on the top o' nothin'. Better men nur me hed gone thet way ter the Kingdom—sevin on 'em wuthin a month—but I detarmined I wouldn't go ef I could holp it; not thet I 'jected ter the journey, only ter goin' afore uv Sally. Ye sees, I hedn't been nigh so good a man as I'd orter be, an' I reckoned Sally—who, ye knows, ar the best 'ooman thet uver lived—I reckoned she, ef she got thar a leetle afore o' me, could sort o' put in a good word wuth the LORD, an' git Him ter shot His eyes ter a heap o' my doin's; an' sides, I should, I know'd, feel a mighty strange loike up thar without har. Wall, I detarmined not ter go, so thet night, as we war camped out on the ground, I slid the coil, stole a nag, an' moseyed off. Howsumuver, I hedn't got more'n a hun'red rods, 'fore the durned Secesh yered me, an' the bullets fell round me thicker'n tar in January. They hit the hoss, winged me a trifle, an' in less nur ten minnits, hed me tighter'n uver. They swore a streak uv blue brimstun', an' said they'd string me up ter onst, but I telled 'em they wouldn't, 'case I know'd I war a gwine ter live ter holp do thet ar' same turn fur Jeff. Davis. Wall, I s'pose my impudence hed suthin' ter do wuth it, fur they didn't hang me—ye mought know thet, Mr. ———, fur, ye sees, I hes a good neck fur stretchin' yit."

"Wall we got ter Chattanooga jest arter noon. The Commission they hed too many on hand thet day ter 'tend ter my case, an' the jail wus chock-heapin', so they put me inter a tent under guard uv a hull Georgy regiment. Things luck'd 'mazin' squally, an' much as I detarmined ter be a man, my heart went clean down inter my boots whenuver I thort uv Sally. I nuver felt so, afore or sence, fur then I hedn't got used ter luckin' at the gallus uvery day.

"Wall, *I* didn't know whot ter do, but thinkin' the Lord did, I kneeled down an' prayed right smart. I telled Him I hedn't no face ter meet Him afore I'd a done suthin' fur the kentry, an' thet Sally's heart would be clean broke ef I went afore har, but, howsumuver, I said, He know'd best, an' ef it war His will, I hed jest nothin' ter say agin it. Thet's all I said, but I said it over an' over, a heap o' times, an it war right dark when I got off uv my knees. The Lord yered me, thet's sartin, 'case I hedn't more'n got up fore a dirty grey-back, drunker'n a member uv Congress, staggered inter the tent. I reckon he thort he war ter home, fur he drapped down onter the ground an' went ter sleep, wuthout so much as axin' ef I wus willin'.

"Then it come inter my head, all ter onst, whot ter do. Ye sees, the critters hed tied me hand an' fut, an' teddered me wuth a coil ter one o' the tent-stakes, so I couldn't move only jest so fur; but the Lord He made the drunken feller lop down jest inside uv reachin'. Wall, when I war shore he war dead asleep, I rolled over thar, drawed out the Bowie-knife in his belt wuth my teeth, an' sawed off my wristlets in no time. Ye kin reckon it didn't take long ter undo the 'tother coils, an' ter 'propriate his weapons, tie 'im hand an' fut loike I war, strip off his coat, put mine onter 'im, swap hats, an' pull the one I guv him down onter his eyes loike as ef he nuver wanted ter see the sun agin. When I'd a done thet, I stopped ter breathe, an' luckin' up I seed a light a comin'. I 'spicioned it war ter 'xamine arter me, so I slunk down inter a corner o' the tent, jest aside the door. They wus a leftenant, an' three privits, makin' the rounds, an' the light showed me nigh onter a army uv sentinels all about thar. Thet warn't no way encouragin', but sez I ter myself: 'Bible,' sez I, 'be cool an' outdacious, an' ye'll git out o' this, yit;' so, when the leftenant luck'd in, an' sayin': 'All right,' put out agin, I riz up, an' jined the fellers as wus a follerin' on him. I kept in the shadder, an' they, s'posin' I war one on 'em, tuck no kind uv notice uv me. We'd luck'd arter three or four pore prisoners loike I war, when I thort I'd better be a moseyin', so I drapped ahind an' arter a while dodged out beyont the second line o' pickets. I'd got nigh onter a patch uv woods half a mile off, when all ter onst a feller sprung up frum a clump uv bushes, yelled, 'Halt,' an' pinted his musket stret at me. I mought hev eended 'im, but I reckoned others wus nigh, an' sides, I nuver takes humin life ef I kin holp it; so I sez ter 'im: 'Why, Lord bless me, cumrad', I didn't seed ye.' 'I s'pose ye didn't. Whot is ye doin' yere?' sez he. 'Only pursuin' a jug o' blue ruin I'se out thar hid under a log,' sez I. 'Ye knows it'r agin rule ter tote it inside, but a feller must licker.' 'Wall, licker up ter-morrer,' sez he. 'We's got 'ticklar orders ter let no 'un out ter-night.' 'Blast the orders,' sez I. 'Ye'd loike a swig yerself.' 'Wall, I would,' sez he. 'Wull ye go snacks?' 'Yas,' sez I; 'an' guv ye chock-heapin' measure, fur I *must* hev some o' thet afore mornin'.'

"Thet brung him, an' I piked off for the ruin. (It warn't thar, ye knows—I nuver totch the dingnation stuff.) Ye'd better b'lieve the grass didn't grow under my feet when onst I got inter the woods. I plumbed my coorse by the stars, an' made ten right smart miles in no time. Then it come inter my head thet I'd a forgot all about the Lord, so I kneeled down right thar, an' thanked Him. I telled Him I seed His hand jest so plain as ef it war day-time, an' thet, as shore as my name war Bible, I'd foller His lead in futur'—an' I'se tried ter, uver sense.

"I'd got ter be right wall tuckered out by thet time—the 'citement, ye see, hed helt me up, but I'd no sooner gone ter prayin' 'fore my knees guv out all ter onst—so, I put fur a piece uv timber, lay down under a tree, an' went ter sleep. I must hev slept mighty sound, fur, long 'bout mornin', some'un hed ter shuck me awful hard, an' turn me clar over, 'fore it woked me. I got up. 'Twar nigh so light as day, though 'twarn't sun-up. Yit I luck'd all round, an' didn't see a soul! Now, whot d'ye s'pose it war thet woked me?"

"Your own imagination, I reckon. You were dreaming, and in your dream you thought some one shook you," I replied.

"No; 'twarn't thet. I nuver dreams. It war the LORD! An' He done it 'case I'd prayed ter 'im. I'se nuver gone ter sleep, or woke up, sense, wuthout prayin' ter HIM, an' though I'se been in a heap uv wuss fixes nur thet, He's got me out uv all on 'em, jest 'case I does pray ter Him."

I did not dispute him. Who that reads the New Testament as Bible reads it—like a little child—*can* dispute him. In a moment he went on with his story.

"Wall, I luck'd all round, an' seed nuthin', but I *yered*—not a mile off—the hounds a bayin' away loike a young thundergust. They wus arter me, an' thet wus the why the GOOD LORD woked me. I luck'd at the 'volver I'd stole from the sodger, seed it war all right, an' then clumb a tree. 'Bout so quick as it takes ter tell it, the hounds—two 'mazin' fine critters, wuth a hun'red an' fifty apiece—wus on me. I run my eye 'long the pistol-barr'l, an' let drive. It tuck jest two shots ter kill 'em. I know'd the Secesh wus a follerin' the dogs, so, ye'd bêtter b'lieve I made purty tall racin' time till I got ter the eend uv the timber.

"Jest at night I run agin some darkies, who guv me suthin ter eat, an' nothin' more happin'd 'fore the next night, when I come in sight o' home. I got ter the edge uv the woods, on the hill jest ahind uv my barn, 'bout a hour by sun; but I darn't go down, fur, ye knows, the house stood in a clarin', an' some uv the varmunts mought be a watchin' fur me. I lay thar till it war thick dark, an' then I crept ter the r'ar door. I listened; an' whot d'ye 'spose I yered? Sally a prayin'—an' prayin' fur *me*, so 'arnest an' so tender loike, thet I sot down on the door-step, an' cried loike a child—I did."

Here the rough, strong man bent down his head and wept again. The moisture filled my own eyes as he continued:

"She telled the Lord how much I war ter har; how she'd a loved me uver sense she'd a fust seed me; how 'fore har father, or mother, or even the chillen, she loved me; how she'd tried ter make me love Him; how she know'd thet, way down in my heart, I did love Him, though I didn't say so, 'case men doan't speak out 'bout sech things loike wimmin does. An' she telled Him how she hed tried ter do His will; tried ter be one on His raal chillen; an' she telled Him He hed promised not ter lay onter His chillen no more'n they could b'ar, an' *she* couldn't b'ar ter hev me hung up as ef I war a traitor: thet she could part wuth me if it war best; thet she could see me die, an' not weep a tear, ef I could only die loike a man, wuth a musket in my hand, a doin' suthin' for my kentry. Then she prayed Him ter send me back ter har fur jest one day, so she mought ax me once more ter love Him—an' she know'd I would love Him ef she axed me agin—an' she said ef He'd only do thet, she'd—much as she loved me—she'd send me away, an' guv me all up ter Him an' the kentry fur uver!

"I couldn't stand no more, so, I opened the door, drapped onter my knees, tuck har inter my arms, lay my head on har shoulder, an' sobbed out: 'The Lord hes yered ye, Sally! I wull love Him! I wull be worthy of sech love as ye's guv'n me, Sally!'"

He paused for a moment, and covered his face with his hands. When he spoke again there was a softness and tenderness in his tone that I never heard in the voice of but one other man.

"Sense thet minnit this yerth hes been another yerth ter me; an' though I'se lost uverythin', though I hes no home, though night arter night I sleeps out in the cold an' the wet, a scoutin', though my wife an' chillen is scattered, though nigh uvery day I'se in danger uv the gallus, though I'se been roped ter a tree ter die loike a dog, though a thousand bullets hes yelled death in my yeres, though I'se seed my only boy shot down afore my vury eyes, an' I not able ter speak ter him, ter guv him a mossel uv comfort, or ter yere his last word, I'se hed suthin allers yere (laying his hand on his heart) thet hes helt me up, an' made me luck death in the face as ef I loved it. An ef ye hain't got thet, Mr. ———, no matter whot else ye's got, no matter whot money, or larnin', or friends, ye's pore—porer nur I ar!"

I made no reply, and after a short silence he resumed his story.

"Jake—thet war my boy—ye remember him, ye hed him on yer knee—he war eighteen an' a man grow'd then: wall, Jake an' me made up our minds ter pike fur the Union lines ter onst. Sally war all night a cookin' fur us, an' we a gittin' the arms an' fixin's a ready—we hed lots o' them b'longin' ter the Guards, hid away in a panel uv the wall—an' the next day, meanin' ter start jest arter sun-set, we laid down fur some sleepin'. Nigh onter dark, Black Jake, who war a watchin', come rushin' inter the house, sayin' the Secesh wus a comin. Thar wus only twenty on 'em, he said, an' one wus drunk an' didn't count fur nuthin', so, we detarmined ter meet 'em. We tuck our stands nigh the door, each on us men—Black Jake, the boy, an' me—wuth a Derringer in his pocket, two 'volvers in his belt, an' a Bowie-knife in the breast uv his waiscoat, an' the wimmin wuth a 'volver in each hand, an' waited fur 'em. Half a dozen on 'em went round ter the r'ar, an' the rest come at the front door, yellin' out:

"'We doan't want ter 'sturb ye, Miss Smith (they's chivurly, ye knows), but we reckons yer husban' ar yere, an' we must sarch the house. We hes orders ter take him.'

"I opened the door stret off, an' steppin' down onter the piazzer—Black Jake an' the boy ter my back, an' the wimmin' ter the winder—I sez ter 'em:

"'Wall, I'se yere. Take me ef ye kin!'

"They wus fourteen on 'em thar, uvery man wuth a musket, but they darn't lift a leg! They wus cowards. It'r nuthin' but a good cause, Mr. ———, thet guvs a man courage—makes him luck death in the face as ef he loved it.

"Wall, they begun ter parley. 'We doan't want ter shed no blood,' said the leftenant: 'but we's orders ter take ye, Mister Smith, an' ye'd better go wuth us, peaceable loike.'

"'I shan't go wuth ye peaceable loike, nur no other how,' sez I; 'fur ye's a pack o' howlin' thieves an' traitors as no decent man 'ud be seed in company uv. Ye disgraces the green yerth ye walks on, an' ef ye doan't git off uv my sheer uv it, in less nur no time, I'll send ye—though it'r agin my principles ter take humin life—whar ye'll git yer desarts, sartin.'

"Then the leftenant he begun ter parley agin, but I pinted my 'volver at him, an' telled him he'd better be a moseyin' sudden. Sayin' he'd 'port ter his cunnel, he done it.

"We know'd a hun'red on 'em 'ud be thar in no time, so,

soon as they wus out o' sight, the boy an' me, leavin' Black Jake ter luck arter the wimmin, struck a stret line fur the timber. We hedn't got more'n four mile—ter the top uv the tall summit ter the r'ar uv Richmond—afore, luckin' back, we seed my house an' barns all a blazin'! The Heaven-defyin' villuns hed come back—shot Jake down in cold blood, druv my wife an' darter out o' doors, an' burnt all I hed ter the ground! We seed the fire, but not knowin' whot else hed happin'd, an' not bein' able ter do nothin', we piked on inter the woods.

"We traviled all thet night through the timber, an' jest at sun-down uv the next day, come ter a clarin'. We wus mighty tired, but 'twouldn't do ter sleep thar, fur the trees wus nigh a rod asunder; so we luck'd round, an' on t'other side uv the road, not half a mile off, seed 'bout a acre uv laurel bush—ye knows whot them is, some on 'em so thick a dog karn't git through 'em. Jake war tireder nur I war, an' he said ter me, 'Dad,' sez he: 'let us git under kiver ter onst. I feels loike I couldn't stand up no longer.' It wus fool-hardy loike, fur the sun warn't clar down, but I couldn't b'ar ter see the boy so, an', agin my judgment, we went down the road ter the laurels. We lay thar till mornin', an' slep' so sound thet I reckon ef forty yerthquakes hed shuck the yerth, they wouldn't hev woked us. Soon as sun-up, Jake riz, an' went ter the edge uv the thicket ter rekonnoitter. He hedn't stood thar five minnits—right in plain sight, an' not more'n two hun'red rods frum me—afore I yered a shot, an' seed the pore boy throw up his arms, an' fall ter the ground. In less nur no time fifty Secesh wus on him. I war springin' up ter go ter him, when suthin' tuck me by the shoulder, helt me back, an' said ter me: 'Ye karn't do nothin' fur him. Leave 'im ter the Lord. Save yerself fur the kentry.' It went agin natur', but it 'peared the LORD's voice, so I crouched down agin 'mong the bushes. I nuver know'd whot it war thet saved me till nigh a y'ar arterwuds. Then I tuck thet leftenant pris'ner,—I could hev shot him, but I guv him his life ter repent in, an' he done it: he's a decent man now, b'longin' ter Cunnel Johnson's rigiment. Wall, I tuck him, an' he said ter me: "I wus aside uv thet pore boy when he war dyin'. He turned his eyes onter me jest as he war goin', an' he said: 'Ye karn't kotch him. He's out o' the bush! Ha! ha!' He said thet, and died. Ter save me, died wuth a lie on his lips! Does ye b'lieve the LORD laid thet agin him, Mr. ——?"

"No, no! I am sure not. It was a noble action."

"It 'pears so ter me, but it war loike the boy. He war allers furgettin' himself, an' thinkin' uv other folk. He war all—all the pride uv my life,—him an' Sally,—but it pleased the LORD ter tuck him afore me—but only fur a time—only fur a time—'fore long I shill hev him agin—agin—up thar—up thar!"

His emotion choked his utterance for a while. When he resumed, he said:

"At the eend uv a fortni't, trav'lin' by night an' sleepin' by day, an' livin' on the darkies when my fixin's guv out, I got inter the Union lines 'bove Nashville."

"And what became of your wife and daughter?" I asked.

"Lettle Sally went ter har sister. My wife walked eighty mile ter har father's. He's one on yer quality folk, an' a durned old Secesh, but he's got humin natur' in him, an' Sally's safe thar. I'se seed har twice ter his house. The old 'un he's know'd on't, but he hain't nuver said a word."

CHAPTER XIV.

BIBLE'S SCOUTING ADVENTURES.

BIBLE'S intimate knowledge of the country, and acquaintance with the loyal men of the district, enabled him to perform more actual service to the Union cause than a regiment of men in the ranks. Hiding in the woods, or secreting himself in the houses of his friends by day, he would sally forth by night, and, penetrating far into the rebel lines, frequently gather information of great importance to our army. Often days without food, sleeping out in the cold and the rain, hunted down with blood-hounds, betrayed by pretended friends, waylaid by whole regiments, the mark for a thousand rifles, and with the gallows ever before him, he went on in his perilous work with a single-hearted devotion to his country, and an earnest, child-like reliance on God, that would do honor to the best names in history.

His scouting adventures would fill a volume, and read more like a romance of the middle ages than a matter-of-fact history of the present time. On one occasion, when about five miles outside of our lines, he came, late at night, upon a party of rebel officers, making merry at the house of a wealthy secessionist. Riding coolly up to the mounted orderly on guard before the door-way, he pinioned his arms, thrust a handkerchief into his mouth, and led him quietly out of hearing. Then bidding him dismount, and tying him to a tree, he removed the impromptu gag, and leveling a revolver at his head, said to him:

"Now, tell me, ye rebel villun, whot whiskey-kags wus ye a watchin' thar? Speak truth, or I'll guv ye free passage ter a hot kentry."

"Nine ossifers," said the trembling rebel; "a cunnel, two majors, a sargeon, two cap'ns, an' the rest leftenants."

"Whar's thar weapons?"

"Thar swords is in the hall-way. None on 'em hain't pistols 'cept the sargeon—he mought hev a 'volver."

"Whot nigs is they round?"

"Nary one, I reckon, more'n a old man thar (pointing to the kitchen-building) an' the gals in the house."

"Wall, I'll let ye go fur this, ef ye's telled the truth. Ef ye hain't, ye'd better be a sayin' yer prayers ter onst, fur the Lord won't yere ye òn the t'other side uv Jurdan."

Fastening his horse in "the timber," and creeping up to the house, he then reconnoitered the kitchen premises. The old man—a stout, stalwart negro of about fifty—sat dozing in the corner, and his wife, a young mulatto woman, was cooking wild fowl over the fire. Opening the door, and placing his finger on his lips to enjoin silence, Bible beckoned to the woman. She came to him, and, looking her full in the eye for a moment, he said to her: "I kin trust ye. Wud ye an' yer old 'un loike ter git out o' the claws uv these durned secesh?"

"Yas, yas, Massa," she replied, "we wud. We's Union! We'd loike ter git 'way, Massa!"

Then awakening her husband, Bible said to him: "Uncle, wud ye risk yer life fur yer freedom?"

"Ef dar's a chance, Massa, a right smart chance. Dis

dark'y tinks a heap ob his life, he does, Massa. It 'm 'bout all hem got."

"Yas, yas, I know; but ye shill hev freedom. I'll see ye ter the Free States, ef ye'll holp tuck them secesh ossifers."

"Holp tuck dem, Massa! Why, dar's a dozen on 'em; dey'd chaw ye up in no time," exclaimed the astonished African.

"No, thar hain't a dozen on 'em; thar's only nine; but—ye's a coward," replied the scout.

"No, I hain't no coward, Massa; but I loikes a chance, Massa, a right smart chance."

Bible soon convinced the negro that he would have a "right smart chance," and he consented to make the hazardous strike for his freedom. Entering the house, he returned in a few moments to the scout, confirming the sentinel's report: the weapons were reposing quietly in the hall, near the doorway, and the officers, very much the worse for liquor, were carousing with his master in the dining-room.

Selecting three of the best horses from the stables, Bible directed the yellow woman to lead them into the road, and to bring his own from where it was fastened in the woods. Then, with his sooty ally, the scout entered the mansion. Removing the arms from the hall, he walked boldly into the dining-room. "Gentlemen," he said, pointing his pistols—one in each hand—at the rebel officers, "ye is my pris'ners. Surrender yer shootin' irons, or ye's dade men."

"Who are you?" exclaimed one of them, as they all sprang to their feet.

"Cunnel Smith, uv the Fust Tennessee Nigger Regiment—one old black man an' a yaller 'ooman," coolly replied the scout.

"Go to ——," shouted the surgeon, quickly drawing his revolver, and discharging it directly at Bible's face. The ball grazed his head, cut off a lock of hair just above his ear, and lodged in the wall at his back. The report was still sounding through the apartment, when the surgeon uttered a wild cry, sprang a few feet into the air, and fell lifeless to the floor! The negro had shot him.

"Come, gentlemen, none o' thet," said Bible, as coolly as if nothing had happened, "guv me the shootin' iron, an' surrender, or we'll sot the rest on ye ter his wuck—rakin' coals fur the devil's funnace,—in less nur a minnit."

Without more hesitation the rebel colonel handed the scout the fallen man's pistol, and then all, followed by the scout and the negro, marched quietly out of the front door. The mulatto woman, holding the horses, was standing in the highway.

"Hitch the nags, my purty gal," said the scout, "an' git a coil. An' ye, gentlemen, sot down, an' say nothin'—'cept it mought be yer prayers; but them, I reckon, ye hain't larned yit."

The negress soon returned with the rope, and while Bible and her husband covered them with their revolvers, she tied the arms of the prostrate chivalry. When this was done, the scout affixed a long rope to the waist of the officer on either flank of the column, and, taking one in his own hand, and giving the other to the negro, cried out:

"Sogers uv the Fust Tennessee! Mount!"

The regiment bounded into the saddle, and in that plight—the planter and the eight captive officers marching on before, the self-appointed "cunnel" and his chief officer bringing up the rear, and the rest of his command—the yellow woman—*a-straddle* of a horse between them, they entered the Union lines.

On another occasion, hunted down by several companies of rebel cavalry, Bible took refuge in a grove of laurel bushes. Among the bushes was a hollow tree in which he had once or twice slept on previous expeditions. It had been overthrown by a tornado, and the soil still clung, in huge bowlders, to its upturned roots. Creeping into this tree, he closed the small opening with earth, and, boring a hole through the trunk with his bowie-knife to admit air, and give him a look-out on his pursuers, he lay there without food for three days and nights. The rebels saw him enter the grove, and at once surrounded it, so that escape was impossible. A party then beat the bushes, and after examining every square yard of the ground, came and sat upon the hollow tree. Listening, he heard them recount some of his exploits, and assert very positively, that he had sold himself to that notorious dealer in human chattels—the devil—who, they thought, had given him power to make himself invisible at will. "An' bein' thet's so, cumrades," very logically remarked one of the number, "doan't it nat'rally foller thet the devil ar' on the Union side, an' moughtent we 'bout so wall guv it up fur a dade beat 'ter onst!"

When the rebel army retreated from Murfreesboro, its advance column came suddenly upon the scout as he was eating his breakfast in an "oak opening" near the highway. There was no chance of escape or concealment, for the "opening" was covered with immense trees standing fifteen and twenty feet apart, with only a short grass growing between them. Bible was disguised in an immense mass of red hair and beard, and wore a tattered suit of the coarse homespun of the district. Knowing he would certainly be discovered, he assumed a vacant, rustic look, and, rising from the ground, gazed stupidly at the soldiery.

"I say, green one, what are you doing thar?" shouted the officer at the head of the column.

"I'se loss my cow-brutes, Cunnel," replied the scout; "two right loikely heffers; 'un on 'em speckle all over, 'cept the tail, an' thet white'n yer face. Ye hain't seed 'em no whar 'long the road, nohow, hes ye?"

"No, I hain't seed 'em, no whar, nohow," rejoined the officer. "Come, step into the ranks; we need just such fellows as you are. Why the devil haven't they conscripted you before. Step into the ranks, I say," he repeated, as Bible, not seeming to comprehend his meaning, remained standing in his previous position. The second command having no more effect on him than the first, the officer directed a couple of soldiers to take Bible between them, and to fall in at the rear of the column. It was not till he was fairly in the road that the scout seemed to awaken to the reality of his condition.

"Why, why, ye hain't a gwine to tuck me long o' ye!" he exclaimed, frantically appealing to the "cunnel." "Ye hain't a gwine ter tuck me long o' ye! Ye karn't mean thet!"

"We do mean that, and you just keep quiet, or, like St. Paul, you'll kick against the pricks," said the officer, alluding perhaps to the bayonets which the two soldiers had unslung and were holding ready to apply to Bible's flanks.

"Why, ye karn't mean thet! ye karn't mean thet, Cunnel!" again piteously cried the scout. "Wh—wh—whot'll become on the old 'ooman—whot'll become on the cow-brutes?"

"D—d the old woman and the cow-brutes," shouted the

officer, riding forward and leaving the new recruit to his fate. And thus Bible marched to the Tullahoma, and thus he enlisted in the second regiment of Alabama Infantry.

He remained a fortnight at Tullahoma, and while there obtained a correct idea of the number and disposition of the enemies' forces, and brought away with him, in his head, an accurate map of the rebel fortifications. Desertions being frequent, the picket lines had been doubled, and when he was ready to leave, it had become next to impossible to penetrate them. But he was equal to the emergency, and hit upon a bold expedient which proved successful.

Restrictions had been laid by the commanding general on the importation of whiskey, and the use of that article, which is a sort of necessity to the Southern "native," had been prohibited within the lines of the army—except on the eve of battle. Then the cold-water generals, themselves, dealt it out—mixed with gunpowder—to every man in the ranks. The regulations concerning it were rigidly enforced in all the divisions except Hardee's. That general—to whose corps Bible belonged—who has, notoriously, a weakness for "spirits" and negro women, winked at the indulgence of his men in those luxuries, when it did not interfere with their strict observance of "Hardee's Tactics."

Knowing his proclivities, Bible, one evening just after sunset, took a tin "jug" under his arm, and sauntered past the general's tent.

"I say," shouted Hardee, catching sight of the long form of the scout, "where are you going with that big canteen?"

"Ter git some bust-head, giniral. Ye knows we karn't live wuthout thet," replied Bible, with affected simplicity.

"Perhaps you karn't: don't you know it's against regulations. I'll string you up, and give you fifty."

"Oh, no! ye woan't do thet, I knows, giniral, fur ye's a feller feelin' for we pore sogers," said Bible. "We karn't live wuthout a leetle ruin; wuthout a leetle, nohow, giniral!"

"Where do you expect to get it?" asked the general.

"Ter Squire Pursley's," said the scout, naming a planter living a few miles outside of the lines. "He's got some on the tallest old rye ye uver seed. I knows him. An' he's the biggest brandy, too, an' the purtiest nigger gal (rolling his tongue in his mouth and smacking his lips,) thar is anywhar round. She's whiter'n ye is, giniral, an' the snuggest piece uv house furnitur' as uver wus grow'd."

"And how do you expect to pass the pickets?" asked the standard authority on "Tactics."

"I reckon' this wull brung 'em," answered Bible, tapping his canteen significantly.

"Well, it won't," replied the general, laughing; "but I'll give you something that will. And here, take this canteen and get me some of that 'big brandy,' and tell the squire I'll be over there one of these days."

The general gave Bible a pass, another canteen, and five dollars of Confederate scrip, to effectually "raise the spirits;" and then the scout, saying, "Ye kin reckon on gittin' sich brandy, giniral, as wull sot ye up so high ye'll nuver come down agin,' walked leisurely out of the rebel lines.

Once, while scouting near McMinnville, Bible was captured by a small party of Forrest's cavalry. One of the Confederates knew him, and he was told he must die. Throwing a rope over the limb of a tree, they adjusted it about his neck, and the rebel officer, taking out his watch, said to him: "You can have five minutes to say your prayers."

"I thanks ye, Cap'n," said Bible; "fur thet shows ye's got a spark uv humin feelin' in ye; an' ef ye'll jest pile a lettle light 'ood on ter thet spark, it mought be it 'ud blaze up, an' make ye a better man nur ye is, or kin be, whiles ye's a fightin' agin' yer kentry. As ter prayin', Cap'n, I doan't need no time fur thet; fur I'se allers a prayin', not wuth words—but silent, deep, down yere"—placing his hand on his heart—"whar I'se allers a sayin' 'OUR FATHER!' *Our* FATHER, Capt'n, *your'n* as wull as mine! An' doan't ye 'spose He's luckin down on ye now, sorry, grieved ter His vury heart thet ye, His chile, thet His own SON died a wus death nur this fur, should be a doin' whot ye is—not a hangin' uv me; I hain't no complaint ter make o' thet, fur it'r His wull, or ye wouldn't be a doin' on it—but sorry thet ye's lifted yer hand agin' yer kentry, agin truth, an' right an' the vury liberty ye talks so much about. Prayin'! I'se allers a prayin', Cap'n, allers been a prayin' uver sense Sally said ter me: 'Pray, Bible, fur it'r the only way ye kin come nigh ter Him: it'r the only way ye kin know, fur shore, thet ye's His raal chile.' An' I does know I'se His chile, 'case I loves ter pray, an' I'll pray fur ye, Cap'n—ye needs it more nur me. It woan't do ye no hurt, an' it mought do ye some good, fur the LORD promises ter yere His chillen, an' He hes yered *me*, over an' over agin."

The five minutes had elapsed, but the Confederate officer still stood with his watch in his hand. At last, turning suddenly away, he said to his men:

"Take off the rope! Take him to the general. *He* may do what he likes with him. I'll be d—d if *I'll* hang him."

Before they reached Forrest's head-quarters at McMinnville, they were set upon by a squad of Union cavalry, who rescued the prisoner, captured a half dozen of the privates, and gave the captain a mortal wound in the side. Bible laid him upon the grass, and, taking his head tenderly in his lap, prayed for him. As the Captain turned his eyes to take a last look at the setting sun, he placed the scout's hand against his heart, and saying, "I'm going now—I feel at peace—I owe it to you—God bless you for it, may God for ever bless you," he uttered a low moan, and died.

While the rebel forces lay encamped around Chattanooga, Bible made them a professional visit. For two days, from the top of Lookout Mountain, he looked down on their fortifications. With the works fully mapped in his mind, so that, in his rude way, he could sketch them upon paper, he started, just at nightfall of a murky, stormy day, to make his way northward. Arriving at the house of a pretended friend, he took supper, and retired to sleep in a small room on the ground floor. It was not far from eleven o'clock, and raining and blowing violently, when a light rap came at his window. He got up—he always slept in his clothes, with his arms about him—and applying his ear to the glass, heard a low voice say:

"Ye is betrayed. Come out ter onst. They'll be yere in a hour."

He lifted the sash, and, springing lightly into the yard, saw—as well as the night would permit—a young octoroon woman standing unprotected in the storm, thinly clad, and drenched from head to foot. Leading him out into the darkness, she said to him:

"This man's son war at master's house not a hour back.

He's telled on ye ter git the reward! They's 'spectin' the calvary uvery minnit. Hark! I yere's 'em now!"

While she yet spoke he heard the heavy tramp of horsemen along the highway. Placing her hand in his, the woman fled hurriedly to the woods. When they had gone about a mile, she paused, and said to him:

"I karn't go no furder. I must git home or they'll 'spect suthin'. When they find ye's gone, the calvary'll make fur the landin'. Ye must go up the river, an' 'bout two mile frum yere ye'll find a yawl. It'r chained, but ye kin break thet. Doan't cross over—a hull regiment is 'camped on t'other side —put up the river so fur as ye kin."

With a mutual "God bless ye," they parted. Bible made his way to the river, and narrowly inspected its banks, but no boat was to be seen! He had spent two hours in the search, when he came to a bend in the stream which gave him an uninterrupted view of it for miles below. All along the river the air was alive with torches hurrying to and fro. He knew his pursuers would soon be upon him, and ejaculating a short prayer, in which he reminded the Lord that the information he carried in his head was of "no oncommon vallu, orter be got ter the giniral ter onst, an' wouldn't be uv no yerthly use" if he were hanged just then, he crept down to the water. Entangled in the underbrush just above him was a large log, the estray property of some up-country sawyer. Dropping himself into the water, he made his way to the log, and, laying down on at it full length, paddled out into the river. When he had reached the middle of the stream, he let himself drift down with the current, and in a short time was among his pursuers. A thousand torches blazing on either bank lit up the narrow river with a lurid glare, and made the smallest object on its surface distinctly visible. Knowing that if he kept his position he would certainly be seen, Bible rolled off into the water, turned over on his back, and, keeping one hand upon the log, floated along beside it. When he came opposite to the landing, he heard one cavalryman say to another:

"See! thar's a log; moughtent the durned critter be on thet?"

"No," replied the other; "thar's nothin' on it. Yer eyes is no better 'n moles."

"Wall, I'll guv it a shot, anyhow," rejoined the first, and fired his carbine. The bullet glanced from the log, and struck the water a few feet from the scout. The one shot attracted others, and for a few minutes the balls fell thickly around him, but he escaped unhurt! The God to whom he had prayed shielded him, and brought him safely out of the hands of his enemies. In six days, after unparalleled hardships, he reached the Union lines.

A few days before I left Murfreesboro, Bible started on another trip into the enemies' lines to establish a chain of spy stations up to Bragg's head-quarters. He succeeded in the perilous enterprise, and, when I last heard of him, was pursuing his usual avocation, doing really more service to the country than many a star-shouldered gentleman who is talked of now in the newspapers, and may be read of centuries hence in history.

If I have outlined his character distinctly, the reader has perceived that he is brave, simple-hearted, outspoken, hospitable, enterprising, industrious, loyal to liberty, earnest in his convictions—though ignorantly confounding names with things—a good husband and father, with a quiet humor which flavors character as Worcester sauce flavors a good dinner, a practical wisdom which "trusts in the LORD, but keeps its powder dry," some talent for bragging, and that intensity of nature and disposition to magnify every thing (illustrated in his stories and conversation) which leads the Southerner to do nothing by halves, to throw his whole soul into whatever he undertakes, to be, like Jeremiah's figs, "if good, very good; if bad, not fit to feed the pigs." Though morally and intellectually superior to the mass of "poor Southern whites," he is still a good representative of the class. They nearly all possess the same traits that he does, and differ from him only in degree, not in kind. That is saying little against them, for one might travel a whole summer's day in our Northern cities, and not meet many men who, in all that makes true manhood, are his equals.

CHAPTER XV.

THE "POOR WHITES."

Professor Cairnes, in his very valuable and generally accurate work on the Slave Power (pages 54, 55), says:

"In the Southern States, no less than five millions of human beings are now said to exist in a condition little removed from savage life, eking out a wretched subsistence by hunting, by fishing, by hiring themselves out for occasional jobs, and by plunder. Combining the restlessness and contempt for regular industry peculiar to the savage, with the vices of the *prolétaire* of civilized communities, these people make up a class at once degraded and dangerous; and constantly re-enforced, as they are, by all that is idle, worthless, and lawless among the population of the neighboring States, form an inexhaustible preserve of ruffianism, ready at hand for all the worst purposes of Southern ambition. . . . . Such are the "mean whites" or "white trash" of the Southern States. . . . . This class comprises, as I have said, five millions of human beings—about seven-tenths of the whole white population."

This opinion of Professor Cairnes is no doubt held by fully nineteen-twentieths of the people of the Northern States and of England. But it is a great—a very great error. Having read of, or seen, the wretched specimens of humanity who loiter about the railway stations, or hover around the large plantations on the great Southern thoroughfares, they have jumped to the conclusion that they represent "seven-tenths of the whole white population" of the South! The very idea is preposterous, for if it were so, one-half of the Southern people would be paupers, and no community could exist which had to support that proportion of non-producers. But it is not so. The great mass of "poor whites" are superior (and I say this with due deliberation, and after sixteen years' acquaintance with them) to every other class of un-cultivated men, save our Northern farmers, on the globe. They *all* were born in this country, and have imbibed from our institutions—distorted and perverted as they are at the South—a sturdy independence, and an honest regard for each other's rights, which make them, though of Scotch, Scotch-Irish, or English descent, better soldiers, better citizens, and better *men* than the over-worked, ignorant, half-starved, turbulent, and degraded peasantry whom England vomits upon the North to create riots, rule in our elections, and support such politicians as Fernando Wood.

There *is* at the South such a class as Mr. Cairnes speaks of. They are appropriately called "mean trash," and "eke out a wretched subsistence by hunting, by fishing, by hiring themselves out for occasional jobs, and by plunder," but they are a comparatively small class. The census shows that they cannot number above half a million.

These people do combine "the restlessness and contempt for regular industry peculiar to the savage, with the vices of the *prolétaire* of civilized communities," are "at once degraded and dangerous," and form a "preserve of ruffianism, ready at hand for all the worst purposes of Southern ambition." In fact, I was about to add that *all* the ruffianism of the South is confined to them and to the "chivalry," but I will not say it, for it would not be strictly true.

To give the reader an idea of what these "mean whites" are, I will glance for a moment at their habits and ways of living. Often their houses are the rude pole wigwams of the Indian—shaped like a sugar-loaf—with merely a hole at the top to let the smoke out, and—the rain in; but, generally, they live in small huts of rough logs, through the crevices of which the wind, in winter, whistles a most melancholy tune. These huts are floored with nothing but the ground—hardened with mauls, and hollowed at the centre, as if to hold the rain that comes in at the roof—and their one apartment is furnished with a few rickety chairs, a pine log—hewn smooth on the upper side, and made to serve as a sofa—a cracked skillet, a dirty frying-pan an old-fashioned rifle, two or three sleepy dogs, and a baker's dozen of half-clad children, with skins and hair colored like a tallow candle dipped in tobacco-juice. In one corner may be a mud oven, half crumbled back to its original earth, and in the others, two or three low beds, with corn-shuck mattresses and tattered furnishings; but the whole aspect of the place reminds one strongly of a tolerably-kept swine-sty or dog-kennel. The character of the inmates of these hovels is suited to their surroundings. They are indolent, shiftless, and thieving; given to whiskey-drinking, snuff-dipping, clay-eating, and all manner of social vices. Brothers intermarry with sisters, fathers cohabit with daughters, and husbands sell, or barter away, their wives, as freely as they would their hounds, or as the planter would his slaves. I have myself met a number of these *white* women who had been sold into prostitution by their natural protectors, for a few dollars or a good rifle.

Their indolence is almost past belief. They are literally "too lazy to come in when it rains." A traveler tells of asking shelter at one of their shanties in a storm. The rain was pouring in at the roof, and the family were huddled about the only dry spot on the floor.

"Why don't you mend your roof?" the traveler asked.

"Stranger," replied the host, "we can't do it—it rains."

"But it doesn't always rain—why not mend it in dry weather?"

"Why, wh—whot's the use o' mendin' it when it doan't leak?" was the very sensible reply.

Still, they have a mortal antipathy to water. They never take it outwardly, unless the roof leaks, or they are caught out in a rain-storm, and never inwardly, unless it is mixed with apple-jack or whiskey. Whiskey is their staple beverage. By exchanging deer or other game (their only currency) at some cross-road doggery, they obtain plentiful supplies of a vile fluid, which is compounded of log-wood, strychnine, juniper berries, and alcohol, and "circulates" among them under the appropriate names of "Tangle-foot," "Blue-ruin," "Red-eye," "Bust-head," and "Knock-'em-stiff." If the vender of this vile stuff did not dilute it freely with water—so freely that it rarely fails to itself "get tight" in cold weather—the race of mean Southern whites" would soon be swept from the earth. As it is, they seem to thrive and fatten upon it; old men, dozing away in the chimney-corner, and little children, tottling about the floor, drink it as if it were water.

A Northern man was once forced to dine at one of their hovels. Missing the customary "whiskey-kag" from the table, he said to the housewife:

"Can't you give me a mug of Knock-'em-stiff?"

"I can't, Stranger," was her reply: "I hain't nary drap ter speer."

"None to spare! Why, I see a barrel of it there in the corner!"

"A barr'l uv it!" exclaimed the woman, "why, whot's thet fur a lone widder an' sevin chillen? We shill be nation dry 'fore winter's over!"

Not one in a thousand of these people can read, and not one in *ten* thousand can write. I have known many who never saw a book or a newspaper, and some who never *heard* of a Bible or a spelling-book. As a consequence of such ignorance, they have very crude notions of God and religious duty. In fact, though they often spend weeks at camp-meetings, shouting "Glory" and groaning "Old Hundred," they have no religion. I once heard one of their preachers deliver a sermon which well illustrated their knowledge of *spiritual* things.

It was at a little church in the shadow of Bald mountain, one of the immense range dividing North Carolina from Tennessee.

The building was a simple structure of logs, with a puncheon floor, and a single opening for a door, but without a window or a chimney. On a bare spot in its centre a huge light-wood fire was blazing, and roaring, and fuming and forcing thick volumes of smoke into the people's eyes till they wept as if they were so many watering-pots. The congregation was seated around this fire on benches of rough logs, and the preacher occupied a small platform, raised a few steps from the floor, and furnished with a single block of wood which officiated as a chair. The women had bare heads and feet, and their only garment (it was the month of November) seemed to be a coarse cottonade gown.

falling straight from the neck to just below the knees. The men had long matted hair and shaggy beards, and wore slouched hats (they kept them on during the services), and linsey trowsers, and hunting shirts, so begrimed with dirt, and so torn and patched in a thousand places, that scarcely a vestige of the original material was left visible to the naked eye. Many of them—owing, no doubt, to their custom of intermarrying—were deformed and apparently idiotic, and they all had stunted, ague-distorted bodies, untanned-leather skins, small heads, round as bullets, and coarse, wiry hair, which looked like shreds of oakum gathered into mops, and dyed with lamp-black.

The preacher's text, which he credited to the *apostle* DAVID, was: "Try the sperrets;" and he showed, to the satisfaction of his auditory, that while Scripture expressly enjoins the taking of "a little wine"—which, he said, was the ancient name for whiskey—"for the stomach's sake," it as expressly requires that we shall "try the sperrets," or, in other words, that we shall drink none but the very best whiskey we can get. He reckoned "thet sech ruin as come from 'Hio, an' could be got ter Jim Decker's—over the mountain ter Jonesboro—fur a coon-skin a gallon, was purty tollable sort o' ruin, an' mought do fur white folk, but sech as Dan Ferguson 'stilled, down thar ter the mill, warn't no way fit fur a hoss ter drink." He belabored bad whiskey, for a time, with savage vehemence, and then opened his batteries upon tobacco. Whiskey was, as the Bible affirms, good for the stomach, and he reckoned the "clar stuff wouldn't hurt no part uv a humin bein'," but tobacco was a vile thing that would kill any living creature but woman; and how she could chaw it, and smoke it, and snuff it, and dip it, as she did, he couldn't see, no how. Its use warn't noway sanctioned by Scriptur,' and nary one uv the Apostles, Prophets, or good men of the olden time uver used it; and while the Bible often spoke of wine and "sperrets, it nuver onst mentioned the name uv terbacker, and that proved it couldn't be good ter take!"

When he had "adjourned the meeting" for a fortnight—PROVIDENCE wullin', an' thar bein' no freshet on the mounting—I ventured to suggest to him that it was possible he had misunderstood his text, and I then learned that he could not read, and that a neighboring planter—one of the chivalry—had given him the text, outlined his subject, told him that the text refers to ardent spirits, and that he must be sure to "pitch powerful strong inter Dan Ferguson's whiskey."

[The men who can thus sport with the best feelings of their fellows, are, as we know, capable of worse things.]

Nowhere but in the Slave States is there a class of whites so ignorant and so degraded as are these people. In every other country the peasantry labor, are the principal producers, the really indispensable part of the community; but the "mean white" of the South does not *know how* to labor; he produces nothing; he is a fungous growth on the body of society, absorbing the strength and life of its other parts, and he would not exist if the Southern system were in a healthy state. And he is the natural product of Slavery, for slavery, which makes the slave the planter's blacksmith, and wheelwright, and carpenter, and artisan of all work, shuts upon the mean white man every avenue of honest toil, and drives him to the barren sand-hills to starve and to die.

He steals the deer from the planter's forests, the hams from his smoke-houses, and the chickens from his hen-roosts, and he vends corruption and bad whiskey among the negroes; but the planter tolerates him for his vote. I have seen a planter march twenty of these wretched caricatures of humanity up to the polls, and when they had voted at his bidding, have had him turn to me and say, with a sneer on his lips:

"This is your boasted Democracy; this trash governs this country; Jefferson gave them the right of suffrage, and they suppose they are voting for Jefferson *now.*"

"But," I said to him, "why do you not let them think? why not give them schools and work?"

"Because," he replied, "if we did, they might not vote for Jefferson!"

To these "mean whites," Mr. Cairnes's description appropriately applies, and it applies *only* to them. The great mass of poor whites, as I have said, are a very different people. The *poor* white man labors, the *mean* white man does not labor; and labor marks the distinction between them. Labor makes one hardy, industrious, and enterprising, a law-abiding and useful citizen; idleness makes the other thieving, vicious, law-breaking, and of "no sort of account" to himself or society.

The *laboring* whites comprise two-thirds of the free population of the South, and they have done more for its material progress than all its "chivalry" and all its slaves. They have done more, because they have worked under the stimulus of freedom, and because they vastly *outnumber* the other classes. The census shows that on the first of June, 1860, there were in the fourteen Slave States, exclusive of Delaware, one million, three hundred and fifty-nine thousand, six hundred and fifty-five white males engaged in agricultural and other out-door employments. Of this number, nine hundred and one thousand, one hundred and two are classed as "farmers"—men who till their own land: two hundred and thirty thousand, one hundred and forty-six are classed as "farm-laborers"—men who till the land of others: and two hundred and twenty-eight thousand, four hundred and seven are classed as "laborers"—men engaged in out-door work other than the tillage of land. The "farmers" are not to be confounded with the planters—men who work large tracts of land and large bodies of slaves, but do not work themselves—for the census takes distinct account of the latter. *They* number only eighty-five thousand, five hundred and fifty-eight, but—such has been the working of the peculiar institution—they own nearly three-fourths of the negroes and landed property of the South. These one million, three hundred and odd thousand of laboring white men represent a population of about six millions; and if we add to them the four hundred thousand represented by the planters, and the one million represented by men in trade, manufactures, and the professions, there can hardly remain, in a total population of less than eight millions, "five millions of human beings who eke out a wretched subsistence by hunting, by fishing, by hiring themselves out for occasional jobs, and by plunder." Half a million—the number I before stated—is vastly nearer the truth.

Little is known at the North of this large working population, for the reason that they live remote from the great traveled routes, and have been seldom seen by travelers. They are scattered over all the South, but are most numerous in the Border States and in Texas. The most of them own small farms, and till the soil with their own hands. Some of them have one or two slaves, and in rare instances the more industrious have acquired ten or fifteen—but they work with the blacks in the fields, and treat them very much as our Northern farmers treat their hired workmen. Before the war the traveler in the interior of North Carolina would have heard the axe of master and man falling, with alternate strokes, in the depths of the evergreen forests, or he would have seen the two "camped out" together in the same tent or pine-pole cabin, drinking from the same gourd—the darky always after his master—eating from the same rude table, and sharing the same bed—the cabin floor—in common. So, too, in Kentucky, Tennessee, Missouri, Western Virginia, and middle and upper Georgia, Alabama, and Mississippi, he would have seen the white and the black ploughing side by side, or, bared to the waist, swinging the old-fashioned scythe, in good-natured rivalry as to which could cut the broadest swath of yellow wheat or waving timothy, or tote the biggest bundle of corn to the evening husking-bee. And when the evening had come, he would have found them gathered in the old log barn, husking, and singing, and shouting, and dancing in company, to the tune of "Ole Virginny," or "Rose, Rose, de coal brack Rose," played by "old Uncle Ned," who "had no wool on de top ob his head," but whose skinny fingers, with handy blows, *could* rap the music out of "de ole banjoes."

The more wealthy of this class sometimes give their children what might be called a fair common-school education, but fully one-half of them never learn to read or write. The reason of this is, there are no schools for the common people at the South. In a village, ten or twenty miles distant, there may be a pretentious "Female College," or "Institute of Learning for Young Men," where "a little Latin and less Greek" is dispensed to the young idea at the rate of four or five hundred dollars per annum, but these prices place their "stores of knowledge" far above the reach of the hard-toiling farmer. Only in Tennessee, so far as I know, are there any free schools, and the scanty State allowance which formerly supported them, was dealt out with a most parsimonious hand by the ruling aristocracy. How much light those institutions gave the people, may be guessed at from the fact that any one was qualified to instruct in them who could "read, write, and do sums in addition."

So many of these people being unable to read, it may be inferred they generally do not "take the papers." They do not. And why should they? Would it be wisdom in the Southern farmer, while his wife and children were barefoot, and the wolf—hunger—was looking in at his door, to waste one-tenth of his only bale of cotton on a wretched hebdomadal, filled with Secession, slavery, and negro advertisements, whose stupid editorial he would be a fortnight in spelling out?

As he does not read, he has to derive his knowledge of current events and political affairs from his wealthier neighbor, who does read, and who is sure to be a slave-owner, and one of the self-baptized "chivalry." At a political barbacue, or a court-day gathering, the farmer may hear, once or twice in the year, the two sides of every national question but the, to him, all-important one of slavery. If that subject is at all touched upon on such an occasion, it is shown to be of divine origin—dating back to the time when Ham first cast a black shadow across his looking-glass, and only to end when the skins of his descendants no longer wear mourning for their forefather's sin.

Thus ignorant, and thus instructed, is it strange that the Southern farmer deems slavery altogether lovelier than freedom? What does he know of freedom? What does he know of what it has done for the poor man of the North? Nothing. He never saw a Northern man in all his life, except, it may be, a Yankee pedlar, and he—my Yankee friends will, I hope, take no offence at my saying this, for I am a Yankee myself—he, when he migrates South, develops into about the meanest specimen of humanity to be found on this planet.

If the Southern workingman knew what freedom is; if he knew what it does at the North; how it builds a free school at every cross-road, while knowledge is saddled with a Morrill tariff at the South; how it makes the Northern laborer comparatively rich, while *he* is wretchedly poor; how it gives the Northern farmer a comfortable home for himself and outbuildings for his cattle, while *he* lodges in a mud-chinked hovel, and stables his cows in the woods; how the Northern workingman travels in luxurious steamboats or velvet-cushioned cars, while *he* journeys on the hurricane deck of a mule, or in that sort of railway train that will climb the steepest grade, if it only has time enough—an ox-cart drawn by a single two-year-old heifer; how the Northern farmer is respected and honored *because* he labors, while *he* is looked down upon and despised for doing the same thing; how the poorest Northern man votes, independently and intelligently, as one of the real "sovereigns of the nation," while he, misled by a stump speech, or bribed by a glass of whiskey, ignorantly casts his ballot for the very men who are robbing him of his birth-right: if he knew all this, would he not crush slavery, and end the rebellion in a day? He would. And slavery will not be effectually crushed, or the Rebellion ended, until he *does* know it. We may overrun the South, we may make its fields a desolation, and its cities heaps of ruin, but until we reach the reason and the hearts of these men, we shall stand ever on the crater of a volcano, whose red-hot lava may at any hour again burst forth and deluge the land with blood and fire! It is idle to talk of conquering a *union* with a disaffected people. It never was done, and never will be done. Ireland, and Italy, and Hungary, ought to convince us of that.

But how, while every able-bodied Southern man is in the Rebel army, can we reach these people? I answer, by fighting them with a sword in one hand and a Union newspaper in the other—by giving them ideas as well as bullets. By scattering loyal publications broadcast over the conquered districts; and by starting a free press wherever we hold a foot of Southern soil. If the men are away in the army, the women will be at home, and will read these things, and that will be enough. If we convert them, the country is saved. Woman, in this century, is every where that "power behind the throne" which is mightier than the throne itself, and the Southern women have been, and are, the mainspring of this Rebellion. Every dollar that we thus plant in the South will spring up a man, in tattered hat and ragged butternuts, it may be, but still a man, hardy, earnest, brave, who, for what he thinks is right, will march straight up to the cannon's mouth, and meet death "as if he loved it."

I have been led into this long digression by an earnest desire to disabuse the Northern mind in regard to these people. For this reason I have drawn, at full length, the portraits of "Long Tom" and "Bible Smith" in this volume, and of "Andy Jones" and the farmer "Barnes" in the book "Among the Pines." They are all representatives of this class. I have endeavored to sketch their characters faithfully—extenuating nothing and setting nothing down in malice—that the reader may believe, what I *know*, that there is not in the whole North a more worthy, industrious, enterprising, honest, brave, and liberty-loving class of people than the great body of poor Southern whites. Take the heel of the man-buying and woman-whipping aristocrat from off their necks, give them free schools and a chance to rise, and they will make the South, with its prolific soil, its immense water-power, and its vast mineral wealth, such a country as the sun never yet looked upon, and this Union such a Union as will be, in truth, "the light of the nations and the glory of the earth!"

CHAPTER XVI.

A DAY WITH ROSECRANS.

THAT afternoon I sent my letters to the Commanding General, and the next morning, after breakfast, taking particular direction from the "culled gemman" who had been my bearer of dispatches, I set out in search of his quarters. On a side street at a little distance from the centre of the town, I found a modest brick building, from the balcony of which a large flag was flying. Before this house a solitary sentinel was pacing to and fro with a musket on his shoulder, and in the court-yard beyond it, in the shade of a group of tents, half a dozen officers were reading newspapers, or lazily puffing away at their meerschaums. Near by, in the door-way of a smaller building,—an edifice about as large as a half grown hen-coop,—with his body balanced on the legs of a rosewood chair, and his feet braced against the door jam, another soldier was indulging in the delightful employments of his superiors. Approaching this soldier, I said to him:

"Are these the General's quarters?"

"Yaw, yaw, General Rosey. Dat is he, dat is he," replied the "adopted citizen," pointing to an officer on a powerful gray, at the head of a squadron of cavalry, which just then was thundering down the road. The escort halted abreast of the principal entrance, and the officer—a straight, compactly built, quick-motioned man, in a rusty uniform, a worn slouched hat, and mud-encrusted cavalry boots—sprang to the ground. A few other officers followed him, and then, without a word being spoken, the cavalry wheeled, and thundered down the road again.

"And that is the General?" I said to the soldier.

"Yaw, yaw, dat is old Rosey. I fights mit him."

"Then, you don't 'fight mit Sigel?'" I rejoined, smiling.

"Yaw, yaw, I fights mit Segel py-me-by (before.) I fights mit Rosey now. Him better as Sigel."

Not pausing to discuss the respective merits of the two commanders, I entered the wide hall of the larger building, and said to an orderly on duty near the door-way:

"Will you take my name to the General?"

"Av coorse, yer honor," replied the soldier, his mouth distending into a good-natured grin; "but as ye knows it an' I don't, hedn't ye better be after takin' it ter him yerself. Ye'll find him in there."

Following the direction in which he pointed, I entered a room at the left, on the door of which were posted, in large letters, the words "Aides-de-Camp." It was a square, spacious apartment, with a huge fire-place surmounted by a wooden mantel, a smoke-begrimed ceiling, dingy walls, covered with gaudy paper hangings, and two wide windows looking out upon the street. A camp cot, dressed in a soldier's blanket, and a pair of jackboots, stood in one corner, and in the others were a miscellaneous assortment of swords, spurs, muskets, knapsacks, and kindred articles known to modern warfare. A variety of dilapidated chairs, and canvas-bottomed stools, straggled about the floor, and between the windows was a large round table, littered over with maps, newspapers, and writing utensils. At this table were two or three young gentlemen in the uniform of staff officers, and addressing one of them, I asked if the General were "visible" so early in the day. He replied that he was then at breakfast, but that the Chief of Staff could be seen at once. Expressing a desire to meet that gentleman, I was conducted into an adjoining room, of smaller dimensions but furnished in much the same manner as the other. In a corner by the window, seated at a small pine desk,—a sort of packing box, perched on a long-legged stool, and divided into pigeon-holes, with a turn-down lid—was a tall, deep-chested, sinewy built man, with regular, massive features, a full, clear blue eye, slightly dashed with gray, and a high, broad forehead, rising into a ridge over the eyes as if it had been thrown up by a plough. There was something singularly engaging in his open, expressive face, and his whole appearance indicated, as the phrase goes, "great reversed power." His uniform, though cleanly brushed, and setting easily upon him, had a sort of democratic air, and every thing about him seemed to denote that he was "a man of the people." A rusty slouched hat large enough to have fitted Daniel Webster, lay on the desk before him, but a glance at that was not needed to convince me that his head held more than the common share of brains. Though he is yet young—not thirty-three—the reader has heard of him, and if he lives, he will make his name long remembered in our history. He glanced at me as I approached, and when I mentioned my name, rose, and extending his hand in a free, cordial way, said:

"I am glad to meet you. I have seen your handwriting —— ——, his (×) mark."

"And I have seen yours," I replied, grasping his hand with

equal cordiality. "But, *you* write with a *steel* pen—epics, in the measure of Hail Columbia.*

I sat down, and in ten minutes knew him as well as I might have known some other men in ten years. Nearly an hour had slipped away in pleasant chat with him, and my intended interview with Rosecrans was almost forgotten, when Garfield reminded me that I had better see the General before he was overrun with visitors. Opening the door of an inner room, he led me at once into another large, square apartment, which had, like the first, a bare floor, and greasy walls, hung round with maps, and decorated with gaudy paper-hangings, done into panels huge enough to have fitted the "grand hall" of the Mammoth Cave. At the right of the doorway was a high-post bedstead, covered with a spotless white counterpane, and about the room, in appropriate places, were a few hard-bottomed chairs, a pine wash-stand, with earthenware wash-basin, and wooden water-pail, and an old-fashioned sideboard, evidently the left-behind property of the previous occupant. On the mantel were a few books, a brace of revolvers, a silver-hilted sword bearing marks of "actual service," and two or three kerosene lamps, which, to all appearance, had done absolutely nothing towards dispelling the darkness of this "benighted world." Against the wall, by the front window, was a large pine table, surmounted by a frame-work of "pigeon holes," and on it were various open maps, several secession newspapers, some bundles of "official documents" done up in "red tape,"

* When about to lead the final charge at the battle of Middle-Creek, General Garfield pulled off his coat, tossed it up into a tree and, turning to his men, cried: "Come on, boys! Give them Hail Columbia." The men threw up their caps with a wild shout, rushed at the enemy, and drove them from the field, General Garfield leading the way.

and a huge pile of unopened letters. There seemed a place for every thing and every thing seemed in its place, but the mingled air of rustic simplicity and faded gentility which pervaded the room, had a most grotesque effect, and only one object in it at all indicated that it was the private apartment of one of the first military men of the time. That one object was Rosecrans himself.

He sat bolt upright in a rosewood arm-chair, covered with faded brocatelle, and sadly out at the elbows; and, with a cigar in his mouth, and a knife in his hand, was rapidly dissecting the letters which lay on the table before him. When my name was mentioned he rose, took my hand, and gave me a quick, searching glance. In that glance—I felt it—he sounded me, took my measure—as accurately as if he had been my tailor—and, with unerring decision, fixed my exact place in the scale of creation. From my first entrance into Kentucky, from high and low, black and white, bond and free, military men and civilians, I had heard nothing but extravagant eulogies of this man, and I had come prepared to be disappointed in him; but that one glance, the indescribable smile that passed over his face, and a certain atmosphere of power which seemed to envelop him, made me feel that, for once, the popular estimate was the true one. And no one ever came within his influence without being fascinated as I was, or without feeling, on the instant, the magnetism of a great nature. Motioning me to a seat, and resuming his letters, he said, while another of those peculiar smiles passed over his face:

"I've been expecting you."

"Expecting *me*, Sir!" I exclaimed in undisguised astonishment. "I've heard you knew every thing. I reckon it's so."

"Not exactly, but I knew you were coming. You've been announced," and continuing to open the letters, he handed me one of them.

It was from the chaplain of an Indiana regiment, whom the red-faced landlord had stowed away in my room one night at Nashville. The worthy gentleman had a plan for educating the blacks in "ten lessons of one hour each," and, not content with boring me with it till two o'clock in the morning, had, without my consent, written Rosecrans referring him to me for "further particulars."

"What do you know of that man?" he asked, going on with his letters.

"Nothing. I never saw him."

"Never saw him!"

"No. I went to bed without a candle, and he left before I awoke in the morning."

"But you formed some opinion of him. What was it?"

"That he knew about as much of the Southern negro, as I know of the moon."

"I thought so. A mere theorist. Only practical men are fit for the work *we've* in hand Mr. ——. What do *you* think of the negro?"

"That he is unfortunate in being black," I replied, smiling.

"Yes, yes, I know. But is he naturally equal to the white man?"

"Measured by the New Testament standard he may be superior—for he is meek enough to be a slave—but measured by *our* standard, he is certainly inferior. He has not the aggressive qualities of the white man."

"Well, what shall we do with him?"

"Let him alone."

"You are right," and for a moment he dropped the letters. "Give him a Bible and a spelling-book, free air, and a chance for something more than six feet of God's earth, and, LET HIM ALONE."

Saying this he dived again into his correspondence.

"This war will give him all that," I replied.

"Yes, and it will give it to every working man, black or white. This is the working man's war. For four thousand years labor has been struggling for its rights—now it will get them. Would to God that every poor man, North and South, could realize this."

He kept on reading, but his fine face flushed, his nervous lip quivered, and his clear, luminous eye actually blazed, as he spoke these words.

"I am glad you sympathize with the working man," I said.

"Sympathize with him! I honor him. He is the true nobleman. Did you never read where it says, 'cursed is the ground for *thy sake?*' Does not that mean that God ordained labor for our good? that it is our highest glory?"

The mass of letters, by this time, had adjusted themselves into several separate heaps, and touching a small bell which stood on the table, he said to a young officer who at once appeared in the doorway: "Tompey, hand these to Goddard, these to Barnett, these to Taylor, and send this to Ducat, and then come here with the Major. I've letters to write. Is any one waiting to see me?"

"Yes, sir; the Medical Director and half a dozen others," answered the aide.

"Ask them in," and turning to me, he added: "Captain Thompson, this is our guest, Mr. ——. Get him a pass to go and come when he likes. Give him a horse, and a squad, whenever he wants to go outside of the lines. He'll stay with us a month or two."

"Say a day or two," I interrupted, laughing, "and you'll come nearer the truth."

"Not a second less than a month. You can't get away till I give you a pass."

The aide disappeared, and the Medical Director, and the "half a dozen others" entered the room.

"Good morning, gentlemen. Be seated," said Rosecrans. "What can I do for you, Doctor?"

"The health of the men, General," replied the Doctor, "with the warm weather coming on, requires more vegetable food. Would it not be well to order potatoes?"

"I ordered them six weeks ago—sent an officer into Ohio, and for seven thousand dollars he bought what would have cost us twenty-one thousand in Nashville. They ought to have been here before now."

"General," said the medical man, with unaffected admiration, "you think of every thing."

"I have to. Good morning, Doctor. Colonel, what can I do for *you?*" added the laconic general, turning to a slightly-built, dark-complexioned young man, and introducing him to me as follows: "Mr. ——, this is one of the McCook's. Colonel Dan. You've heard of him."

At this moment the aides came in, and seated themselves at the two opposite corners of the pine table. An orderly also entered, and handed the General a note from one of the Corps commanders. Rosecrans introduced me to "the Major"—the other aide—dictated to him a reply to the note, and in the same breath said to McCook:

"Now, Colonel, what is it?"

"My men," said McCook, "in half an hour yesterday, subscribed four thousand dollars to get the Henry rifle. I want liberty to use it."

While the Colonel was speaking, the General took up the pile of letters remaining on the table, and began dictating to the two aides.

"Can they hit an elephant at a hundred paces?" he asked.

"Two hundred of them can hit the head of a candle box three times in five, at three hundred yards," rejoined McCook, a flush of pride on his face. A discussion as to the merits of the different kinds of rifles ensued, but not understanding it then, I cannot report it now. Meanwhile the General was dictating as fast as the two aides could write, and addressing an occasional remark to me. McCook had done speaking, when a very tall, ungainly man, with stooping shoulders, and long white hair, entered the room, and stalking directly up to the General, and taking his hand, said:

"I'm going by the train. Good-by."

"Good-by, and God bless you," returned Rosecrans, rising. "If you ever want to come back, we'll find a warm place for you."

"I know you will. I've had experience of your warm places," rejoined the veteran, smiling.

"And he likes them," said the General, turning to me. "At Stone River, in the hottest fire, when his men were hugging the ground as if they'd bury themselves, the Parson got up and made them a speech, and they do say, he told them—"

"No, I didn't. Don't traduce your friends, General," rejoined the Parson, laughing. "Good-by."

"Good-by, and God bless you," said the General.

"Good-by, boys, all of you," said the Parson, warmly. Every officer in the room grasped his hand, and amid a chorus of "God bless yous" he went out. It was "the fighting Parson," Colonel Moody of the 74th Ohio.

A half a dozen others now crowded around and addressed Rosecrans, who replied to each, and at the same time kept on dictating, his words all the while pouring forth in quick, terse sentences, his luminous eyes smiling, and his nervous fingers thrumming an odd accompaniment on the ragged arm of his chair. In all this he manifested no effort. I thought he could have done twice as much had it been possible for words to flow faster. His mind seemed to act with lightning rapidity, *flashing* from premise to conclusion, and grasping with ease half a dozen subjects in almost instantaneous succession. At last I said to him:

"I have seen business men turn off work, but never any who did it half so fast as you."

"I have been a business man. There are some relics of my business career. I have credit for those at the Patent Office," he replied, pointing to the lamps on the mantel-piece. They were the "Patent Kerosene Burners, warranted to give out neither smoke nor odor," which every American housewife values, but which every American housewife may not know she owes to a Major-General.

Another aide then entered, and announced that several ladies of the Sanitary Commission, about to depart by the train, desired to take leave of the General. "Show them in," he replied, rising, and taking a single turn up and down the room. This seemed a well understood signal, for all present except the aides at once left the apartment. I was rising to follow when he said to me: "Don't go. Stay, and after lunch we'll ride out to Sherridan's."

The ladies came in, and the General entered into conversation with them in a free and vivacious manner, as if the interests of a vast army, and movements involving the lives of thousands had not, the moment before, engaged his attention. They were all "on the shady side of forty," and one was not a day younger than fifty; but he addressed them throughout the interview as "young ladies." When they had gone, I said to him: "Don't consider me impertinent, but I am curious to know why you called your visitors '*young* ladies.'"

"Because they *are* young. Any woman who comes a thousand miles to attend on sick and dying men must be young—young of soul—and, no matter how old she grows, she'll *always* be young."

The letters were written, the two aides had disappeared, and another knot of officers had gathered around the General, when a short, stout, thick-necked man, with puffy cheeks, coarse, heavy features, and very much the air of a Bowery boy rigged out in regimentals, swaggered into the room with his hat on. Giving no heed to the galaxy of generals and major-generals about me, he stalked up to Rosecrans, and said to him: "Can I see you?" They passed to the farther corner of the apartment, and I asked the gentleman nearest me: "Who is he?" "General McCook," was the answer.

It was Major-General Alexander McDowell McCook—the "fighting McCook"—who never fought without being beaten, and has probably wasted more lives than any ten generals in the army.

"Why do you always attack McCook?" I asked Captain Firman, the rebel General Wheeler's aide, a short time afterwards. "Because we are always sure to whip him," was his reply.

While the two generals were in conversation, a spare, sallow-faced, dark-haired man, who had the air and manners of a gentleman, entered the room, and bowing to the officers about me, joined the two in the corner. "That is Crittenden," said the officer. "They are here for consultation. We must leave."

We all passed into General Garfield's apartment, and every chair and stool in the room, and the low camp-cot in the corner, were soon filled with "sitters"—and sitters who would grace any portrait-gallery in the world.

The reader has heard of every one of them. The stout, full-faced, florid-complexioned man, leaning against the wall by the window, was the "old Russian" Turchin. The very tall, slim young man, with long, dark hair and flowing beard, just then canted back in his chair, with his long legs perched on the window-sill, was the Chief of Cavalry—Stanley. The handsome man next to him, with wavy, brown hair, and face so much like Lowell's, was St. Clair Morton, who might be a poet, and *is* a hero. The scarred warrior on his right, with long, white beard, thin, gray tufts on the sides of his head, and spectacles on his nose, was Van Cleve; and leaning against the wall, at his back, the dark man, with keen, intense eyes, heavy black beard, and coarse, wiry hair, starting up into a sort of pyramid on the top of his head, was Jeff. C. Davis, who killed Nelson. The plain, farmer-like, plucky-looking man on my right, was Palmer—now commanding the Fourteenth Corps. The tall man next to him, in rusty uniform and big boots, with a full, clear eye, and expressive face, was Negley; and in other parts of the room were Hazen, Lytle, Reynolds, Harker, King, McKibben, and others, "too numerous to mention."

Thrusting his pen behind his ear, Garfield wheeled about on his stool, and opened the conversation. It soon turned upon the rebellion, which he compared to the conspiracy of Catiline. It had, he said, the same origin and objects, and was set afoot by a similar class of bankrupt scoundrels. A discussion followed, and in it, Garfield—who, at fifteen, drove horses on a canal, and worked his way through College with a saw and a jack-plane—displayed a classical knowledge that would have done credit to any Harvard professor. At its close, a singularly quiet, unassuming man, in plain pants, loose, blue sack, and every-day boots, entered the room, and took a seat on the window-sill, by the side of Stanley. He was below the medium height, slightly built, with closely-cut hair and beard, and a dark, sun-browned face. There was nothing about him to attract attention, except his eye, but that seemed a ball of black flame. "How are you, Phil?" "Good morning, Sherridan," greeted him from various parts of the room, and Garfield, turning to me, said: "Mr.——, this is General Sherridan."

It was the youngest corps commander in the army—the man who, when McCook was routed, stood so like a wall at Stone River; who led the desperate assault on Mission Ridge, and has recently made the brilliant cavalry campaign in Virginia.

"Do you remember Pope's thirty thousand muskets and ten thousand prisoners?" asked a young officer near me.

"Yes, very well," I replied.

"I took the muskets, and Sherridan took the men. How many were there, Sherridan?"

"I don't remember," answered the quiet general.

"Well, I remember the muskets; they counted nine hundred and thirty—not one more or less."

"I was with Pope at the second battle of Booneville," said another general, "when Sherridan rode up and reported sixty-five prisoners. 'Why don't you say five hundred?' said Pope. 'Because there are only sixty-five,' said Sherridan. 'There ought to be five hundred—call them five hundred, any way,' said Pope; and five hundred they were—but not in *Sherridan's* report."

A general laugh followed, but the quiet hero said nothing, and, in all I saw of him afterwards, I never heard him speak disparagingly of any one.

"You got through at last, Sir," just then said a voice at my elbow. Turning round, I saw a thin, spare man, with bushy, gray hair, and about the keenest eye I ever saw, looking in at the window. He was dressed in citizen's clothes, and had under his arm a paper box filled with letters.

"Oh, yes," I replied, "I got through. But where have I met you, Sir?"

"Probably nowhere, but I know you," he replied, smiling; "you see I have to look after suspicious new-comers."

There was a general laugh at my expense, and Stanley, glancing at the box of letters, said to the civilian:

"Robbing the mails again, eh, Colonel?"

"Yes, bagged two thousand dollars this morning;" and, addressing me, he added: "Some of your New York gift-book and bogus-jewelry concerns, tempt our boys to waste money on their worthless trash. I head them off by watching the mails. I've stopped seventeen thousand dollars within a fortnight—sent it back to the boys with a little good advice, gratis."

"You deserve the thanks of every soldier's wife and mother in the country," I said warmly.

But he has not received even *their* thanks, and his great services have had the poorest possible recognition from the Government. It was "Colonel" Truesdail who organized the admirable spy-system of the Cumberland army, which gave Rosecrans such perfect information of the movements of the enemy.

Just then the inner door opened, and McCook, looking for all the world as if he had the universe on his shoulders, and found it decidedly heavy, passed through the apartment, and soon Rosecrans and Crittenden appeared, and we went in to lunch.

At Stone River, during the second day's fight, a young cavalry officer rode up to General Thomas for orders. "Report to Morton—at the front," said the General, and shouting to his men, the young man dashed on to where the battle was raging hotly. Morton was not there. On he went again to where Palmer was rolling back the red waves on the left, but—Morton was not there. On again he went, through the thick smoke and the hurtling fire, to where Hazen was reaping a harvest of death on that terrible "half-acre;" but—Morton was not there. "Where is Morton?" he cried. "At the front!" came back from out the smoke, and again he rode on —rode on past the "Burnt House"—past where Rosecrans sat like a statue amid a hailstorm of fire—past where a reeking funeral pile marked the outer line of intrenchments—on to the cannon-ploughed, death-strewn cotton-field! "Is he mad? Call him back! Call him back!" shouted the General, but the bugle was drowned in the awful uproar, and still he rode onward. Amazed the rebel gunners stood at their pieces, but straight at them he rode with his handful of men. "I say, Rebs," he shouted, "where is Morton?" "Gone where you are going," they answered, and the cannon echoed "Gone," and he went—back again, not a man wounded.

That young officer—Lieutenant Kelley, 4th U. S. Cavalry—and the men who rode in that terrible ride, escorted us out to Sherridan's.

As we entered the forest encircling the town, Garfield broke out with Hosea Bigelow's poem:

"I du believe in Freedom's cause,"

and if the "down-east poet" would have any appreciation of his own lines, he should hear them in some such grand old woods, the words echoed back from the great spreading trees, and set to the music of a hundred horse's heels. He had scarcely ended, when the General began to tell how:

"Zekle crep' up, quite unbeknown,
An' peeked in thru the winder;
While there sot Huldy all alone,
'ith no one nigh to hender."

"What would you give to have written that?" he said, as he finished the recitation.

"All the castles I ever built in the clouds," I replied.

"So would I. You know what Wolfe said before his great battle?"

"That he would rather have written Gray's Elegy than take Quebec. Would *you* have said that before Stone River?"

He hesitated a moment, and then answered: "No; for now we need victories more than poems."

"As I came down, I saw the battle-field—what were your sensations when under fire so constantly all of that day?"

"I had no sensations. I was absorbed in planning how to beat them."

Just then an opening in the trees showed us several thousand men under review, in a field off at the left.

"It is Negley's division. Let us ride over there, General," said Garfield.

We turned our horses and galloped off through the forest. The underbrush was cleared away, and a rich sward of "blue grass" covered the ground, but every here and there a great tree felled for the fortifications, obstructed our way. One of these trunks—eighty feet long and nearly ten feet thick at the base—lay directly across our path. Garfield and I, who rode on either side of the General, reined our horses around its two ends, and the rest of the party divided and followed us, but Rosecrans spurred "Toby" directly at the trunk, and cleared it at a bound.

"Well done, General," I shouted; "you fire straight at the mark."

"It's the surest way to hit it," he replied, smiling.

Clearing a low fence into a cotton field, we soon "turned" a small hill, and were abreast of the division. As the well-known "gray" came in sight, the soldiers set up a loud shout, and uncovering his head, the General rode down the lines. Halting every now and then he spoke to the men. "You keep yourself tidy, Patrick. You can fight," he said to one. "I kin fight for *ye*, Giniral, be Jabers." "Leave out the hard words, my man. Brave men never swear." Passing before a company of Tennesseans, he said: "You've had mountain air; there's not a pale face among you." "Ye've guv'n us exercise, Gen'ral. Guv us more on it," was the answer. "I'll give you enough—never fear." To a mere boy, he said: "I saw you at Stone River—you fought like a man." "They've made a man of me, sir," said the soldier, pointing to the stripes on his arm. "I saw *ye* thar, Gen'ral," said another. "My old 'ooman prayed fur ye, an' thet's the how ye 'scaped." "Tell her for me, God bless her," said Rosecrans as he rode on.

And so we went down the lines, the General halting every few minutes to say some free word to the soldiers, and greeted, at every step, with cheers and "God bless yous." That ride showed me why his men worship him.

As we reined our horses again towards the woods, he said to me: "Do you see that young man yonder?" "That quiet, modest looking Brigadier?" I asked. "Yes. It's Carlin. At Stone River he sat his horse as coolly as he does now."

At Sherridan's I saw Rosecrans unbent. The bow which is always strung loses its power: so workers, such as he, wear out by constant working. The hour of relaxation is the time to learn any man, and then I tried to study him. Sherridan had invented a game he called "Dutch Ten-Pins." On the lawn in front of his quarters, between two immense elms, he had suspended a long rope, and to the end of it attached a small cannon-ball. On the ground, midway between these trees, was a square board which held the ten-pins. The game lay in throwing the ball so that it would miss the pins in going out, and strike them in coming back. To do this, a peculiar twist had to be given to the rope by bending the wrist, and it seemed almost impossible to avoid hitting the pins on the direct throw. Three "throws" were "a game," and only thirty "strokes" could be made. Sherridan, by much practice, had become expert at the play, and could make, pretty regularly, twenty "strokes," but a novice did well if he made ten. He soon challenged Rosecrans, and the dozen officers with him, to enter the lists. Sherridan opened the play, cleared the board twice, and missed it altogether the third throw. "Twenty," cried the "scorer," and another player took his place. He did indifferently well. Others followed with more or less success, though none came up to Sherridan's "score."

"Now for the General," shouted "the Major," laughing, as Rosecrans took his place. "He'll score thirty, sure."

"Don't laugh till *you* win, my boy," answered the General, with his peculiar smile.

Calculating deliberately the motion of the ball, he let it go. Every pin fell, on the direct throw, and a general laugh followed. Not at all disconcerted, he tried again and again, till he had played three or four "games," with scarcely better success. Amid the mock congratulations of the whole assemblage he at last sat down, and Garfield entered the lists. "It's nothing but mathematics," said Garfield; "you only need an eye and a hand," and carelessly throwing the ball, he cleared the board and scored twenty-three!

"You can't do that again."

"I'll try," answered the modest Brigadier, and he did do it, several times in succession.

"I can do better than *that*," said Rosecrans, again taking the ball. A shout of derision followed the boast, but he quietly set himself to work, and, half a dozen times in succession, made from twenty-five to thirty "strokes." As he resumed his seat, I said to him:

"That leap over the tree, and the way you've won this game, have shown me what made you conquer at Stone River."

"What was it?" he asked, smiling.

"Directness—firing straight at the mark—and a kind of persistence which makes you hold on till you succeed." And those two qualities, with untiring work, have made him the great man and the great general that he is.

For hours after dinner, and far into the night, the General was as intensely occupied as during the morning. Despatches were read, letters dictated, orders given, visitors received, and grave questions disposed of, with a celerity that taxed his aides to the utmost, and made the head of a looker-on almost swim with excitement. "Give me young men for work," he said, glancing at "the Major"—his senior aide, Frank S. Bond, of Cincinnati—"these sandy-haired fellows, who can drive a quill like lightning."

"But they soon wear out," I answered, "and even dark-haired men couldn't long stand the work you give them."

"Well, they do well while they last, and you know we live in deeds, not years."

At the battle of Iuka, an officer of General Ord's staff, seeing a division of rebels about to flank one of our regiments, rode up and informed Rosecrans of the danger. "Ride on and warn Stanley, at once," said the General. An acre on fire, and showered with bullets, lay between them and the menaced troops. The officer looked at it, and said: "General, I have a wife and children."

"You knew that when you came here," said the General, coolly.

"I'll go, sir," was the only answer.

"Stay a moment. We must make sure of this," and hastily writing some despatches, the General called three of his orderlies. Giving a despatch to each, he said to the officer: "Now go." He started, and at intervals of about fifty yards, bearing a similar message, the orderlies followed. The officer ran the fiery gauntlet, and, his clothes pierced with bullets, and his horse reeling from a mortal wound, reached Stanley,—the orderlies found their graves on that acre of fire!

To that officer, Lieutenant Colonel Arthur C. Ducat, Inspector-General of the Cumberland army, and General Thomas, I was, about midnight of the day I am describing, illustrating the superior advantages of slavery as a bleaching process, when Rosecrans approached, and laying his hand on General Thomas's chair, said:

"Speaking of white blacks, reminds me of two who came within the lines a few weeks ago. They were as white as I am —a little boy and girl, belonging to 'General' Chambers, a rich planter and a 'strong Union man,' living some twenty miles from here. Chambers called on me the other day, and feeling it my duty to be courteous to 'our friends,' I asked him to dinner. Every moment I expected he would broach the subject of his slaves, but he left without saying a word about them. However, he came back in a few days. I invited him again to dinner, and he declined, but said:

"Gen'ral, some on my property has come inter yer lines. I know'd they was har when I seed yer afore. I was telled ye'd yered they wus my children,—ye sees they's as white as I is—an' I felt sort o' delicate like 'bout axin' yer fur 'em till I could show, fur sartin, they wasn't. They is my nevye's—yere's the papers ter prove it."

"I don't see what difference it makes whether they are *your* children or your nephew's," I answered. "But I suppose you've come to claim them?"

"That *is* what I'se come for, Gen'ral—I s'pose ye'll guv 'em up?"

"Of course," I replied; "we are not negro-stealers. Every man shall have his rights within my lines."

"I am obleeged ter ye—much obleeged ter ye, Gen'ral," he said, showing strong symptoms of hugging me. "I war telled ye wus a blasted ab'lishioner, an' wudn't guv 'em up, an' I'm right glad ye does, fur it'll do a heap uv good; it'll cunciliate the loyal peeple round yere, mightly. Whar is they, Gen'ral?"

"I don't know—Major Bond can tell you."

"Won't it 'quire an order frum ye ter git 'em, Gen'ral?"

"Oh, no; you only need to ask them to go—slavery is so benign a thing that even white children must love it."

"An' karn't I hev 'em 'less they'll go peacerbly," he exclaimed, in consternation.

"Of course not; you must use no force. We neither steal negroes nor *catch* them."

"With a big flea in his ear, he left, no doubt cursing me for a 'blasted ab'lishioner.'"

To appreciate this action, the reader needs to remember that our Government was then pursuing the "conciliatory policy," and that nearly every department commander was returning fugitives. Rosecrans sent the children North, and, I am told, is now having them educated at his own expense.

The clock had struck one when I rose, and General Thomas said to me: "Come to my quarters to-morrow; I want to introduce you to one or two of the prominent Union men of the district."

I remained with Rosecrans nearly a month, and in that period saw much of him, meeting him every day. During all of that time, I saw nothing of the brandy-drinking or opium-eating with which his enemies have charged him—and I should have seen it, had it existed. In all our intercourse, I found him as earnest a patriot, as honest a man, as true and Christian a gentleman as, I think, ever lived; and I should be false to my convictions of right if I omitted to say, that those who, at such a time as this, have been instrumental in burying his great military talents in a mere civil employment, have done immense wrong to the country. It is not our most excellent President who has done this. He, I know, thinks of Rosecrans as I do. Nor was he removed because of the repulse at Chickamauga. The Government has exonerated him from blame in that affair; and those best informed have told me that, had the information on which he acted been correct, we should have lost Tennessee and Kentucky, had he done differently from what he did. Time is said to take its revenges; it also bestows its rewards. It will reward Rosecrans, by placing his name among those of the best and truest men in our history.

CHAPTER XVII.

VIEWS OF SOUTHERN MEN.

AT General Thomas's quarters, on the following day, I met several leading men of the district, who had "suffered the loss of all things" rather than deny the Union. One of them—Colonel Wisner, of the County of Bedford—was the only member of the Tennessee Legislature who, to the very end, voted against the schemes of the secessionists. He had the moral courage, at the time of the June election, to canvass his district in the face of a thousand rebel bayonets. The soldiers often attempted to break up the meetings, but the unarmed people gathered around the stands, kept off the soldiery, and bade him "go on." The result was, a large majority of the votes of his county were cast against "separation." He was ordered away by the Confederate authorities, but refused to go, and only went at last on being taken from his bed by a squad of soldiers. He was bound to a horse—he refused to mount, or to keep mounted—and driven in that plight within our lines.

He said to me: "The Southern *people* are at heart loyal to liberty. They think they are fighting for it. Disabuse them of the error, and all of them will be Union men. Give me free speech, and in six months I will revolutionize one-half of this State. Bosson will do the other half."

"But the Emancipation proclamation must stand. Will the masses come cordially back if the blacks are freed?"

"They will, unless you attempt to give the slaves suffrage. If you do that, the poor whites will fight until not a man is left. They think themselves superior—they *are* superior to the negroes, and they will never consent to blacks making laws for whites."

"But the abolitionists," I said, laughing, "have hit upon a plan for bleaching the blacks—making good white men of them."

"That is absurd. You know the black does not seek the white, but the white the black. Free the negro, give him control of his own person, and amalgamation will totally cease."

"I think so; and that, to me, is one of the strongest reasons for abolishing slavery. But if the blacks are all emancipated, what state of things will follow?"

"There would be no change at first. The South needs labor, and the blacks would give it. Gradually the more enterprising and ambitious would emigrate to some new territory, and found a community of their own, like the Mormons. The less enterprising would stay here, and finally die out."

"Why die out?"

"Because they cannot compete with the white man.* Remove the odium attached to white labor—abolishing slavery will do it—and you would call out the energies of the poor whites. One of them would earn a dollar, where a negro would earn fifty cents. The consequence would be,

* This is a new view for a Southern man. The slaveocracy has always insisted that white labor cannot compete with black, in a hot climate. Observation has satisfied me that the contrary is true. The severest work at the South, ditching and clearing swamp lands, has always been done by whites.

poverty and starvation for the negroes; and those that stayed here would in time die out."

"Some of our wisest statesmen advocate black-suffrage as a means of insuring a Union strength at the South. What do you think of it?"

"That it would not be a strength, but a weakness. The black are ignorant, docile, and accustomed to being led. Their votes would be controlled by a few demagogues, and all over the South, you would have the state of things you now see in New York city."

Another of these gentlemen—Mr. Bosson, of White County, who before the war was largely identified with the railway interests of the State, and a prominent actor in its politics, gave me so interesting an account of the rise of the secession movement in Tennessee, that I am tempted to repeat it. His views of the real feeling of the masses, and of what should be done with them and their leaders, are entitled to great respect, for he is largely experienced in public affairs, and thoroughly acquainted with all classes of the Southern people.

"During the Presidential canvass of 1860," he said, "I clearly saw that the purpose of the Secessionists was to precipitate the South into rebellion. I communicated my impressions to our Bell and Everett elector, and advised him to so conduct the discussion as to arouse the people to the coming issue. The month of November came, and with it the action of the South Carolina Legislature, initiating the Rebellion. Our legislature was then in session, and under the guidance of Governor Harris, and other leading advocates of Southern rights, its proceedings assumed a direction that tended to strengthen the purpose of the Secessionists. When I perceived this, with a view to awaken the people, and prepare them for the great issue, I inaugurated a series of meetings in the counties along the mountains. They were largely attended, and the people seemed unanimous for the Union.

"On the third of January, 1861, the legislature reported and passed a resolution authorizing a vote to be taken in the month of February following. The issue: 'For a Convention or against it,' and, 'For delegates to the Convention.'

"The election was held, and resulted, throughout the State, in a large majority against a convention, and a still larger majority—65,000—for the Union candidates to the convention. In the county of White—where I resided—out of sixteen hundred votes, the secessionists polled only a hundred and twenty-nine; and there, Judge Gardenhire and Colonel Colms, both popular speakers, took the 'stump,' and spoke for Separation; and hand-bills and circulars, breathing the bad spirit of secession, were widely scattered. The people were rejoiced at the result, and when I announced the vote at our precinct, they unanimously resolved never to support a man for any civil office who that day had voted for a disunion candidate. The Secessionists were rebuked, and, receding from the high ground they had taken, proposed 'Neutrality' as the true policy.

"Fort Sumter surrendered, and the call for seventy-five thousand men gave encouragement to the leading disunionists. They at once sounded the alarm that the Government meant to *coerce* the South. The Legislature was immediately convened, and on the recommendation of Governor Harris, it resolved to place the forces of the State on a war footing, authorized the raising of volunteers for State defence, and made large appropriations for that purpose. It also matured a plan, and passed a law for an election in the following June, to vote 'Separation or no Separation,' 'Representation or no Representation.'

"Then, all over the State, allured by the novelty of the enterprise, the young men responded to the heated declamation of the secession speakers, and with fife and drum, the demagogues accomplished what they could not have done with argument. No speaker of loyal proclivities was allowed to participate in the discussions. At each meeting squads of armed volunteers, with drums beating and flags flying, escorted the speakers and overawed the loyal voters.

"Election day—the 8th of June—arrived, and threats were widely made that no black republican would be permitted to approach the polls. I regarded the action of the Legislature as contrary to the Constitution, but I resolved to vote. On the morning of the election, with four gentlemen who thought as I did, I went to the precinct. Soldiers were within and around the building, and no Union man had dared to enter; but we quietly elbowed our way through the crowd, wrote our ballots in the sight of the multitude, and gave our votes to the officer. A profound silence prevailed as our votes were read, and when we turned and looked on the secession crew, not a word was spoken, not a gesture made. They were cowed by five honest men! On my return, the meeting with my wife and children was an affecting one. They had not expected to see me again alive.

"The vote in the State at the February election was 155,000, and the Union majority 65,000. In June, the total vote was only 115,000, and the separation and representation majority about 36,000. The vote fell short of the vote in February 40,000.

"Timidity overcame loyal men, and those disposed to be loyal, and they stayed at home; besides, all were told that if they supported 'No Separation,' they would vote a halter to the necks of their own and their neighbors' sons, who had volunteered. Could we have had free speech, we might have rallied the moral strength of the loyal, and defeated 'Separation;' but our leaders had deserted the Union: Brown, Bell, Ewing, and others were either committed to the rebel enterprise, or alarmed into acquiescence by the merely apparent popularity of the secession movement. The people did not want separation. They were content with their political condition; but, abandoned by their leaders, appealed to by a variety of bad influences, and surrounded by an armed mob—headed by the Governor of the State—they yielded to the sweeping storm. Wherever there was free discussion, the Union was sustained. In Bedford County, where Colonels Wisner and Cooper boldly discussed the question, the people voted against separation. And so it was in that portion of Smith County which was canvassed by Dr. Gordon and W. B. Stokes; and so, if we could have had free speech, would it have been all over the State. The action of East Tennessee proves this.

"The first Wednesday in. August was our Gubernatorial election. The aggregate vote then was 116,000—Harris beating Polk 33,000, and the ballots at this election fell short o. February, 39,000 votes.

"Then I saw the storm that was coming, and remained at my home in White County, to gather up my scattered means, and prepare for the inevitable and terrible future. General Buell reached Nashville in May, 1862. As soon as I heard of it I passed the rebel pickets in the night, to look once more on the glorious flag of my country. I stayed at Nashville till Buell advanced to the Tennessee River, and then returned home, defying the threats of my rebel neighbors. In July, Forrest encamped on my plantation, and there planned the capture of Murfreesboro. He returned there with his prisoners and plunder, cannons, guns, horses and mules, and left his sick at my house. I was known to him and his officers as a Union man, but they treated me with respect. I showed them the commission of my father, signed by John Hancock, and they admitted I could not be false to his principles. I found many Union men in the rebel regiments. They would come to me and say they loved me, because I dared to stand up for the old flag.

"Forrest took my stock, corn, hay, and oats, and made requisition on me for bread and meat, offering pay in Confederate money. I refused to take it, telling him it was tainted with treason. I then became the object of persecution. My letters had been opened and examined long before; but then I was waited on by a self-constituted committee, who told me they were my friends, and used many arguments to make me a rebel. The South, they said, was sure to come gloriously out of the contest, when Tennessee and the border States would be the New England of the Confederacy, and my large water-power would become immensely valuable. I answered that my loyalty was not in the market, and consequently could not be bought. This exasperated them, and they said I must immediately leave the county—that if I went at once, no personal harm should come to me. I replied, that I should leave when convenient—not before; that the property about me was my own—earned by my own industry; but I would abandon it all rather than abandon the Union. Then they told me that they would not be responsible for my personal safety, and left—I telling them, as they went away, that though my hair was gray, I could defend myself.*

"Rebel soldiers, in citizens' clothes, then waylaid and attempted to shoot me, and, at last, yielding to the entreaties of my wife, I fled at night, and joined our good General (Thomas, who was then present) at McMinnville. I went with him to Nashville, and remained there till after the battle of Stone River, when I joined him again at Murfreesboro. My wife said to me, when I left her: 'I have nothing to give to the Union but you. I give *you*, and God will accept the sacrifice' (and here the cool, collected man paused, and while every one was silent, wept). She and the children are still within the Rebel lines. My plantation and mills are occupied by rebel soldiers, and I have turned my back upon a home that, before the rebellion, was one of peace and plenty—and I say to you, Sir, the rebels are more wicked, more malicious, and more dangerous than any foreign enemy could be. We must exterminate the leaders wholly. The poor, simple people have been misled: and, mortified and humiliated, they would, the most of them, now come back to their allegiance, and become again good citizens. We must deal with them gently, but the leaders—every man who has taken a prominent part in promoting the rebellion—must be expatriated—placed where he

* This is the language of every Southern Union man. If the reader would have his Unionism invigorated, he should make the acquaintance of some of those men.

can no longer deceive the people. The *people* of Tennessee never desired the destruction of the National Government. They did not appreciate its blessings till they lost them; but now, in mortification and astonishment, they have awakened to its blessings, and see the ruin they have caused. Remove the leaders, and the masses will joyfully return to obedience. I hold the perpetuation of the Union above all other considerations. I have sacrificed every thing for it, and I have no ill-will against those who would destroy it, but I counsel the removal of every impediment that stands in the way of re-establishing its power and authority. It cannot be expected that all the Union men in the slave States will approve of the destruction of slavery—but the number who will not is small. It *must be* destroyed.

"*I* say, if slavery, property, or persons stand in the way of restoring the Union, remove them all. Save the life of the Nation. Preserve that, whatever else is lost.

"To a careful observer, who has resided long in the South, the truth is apparent that slavery has moulded all its manners, customs, and interests, its social, moral, and religious institutions. Our people are not a reading people; few books or newspapers are seen among them, and their educational interests have been shamefully neglected; therefore, the non-slaveholders have yielded a ready obedience to the slaveholders, who have controlled all legislative action. They have controlled every thing, and therefore we must crush them. Crush *them* as well as slavery, for until we do that, we can have no lasting peace."

These are the words of a loyal Southerner. I have met many of them, but I never met one who did not feel and talk as he did. *They* advocate no halfway measures: they would strike at the root of the tree. They know that this is a life and death struggle between two great principles; between Democracy and Aristocracy; between a Republic and a Despotism; and that one or the other must perish. Would to God that the loyal men of the North realized this as they do. If they did, Copperheads and peace-men would now be things of history.

CHAPTER XVIII.

A PROJECTED INSURRECTION.

I PASSED, as I have said, several weeks at Murfreesboro, and I could fill a volume with what I saw and heard, but the fear of compromising public interests holds my pen. Some day, when "this cruel war is over," I may be at liberty to write what I know. Then, if not before, the American people will say to Rosecrans: "Well done, good and faithful servant."

But now, when the rebels are raising the black flag, and butchering our troops, black and white, in a spirit unknown to even savage warfare, there is one thing which should be told.

One day, as I was sitting alone with Rosecrans, an aide handed him a letter. He opened it, ceased doing half a dozen other things, and became at once absorbed in its contents. He re-read it, and then, handing it to me, said: "Read that. Tell me what you think of it." I read it. Its outside indicated it had come from "over Jordan," and had "a hard road to travel," but its inside startled me. It was written in a round, unpractised hand, but though badly spelled, showed its author familiar with good *Southern* English. Its date was May 18th, 1863, and it began thus:

"GENERAL:—A plan has been adopted for a simultaneous movement or rising to sever the rebel communications throughout the whole South, which is now disclosed to some general in each military department in the Secesh States, in order that they may act in concert, and thus insure us success.

"The plan is for the blacks to make a concerted and simultaneous rising, on the night of the first of August next, over the whole States in rebellion. To arm themselves with any and every kind of weapon that may come to hand, and commence operations by burning all railroad and county bridges, tearing up all railroad tracks, and cutting and destroying telegraph wires,—and when this is done take to the woods, the swamps, or the mountains, whence they may emerge, as occasions may offer, for provisions or for further depredations. No blood is to be shed except in self-defence.

"The corn will be in roasting ear about the first of August, and upon this, and by foraging on the farms at night, we can subsist. Concerted movement at the time named would be successful, and the rebellion be brought suddenly to an end."

The letter went on with some details which I cannot repeat, and ended thus:

"The plan will be simultaneous over the whole South, and yet few of all engaged will know its whole extent. Please write '1' and 'approved,' and send by the bearer, that we may know *you are with us.*

"Be assured, General, that a copy of this letter has been sent to every military department in the rebel States, that the time of the movement may thus be general over the entire South."

I was re-reading the letter when the General again said: "What do you think of it?"

"It would end the rebellion. It taps the great negro organization, of which I speak in 'Among the Pines,' and, cooperated with by our forces, would certainly succeed, but—the South would run with blood."

"Innocent blood! Women and children!"

"Yes, women and children. If you let the blacks loose, they will rush into carnage like horses into a burning barn. St. Domingo will be multiplied by a million."

"But he says no blood is to be shed except in self-defence."

"He says so, and the leaders may mean so, but they cannot restrain the rabble. Every slave has some real or fancied wrong, and he would take such a time to avenge it."

"Well, I must talk with Garfield. Come, go with me."

We crossed the street to Garfield's lodgings, and found him bolstered up in bed, quite sick of a fever. The General sat down at the foot of his bed, and handed him the letter. Garfield read it over carefully, and then laying it down, said:

"It will never do, General. *We* don't want to whip by such means. If the slaves, of their own accord, rise and assert their original right to themselves, that will be their own affair; but we can have no complicity with them without outraging the moral sense of the civilized world."

"I knew you'd say so; but he speaks of other department commanders—may they not come into it?"

"Yes, they may, and that should be looked to. Send this letter to ——, and let him head off 'the movement.'"

It was not thought prudent to intrust the letter to the mails; nor with the railway infested with guerillas, was it a safe document to carry about the person. A short shrift and a long rope might have been the consequence of its being found on a traveller. So, ripping open the top of my boot, I stowed it snugly away in the lining, and took it North. On the 4th of June following, Garfield wrote me that he had just heard from the writer of the letter; that five out of our nine department commanders had come into the project, and, subsequently, that another general had also promised it his support.

But I can say no more. All the world knows that the insurrection did not take place. The outbreaks in September, among the blacks of Georgia and Alabama, were only parts of the plan, the work of subordinate leaders, who, maddened at the miscarriage of the grand scheme, determined to carry out their own share of the programme at all hazards. It was a gigantic project, and the trains were all laid, the matches all lighted, and two centuries of cruel wrong were about to be avenged in a night, when a white man said to the negro: "You will slaughter friends and enemies. You will wade knee deep in innocent blood; God cannot be with you in midnight massacre!" A white man said that, and the uplifted torch fell from the negro's hand; and saying: "I will 'bide my time; I will leave vengeance to God," he went back to his toil and his stripes.

The time has not come to write the history of this, and I have said what I have, only to show that while Southern men were starving our prisoners, butchering our wounded, and desecrating our dead, we were supplicating the destroying angel to pass over their homes, and save their wives and little ones from a swift destruction. In the day when "He maketh inquisition for blood," on whose garments, my Southern brother, think you, He will find the stain?

CHAPTER XIX.

COLONEL JAMES F. JAQUESS.

ONE morning, not many days after the events recorded in the last chapter, General Rosecrans handed me another letter, saying, as he did so, "Here is an application from one of my officers for a furlough. It explains itself. I have to be at the front all day, and I wish you would stay and see him. If you think well of it, I will telegraph the Department for the furlough. The Colonel was a prominent member of the Western Methodist Church, and, though a clergyman, is one of my best and bravest officers. You will be glad of his acquaintance."

I cheerfully assented to the request, and an orderly was at once dispatched to his camp for the officer. Meanwhile, I read the application. It was as follows:

"HEAD-QUARTERS, 73D REGIMENT ILLINOIS INFANTRY,
CAMP NEAR MURFREESBORO, 19TH MAY, 1863.

"GENERAL:—I feel it to be my duty to lay before you the following facts, considerations, and proposition:

"Situated as we are, it is no matter of astonishment that the great eye of the world is intently fixed upon us. The truth is, we are intrusted with the dearest interests of humanity, with the solution of the grandest problem that ever inspired the hopes or engaged the attention of man. It is the problem of his capacity for self-government. And, if we fail, which we shall do most signally if we do not suppress this rebellion, man's emancipation from tyranny and oppression, and human liberty and self-government, are failures.

"The question that Heaven has called us to decide in blood, with the weapons of war, and amid the slaughter of the battle-field, is not one of a political character only. It is not simply a question of latitude and longitude; it is, whether we are a Christian or a heathen people.

"On both sides of Mason and Dixon's line we claim to be Christian men. We speak the same language, read the same Bible, and worship God with the same forms and ceremonies. We appoint days of fasting and prayer, and observe them with a zeal worthy of a Christian people, and, independently of man's design, these appointments often fall on the same days, North and South. Resolving to 'trust in God, but keep our powder dry,' we have risen up from our devotions, grasped again the weapons of death, and rushed into the thickest of the fight, without stopping to reflect that God has other means than the sword to subdue his enemies.

"It is well known, that before the Southern States seceded, the Methodist Church in the United States was separated on the very questions which have since divided the nation. It is also known that 'the Methodist Episcopal Church, South,' was a leading element in the rebellion, and has been a prominent power in the prosecution of the war.

"A considerable part of the territory occupied by 'the Methodist Episcopal Church, South,' at the time of the separation, and up to a recent date, is now in possession of our armies. This has brought a large number of the ministers and people of that communion within our lines. Some of these persons were prominent in the movement that separated the Church, and were most bittei and uncompromising on the questions of difference.

"From these persons I have learned personally the following facts, viz.: That they consider the rebellion has destroyed the 'Methodist Church, South;' that it has virtually abolished slavery, and obliterated the other prominent questions of difference; that they are sincerely desirous of returning to the 'Old Church;' and that their brethren within the rebel lines are most heartily tired of the rebellion, and most ardently desire peace and the privilege of returning to their allegiance to Church and State, and will do so whenever they are assured of amnesty for the past.

"My attention has been called to these facts, and to others of a like character, frequently of late; and from these considerations —though not from these only, but because God has laid the duty upon me—I would submit to the proper authorities the following proposition, viz.: *To go into the Southern Confederacy, and return within ninety days, with proposals of peace that will be acceptable to our Government.*

"I shall propose *no compromise* with traitors, but their immediate return to their allegiance to God and their country. It is no part of my business to discuss the probability or the possibility of my accomplishing this work. I propose to do it in the name of the Lord, and to leave results with Him.

"If He puts it into the hearts of my superiors to allow me to go, I shall be thankful; if not, I have discharged my duty.

"Your obedient servant,

"(Signed) JAMES F. JAQUESS,

"*Col. Comd'g 73d Reg't Ill. Inf'ty.*

"To Brig.-General GARFIELD, *Chief of Staff,*

"*Department of the Cumberland.*"

A little more than an hour after the departure of the orderly, an erect, spare man, in the undress uniform of a colonel of infantry, entered the inner room of the General's quarters, where I was seated. He seemed rather more than forty, and was a little above the medium height, with gray hair and beard, a high, broad, open forehead, and a thin, marked face, expressing great earnestness, strength, and benignity of character. He came directly up to me, and, bowing rather stiffly, said:

"Is this Mr. Kirke?"

"That is a name I sometimes go by. You are Colonel Jaquess. I am very glad to meet you," and I took his hand very cordially.

"I am very glad to meet you," he replied, taking my hand, and the stiffness disappearing from his manner; "I feel that I know you. My little boy, only this morning, was speaking of you. We were riding through a piece of woods, when he said to me: 'Father, don't this remind you of "Among the Pines?"' He has the story all by heart."

Was not that fame? To be talked of by a Western boy in the wilds of Tennessee! Reader, I have my "weaknesses," as well as yourself. One of them was touched then—I confess it. The Colonel must have observed it, when I replied:

"You gratify me. And you've brought your little boy out here to see the South as it is?"

"Yes, to see the reality of slavery. I want him to hate it as I do. But the General has sent me word he has referred my application to you."

"He has asked me to hear what you have to say, and you know he is very busy."

He then explained at some length, the objects he had in

view in his proposed visit among the Rebels. He had been, it appeared, for many years a prominent clergyman of the Western Methodist Church, and in friendly and familiar intercourse with the leading divines of that communion in the South. He was a member of the Nashville Convention, which divided that denomination into the "Church North" and the "Church South," and there did all in his power to defeat that unfortunate measure, which, undoubtedly, was the entering-wedge that rent the Union. On the breaking out of the war, he resigned the Presidency of Quincy College—leaving home, ease, and honors—to accept the chaplaincy of the Sixth Illinois Cavalry. After the battle of Pittsburg Landing, for brilliant services in that engagement—this is not his own account of himself—he was solicited by Governor Yates to raise and take command of a regiment. After repeated and urgent entreaty from the Governor, he consented to do so, and the result was, that within three weeks the Seventy-third Illinois Volunteers, known as the "Preachers' Regiment"—nearly every officer in it being a clergyman—was in the field. With this regiment he had served throughout the campaigns in Kentucky and Tennessee, and during that service had met many of his most active and zealous opponents in the Nashville Convention. Without exception, they all had told him they regarded slavery—the sole cause of their schism—as virtually abolished, and had expressed a wish to come back to the Church and the Union. Through them he had corresponded with a number of leading divines within the rebel lines, and they, too, had said they desired to return to their allegiance to the Church and the country. He thought the Methodist people of the South sympathized in this with their leaders, and he added:

"I want to go to them—to offer them the olive-branch—to tell them, in the name of God and the country, that they will be welcome back."

"The Methodist element, I know, Colonel," I replied, "is a strong element at the South; but I fear the peace part of it is not strong enough to control the politicians. They, if I know them, care little about church or country. They have other views than submission. They mean to establish an independent government, *at all hazards*."

"I don't know what their views are. It is not my business to ask. I feel that God has laid upon me the duty to go to them, and go I must, unless my superiors forbid it."

"But how will you go? The Government, I feel sure, will give you neither authority nor protection. How, then, will you go?"

"Openly; in my uniform; as the messenger of God."

"I fear the rebels, like the people of old, will not recognize the Lord's messenger. They'll shoot or hang you as a spy."

"It is not for me to ask what they will do; I have only to go."

"Well, I'll report what you say to the General, but I must be frank with you: if he asks my opinion, I shall advise him not to apply for the furlough. I have heard of you before, and your life, in my judgment, is altogether too valuable to be wasted on such an embassy."

"That is not for you to judge. But I want more than a furlough; I want an interview with Mr. Lincoln, to learn the terms on which he will give amnesty to the Rebels. You will say this to the General?"

"Yes; and, as I told you, advise him to do nothing about it."

At this the Colonel laughed, good-humoredly.

"What amuses you?" I asked, a little annoyed.

"I was only thinking how little we know what we will do. Now, I shall not only go, but *you* will help me."

"How do you know that?"

"You'll think me superstitious if I tell you."

"Not till I hear you."

"Well; when I called on General Garfield, yesterday, and opened my project to him, he told me to put it in black and white, and he would submit it to the General. I went back to camp, and did so—wrote the letter you have in your hand. I had thought of this for several months, but, until I spoke to General Garfield, had said nothing to any one about it. This morning, however, just after sunrise, it occurred to me to talk it over with my Chaplain, who is my intimate friend. Taking the letter with me, I went to his tent. He was just coming out of it; and he said, as he saw me:

"'Ah, Colonel, I was about to go and see you. I had a strange dream about you last night.'

"'Did you? What was it?'

"'I dreamed that you were in a small room with Jeff. Davis and two other gentlemen. I couldn't hear what was said, but you all seemed in very earnest conversation. What did it mean?'

"I then told him of my intention to visit Mr. Davis, and read him my letter. We both thought it very singular. About an hour afterwards, as we were riding in the woods, my little son mentioned your name. At once it occurred to me that you were here—I did not *know* you were—and here to help me. Now, I have no faith in dreams—I believe God has 'sealed up the vision and the prophecy,' but the impression is strong upon me—stronger than my reason, I cannot shake it off—that I shall see Jeff. Davis, and *you* will help me."

"Well, I *may*. As you say, we cannot tell what we may do."

I kept my word with him; that is, I reported the interview to General Rosecrans, and recommended that he should do nothing about it.

"Why not?" asked the General.

"Because he could accomplish nothing, and would throw his life away."

"I know, if he talks peace to the people the leaders will hang him; but he'll not do that. He'll go to the leaders themselves. The terms he will offer may not be accepted, but it will strengthen our moral position to offer them. It will show the world that we do not seek to subjugate the South. As to his life —he takes the right view about that. He considers it already given to the country. If you had seen him at Stone River, you'd think so. He is a hero—John Brown and the Chevalier Bayard rolled into one, and endowed with common sense, and a knowledge of Greek, Latin, and the mathematics."

That evening the General sent a telegram to Washington, stating the Colonel's objects, and asking for him a four months' furlough, and an interview with the President. Answer came in the morning, declining the requests, but asking a fuller explanation of Colonel Jaquess's purposes, by mail. The message was sent out to the Colonel's camp, and in a few hours he appeared at head-quarters. I happened to be with the General at the time. He was as busy as usual, but, as Jaquess came in, looked up, and said:

"Well, Colonel, you've got your sentence."

"I don't think so, General. I never give up with one trial."

"That's right; but what's to be done now?"

"Try again. Mr. —— must go to Washington. I've known Mr. Lincoln twenty years, but I might write him forty letters, and accomplish nothing. Writing won't do it. Mr. —— must go."

This was spoken with such inimitable coolness, that I burst into a hearty laugh.

"Yes," said the General, also laughing; "that's it. You must go. You've been talking of going every day for a week—now you must go, and take Washington on your way. I've some other business I want attended to; and you will do it—to oblige me."

"Well, to oblige you, I will." And thus so much of the Colonel's presentiments were realized. About the rest, the reader will learn before this book is ended.

I was to start the next afternoon, and in the morning Jaquess came into town to bid me good-by. As we parted, he took my hand, and said to me:

"I know I shall go on this mission, but whether I shall return or not, is uncertain. But if I do not—if I go to the other side of Jordan before you, be sure I shall be the first man to take you by the hand when you get there."

This sentence displays the whole character of the man. He "walks by faith, not by sight." To him the curtain which hides the other life from ours is already lifted—the two worlds are already one.

A few days thereafter, with a bundle of "dispatches" in my pocket, I landed in Washington. Among these "dispatches" was one, of which the following is a copy:

"HEAD-QUARTERS, DEPARTMENT OF THE CUMBERLAND,
"MURFREESBORO, TENN., *May* 21, 1863.

"To His Excellency,

"THE PRESIDENT OF THE UNITED STATES:

"The Rev. Dr. Jaquess, Colonel commanding the 73d Illinois, —a man of character,—has submitted to me a letter proposing a personal mission to the South. After maturely weighing his plan, and considering well his character, I am decidedly of opinion that the public interests will be promoted by permitting him to go as he proposes.

"I do not anticipate the results that he seems to expect, but believe that a moral force will be generated by his mission, that will more than compensate us for his temporary absence from his regiment.

"His letter is herein enclosed, and the bearer of this, Mr. ——, can fully explain Colonel Jaquess's plans and purposes.

"Very respectfully,

"W. S. ROSECRANS, *Major-General.*"

Enclosing this and the other papers in an envelope, I sent them, with a note, asking when I could have a private interview with the President, to the White House.

"Come at half-past seven this evening, and I'll be glad to see you," was the answer.

I went at the appointed time, and my friend, Mr. Nicolay said to me:

"Mr. Lincoln is expecting you, but, just now, he's engaged with Reverdy Johnson. Take a seat in my room, and he'll call you when he's ready."

I did as I was bidden, and in about half an hour, the homely, humane face, with which everybody is familiar, looked in at the door, and a kind, benevolent voice said to me: "Sorry to have kept you waiting. Come in. Do you know, I can't talk with you about that Jaquess matter?"

"Why not, Sir?" I asked, following him into the room.

"Because I happen to be President of the United States. We can make no overtures to the Rebels. If they want peace, all they have to do is to lay down their arms. But never mind about that; you've been to Tennessee, and I want to see you. So sit down, and tell me all you know,—it won't take you long."

It did take me three whole hours; and, while I told it, I took advantage of my position as one of the "sovereigns" to find a little fault with the War Department. Mr. Lincoln heard me patiently, parrying my thrusts with a smile or a humorous story, and, when I concluded, said: "Well, it's lucky that you're 'one of the people.' You escape all this."

"I know I do; and that reminds me—I received a letter this morning, which I want to read to you. It's from a young woman you've heard of. Long ago she gave herself to the Lord, and that, you know, means the country; so, she's a right to speak."

Then I read the letter. It was as follows:

"You write that you are going to Washington, so, I know you'll see 'Old Abe.' Now, don't *you* find any fault with him. I know your impatient disposition—I know you think he ought to have done a good deal more than he has done. But, remember, that he has had an untried way, difficulties all about him, conservatives advising one thing, radicals another, and all deceiving him. So, don't *you* find fault with him, but bid him 'God speed.' Tell him that all good men and women, everywhere, are with him—that they pray for him, and bless him for what he has done, and will yet do. One word, from a man he knows has nothing to ask for, may cheer him—cheer him more than you know—and don't you fail to say it. As you love truth and God, say it, for it is true, and you *ought* to say it."

It would not be true if I said there was "a tear in his eye" when I read this. There was not. He is not "given to weeping," but his voice had a mellower, softer tone, as he asked:

"Who is she?"

I told him.

"Tell her," he said, "that I thank her—that I hope God will bless her."

That was a year ago; but what that young woman then said might as well—might better—be said now by every man and woman in the country.

As I rose to go, he asked me:

"When do you go home?"

"In the morning."

"Can't you stay another day, and come to see me to-morrow evening? I want to think more of that Jaquess matter."

"Yes, Sir, I'll do so," and on the following evening I called on him again.

Grant had then "watered his horse in the Mississippi." Vicksburg was beleaguered, but Pendleton was inside of it with twenty-five thousand men, and Johnston outside of it with thirty thousand. Grant had only thirty thousand. Re-enforcements had not then reached him. Might he not be crushed before they arrived?

The President was very anxious. He showed none of his

usual humor and vivacity. Dispatch after dispatch came in from the War Department, and he opened them, glanced at their signatures, and then, laying them down unread, said: "Only from Hooker;" or, "Only from Burnside;" or, "Only from Rosecrans. Nothing from Grant yet! Why don't we hear from Grant?"

If the life of his own son had been quivering in the balance at Vicksburg, he could not have shown more anxiety. I had not voted for him. I had not admired or even supported him; but that night I regretted that I had not, for what I saw satisfied me that there is not a drop in Abraham Lincoln's veins that does not beat for his country.

It was hard to get him to the subject, but at last I did do it; and then he told me, in a clear, direct way, the terms he would give the Rebels. A portion of these terms have since been included in the Amnesty Proclamation; the rest I do not feel at liberty to make public. They are all, however, embodied in a few of his words:

"The country will do every thing for safety—nothing for revenge."

If Washington ever uttered a grander, or a nobler sentence than that, I have not read it.

Finally, he said:

"You can write what I say to General Rosecrans, and he can communicate as much of it as he thinks best to Colonel Jaquess; but the Colonel must not understand that he has these terms from me. We want peace, but we can make no overtures to the Rebels. They already know that the country would welcome them back, and treat them generously and magnanimously."

It was nearly twelve o'clock when I rose to go. As I did so, he said:

"Don't go yet. I shall stay here until I get something from Grant!"

The next morning I wrote to Rosecrans, and, within ten days, Colonel Jaquess started for the South. At Baltimore he reported to General Schenck, who forwarded him on to Fortress Monroe. Arriving there he explained his business to General Dix, and he, after some delay, allowed him to smuggle himself on board a flag-of-truce boat going to the Rebel lines. He was in his uniform, but the Rebel officer who met our flag said to him:

"Go where you please, and stay as long as you like."

Any one can see the great risk he ran. He had no credentials; nothing to show who he was, or why he came; and there were ten chances to one that he would be taken as a spy. But what was that to him? He was about his MASTER's work, and his trust in the MASTER, which "whoever runs may read" in his face, carried him safely through.

He went to Petersburg, and there they came to him. As Nicodemus came to the great PEACE-MAKER, so the Rebel leaders came to him, by night. Disguised, and under false names, they sought him to ask the way to peace.

"Lay down your arms; go back to your allegiance, and the country will deal kindly and generously by you," he said to all of them.

From all he had the same answer:

"We are tired of the war. We are willing to give up slavery. We know it is gone; but so long as our Government holds out, we must stand by it. We cannot betray it and each other."

And this is *now* the sentiment of the Southern people, and of a vast number of the Southern leaders.

He remained at Petersburg several weeks and then returned to Baltimore. From there he wrote to the President, but received no answer. He waited there a long time; but, no answer coming, finally returned to his regiment. Then he wrote me, stating the result of his visit, and saying he wanted to go again, with liberty to see Jeff. Davis. [Other leaders he had seen, but Davis he had not seen.] This letter came just as I was setting out on a long journey; and, naturally concluding that if he had not answered Jaquess, he would not answer me, I did not write to the President. Thus the affair rested till I returned from my journey. Then I went to Washington, and, calling on Mr. Lincoln, asked him why he had not answered Jaquess.

"I never received his letter," was the unexpected reply.

"Well, it's not too late. Those people are ripe for peace now. I know that from many of them. Let Jaquess go again. There is no telling what he may accomplish."

The President turned about on his chair, and on a small card wrote the following:

"*To whom it may concern:*

"The bearer, Colonel James F. Jaquess, Seventy-third Illinois, has leave of absence until further orders.

"A. LINCOLN."

In a few weeks Jaquess joined me in Baltimore. Going with him to Washington, I then learned that unexpected obstacles were in the way of his further progress. These obstacles could be removed by my accompanying him, and that and other reasons finally led to our visiting Richmond together.

CHAPTER XX.

WHY I WENT TO RICHMOND.

I HAVE, in the preceding chapter, related the fact of Colonel Jaquess' first visit within the Rebel lines, and the circumstances which led to his setting out on a second journey thither; and the reader may now ask why I, a "civil" individual, not in the pay of Government, and having no sort of influence in "the Methodist Church South," accompanied him on this second expedition, and, at a season when all the world was rushing North to the mountains and the watering-places, journeyed South for a conference with the arch-Rebel, in the hot and dangerous latitude of Virginia.

I could give half a dozen good reasons for undertaking such a journey, and any one of them would prove that I am a sensible man, altogether too sensible to go on so long a trip, in the heat of midsummer, for the mere pleasure of the thing; but I will content myself with enumerating a smaller number, and the reader may believe that any one, or all of them, had a greater or a less influence, or no influence at all, in determining my movements.

First: Very many honest people at the North sincerely believe that the revolted States will return to the Union if assured of protection to their peculiar institution. The Government having declared that no State shall be readmitted which has not first abolished slavery, these people hold *it* responsible for the continuance of the war. It is, therefore, important to know whether the Rebel States will, or will not, return to their allegiance, if allowed to retain Slavery. Mr. Jefferson Davis could, undoubtedly, answer that question; and that may have seemed a reason why I should go to see him.

Second: On the second of July last, C. C. Clay, of Alabama; J. P. Holcombe, of Virginia; and G. N. Sanders, of nowhere in particular, appeared at Niagara Falls, and publicly announced that they were there to confer with the Democratic leaders in reference to the Chicago nomination. Very soon thereafter, a few friends of the Administration received intimations from those gentlemen that they were Commissioners from the Rebel Government, with authority to negotiate preliminaries of peace on something like the following basis, namely: A restoration of the Union as it was; all negroes actually freed by the war to be declared free, and all negroes not actually freed by the war to be declared slaves.

These overtures were not considered sincere. They seemed concocted to embarrass the Government, to throw upon it the odium of continuing the war, and thus to secure the triumph of the peace-traitors at the November election. The scheme, if well managed, threatened to be dangerous, by uniting the Peace-men, the Copperheads, and such of the Republicans as love peace better than principle, in one opposition, willing to make peace on terms inconsistent with the interests and safety of the nation. It seemed, therefore, important to discover—what was then in doubt—whether the Rebel envoys really had, or had not, any official authority.

Within fifteen days of the appearance of these "Peace Commissioners," Jefferson Davis had said to an eminent Secession divine, who, late in June, came through the Union lines by the Maryland back-door, that he would make peace on no other terms than a recognition of Southern Independence. (He might, however, agree to two governments, bound together by a league offensive and defensive—for all external purposes, *one;* for all internal purposes, *two;* but he would agree to nothing better.)

There was reason to consider this information trustworthy, and to believe Mr. Davis altogether ignorant of the doings of his Niagara satellites. If this were true, and were proven to be true—if the *great* Rebel should reiterate this declaration in the presence of a trustworthy witness, at the very time when the *small* Rebels were opening their Quaker guns on the country—would not the Niagara negotiators be stripped of their false colors, and their low schemes be exposed to the scorn of all honest men, North and South?

I may have thought so; and, if I did, that may have seemed another good reason why I should go to Richmond.

Third: And this, to very many, may appear as potent as any of the preceding reasons:—I had in my boyhood a strange fancy for church-belfries and liberty-poles. This fancy led me, in school-vacations, to perch my small self for hours on the cross-beams in the old belfry, and to climb to the very top of the tall pole which still surmounts the little village green. In my youth, this feeling was simply a spirit of adventure; but as I grew older it deepened into a reverence for what those old bells said, and a love for the principle of which that old liberty-pole is now only a crumbling symbol.

Had not events shown that Jeff. Davis had never seen that old liberty-pole, and never heard the chimes which still ring out from that old belfry? Who knew, in these days when every woodsawyer has a "mission," but *I* had a mission, and it was to tell the Rebel President that Northern liberty-poles still stand for Freedom, and that Northern church-bells still peal out, "Liberty throughout the land, to *all* the inhabitants thereof?"

If that *was* my mission, will anybody blame me for fanning Mr. Davis with a "blast" of cool Northern "wind" in this hot weather?—and might not that be reason enough why I should go to Richmond?

But enough of mystification. The straightforward reader wants a straightforward reason, and he shall have it.

I went to Richmond because I thought I could render material aid to Colonel Jaquess, in paving the way to negotiations that might result in peace.

If we should succeed, the consciousness of having served the country would, I thought, pay our expenses. If we should fail, but return safely, we might still serve the country by making public the cause of our failure. If we should fail, and *not* return safely, but be shot or hanged as spies,—as we might be, for we could have no protection from our Government, and no safe-conduct from the rebels,—two lives would be added to the thousands already sacrificed to this rebellion; but they would as effectually serve the country as if lost on the battle-field.

These are the reasons, and the only reasons, why I went to Richmond.

CHAPTER XXI.

ON THE WAY TO RICHMOND.

HAVING decided on accompanying Colonel Jaquess, I procured a pass to General Grant's head-quarters, and, on a pleasant afternoon in July, went with him on board of one of the small steamers plying between Washington and City Point. As we stepped upon the gangway, a civil young gentleman, in linen trousers and the undress coat of an infantry captain, said to me:

"Your pass, sir."

I produced the required paste-board, and coolly putting it in his pocket, he remarked:

"All right, sir."

"Not exactly all right, my dear fellow. It will be when you return me the pass."

"But I'll see you safely to the General's. This is a kind I don't often get, and I want to keep it."

"And I prefer you shouldn't—perhaps for that very reason. So deliver."

He did "deliver," but very reluctantly. However, he made amends for the slight incivility by uncommon attention during the passage.

The boat was crowded with passengers—officers returning from furlough, recruits going to the field, convalescent veterans rejoining their regiments, and country clergymen entering on the good work of the Sanitary and Christian Commissions—and the trip was fruitful in incidents characteristic of the war, and illustrative of the mighty transition which is regenerating the nation. But we are going to Richmond, and the reader will not thank me if I linger by the way.

It wanted several hours of sundown on the following day, when the boat rounded to under the abrupt promontory which bears the name of City Point. A large flag was flying among the trees which crown the higher part of the headland, and, making our way to it, we asked for the quarters of the General.

"Yonder, in that tent. He is sitting there, you see," replied the adjutant.

Without more ceremony, we passed down the grassy avenue, and presented ourselves before him. He was seated on a camp stool, smoking a cigar, and listening to the reading of a newspaper by General Rawlins. A few other officers sat near, and something which had just been read appeared to amuse them greatly. The General looked up as we approached, and, as he espied my companion, rose rather hastily.

"Ah! Colonel," he said, extending his hand, "I am glad to see you. It's a long time since we met. Not since—"

"Pittsburg Landing, I believe, General. I think we met there," returned my companion.

"Yes, I remember. I remember the work you did there for the wounded. When did you leave Sherman?"

"About ten days ago. I brought dispatches from him to the War Department."

"I have heard from him later than that. He is doing splendidly—handling his army most magnificently."

Meanwhile, the Colonel had introduced me to the General, and at this break in the conversation I said to him:

"We want your ear, Sir, privately, for a few moments."

"Certainly; walk in this way." And rising, he led us into his sleeping apartment—a square tent, with a single strip of carpet on the ground, a low camp-cot in one corner, and a portable desk, covered with open papers, in the other.

Handing him, then, a note I had with me, I briefly explained our wishes.

"I don't believe the rebels will receive you. They have not answered a flag for a month. However, I will send one. I shall have to address General Lee. Shall I say you want to meet Judge Ould?" he asked, drawing his stool to the desk.

"If you please, and suppose you add, that if there appears to Lee any objection to Ould's meeting us, you would like to have him refer our request to Jeff. Davis."

"I'll do so," and he began the note. While he was writing it, I noted more particularly his appearance. He is of about the medium height, with a large head, a compact frame, and a deep, broad chest and shoulders. His hair is brown, his eyes clear, deep gray, and his features regular, and of a cast that might be called "Massive, Grecian." Though his first meeting with the Colonel was decidedly cordial, his usual manner is cool and undemonstrative; but with this coolness is a certain earnest simplicity, that impresses one very favorably. In his face is the unyielding persistency which has won him so many battles, but there is nothing else remarkable about him. He does not at once magnetize a stranger with a sense of his genius, as does Rosecrans.

The note finished, he read it to us. "Will that do?" he asked.

"Yes, Sir, when can it go off?"

"At once. It'll go by boat to Point of Rocks, and from there to the Rebel lines; but, at the earliest, you'll not get a reply before to-morrow night."

The conversation then took a general turn, and in a clear, simple way he explained the military position, expressing the opinion that the fall of Richmond and the defeat of Lee, though they might be delayed, were inevitable events.

As we rose to go, he said:

"Where do you sleep to-night?"

"We've engaged lodgings on the steamer. We hope to leave you to-morrow."

As we passed down towards the wharf, we met a number of officers just landed from a small steamer. One of them, though I had never seen him before, I knew at once to be General Butler. Obeying a sudden impulse, I halted as he came abreast of us, and said to him:

"I want to take you by the hand; I am, myself, a live Yankee," and I mentioned my name.

Giving me a cordial grasp, he replied, "I'm delighted to meet you. Come up and see me. Take the 'Gazelle' to Point of Rocks—don't go to Bermuda. Come to-morrow."

I then introduced the Colonel, and the General again urging us to visit him, we promised to do so.

Reporting our intended absence to General Grant, and requesting him to forward Lee's answer to us by telegraph, we set out on the following morning for the head-quarters of "Our Massachusetts General." We found them about a mile distant from the Appomatox river, in a worn-out tobacco-field, flanked on two sides by dense woods, and hemmed in on the others by "moving" banks of Virginia sand. It was a dreary spot, but we forgot that, the moment we entered the General's tent, and he accosted us with:

"I'm glad you've come. There are two cots in the corner. They are yours. I sent your flag this morning. It may not be back for some days. In the mean time make yourselves at home. Go and come when you like, and do exactly as you please."

We remained with the General nearly three days, and they were among the most agreeable days I ever passed. We rode with him about his lines, witnessing his reviews of the black troops, and his various experiments in "Greek fire," "Proclamation kite" flying, and "infernal shell" shooting, which are proving so valuable to the army; or, when not so engaged, sat with him in his tent, listening to his interesting political and military experiences, and getting such inside glimpses of "Butler in New Orleans" as are not to be found even in Parton's admirable book. With a keen sense of humor, an inexhaustible fund of anecdote, and a ready, comprehensive intellect, he is about the most interesting and entertaining conversationalist I ever knew. In hearing him, one loses the "power of speech," and only sits still and listens. He knew our object in visiting Rebeldom, and one morning I said to him:

"General, you know Jeff. Davis. Tell us, how shall we approach him?—what shall we say to him?"

Drawing one leg over the other, and dilating his nostrils in a way peculiar to himself, he answered:

"Do you really want to know? Well, I'll tell you," and, throwing himself into an attitude, he gave us for half an hour an imaginary conversation with the Rebel leader, personating first him, and then the Colonel and myself, and "doing" us so admirably that I almost fancied we ourselves were actually speaking. As he was about concluding, General Meade entered the front tent, and as he rose to receive his visitor, he turned on his heel, and—still speaking as Jeff. Davis—"finished us" as follows:

"Now, gentlemen, I've said my say, and if you don't clear out, and take your Yankee notions to some other market, I'll hang you to the first tree—I will, as I'm a Christian!"

Afterwards, when listening to the much more serious words of the Rebel leader, I had often to smile as General Butler's inimitable personation of him recurred to me; and when again, late at night, we returned from the Rebel lines, and stiff with long riding, and exhausted with fatigue and illness, I staggered into his tent, and threw myself on a cot in the corner, I almost died with laughter while the Colonel recounted to him the Richmond interview—it was so like the advance representation he had given us. If we had known Jeff. Davis as General Butler knows him, I very much question our having gone to Richmond.

The next morning the flag-of-truce officer came into camp with a dispatch, of which the following is a copy:

"WAR DEPARTMENT, RICHMOND, VA., *July 12th*, 1864.

"*To the Officer commanding*
the United States Forces at Deep Bottom, Va.:

"SIR:—A communication from Lieut.-General U. S. Grant to General R. E. Lee, requesting that —— ——, Esq., and Colonel James F. Jaquess, be allowed to meet the undersigned at such place between the lines of the two armies as may be designated, having been referred to the War Department, I am directed to request you to notify Lieut.-General Grant that I will be in attendance at some convenient point between Deep Bottom and Chaffin's Bluff (say at Mrs. Grover's), on Thursday, the 14th inst., at one o'clock P. M., to receive any communication the above-named parties have to make.

"Respectfully,

"Your obedient servant,

"Ro. Ould,

"*Agent of Exchange.*"

At the appointed time we rode up to Mrs. Grover's, a modest plantation mansion, about midway between the two armies on the James River. Our "Southern friends" were not there; but in the edge of a grove of cedars, a few hundred yards distant, we saw a white flag aflying. Galloping rapidly across the intervening wheat-field, we soon caught sight of a pair of horses hitched to an open, two-seated wagon, and near it saw three gentlemen seated on a log in the shade of a huge tree. These gentlemen rose as we approached, and one of them—a courteous, middle-aged man, in a Panama hat and a suit of spotless white drillings—said to Major Mulford, the Union Commissioner, who accompanied us:

"I'm glad to see you, Major. It's some time since we met."

"Yes, it is. I've come now to deliver to you these gentlemen, to be shot or hanged—whichever you like."

The Judge—for it was Judge Ould—laughed, and then introduced us to his companions—Captain Hatch, of the Commission, and Major Henniken, of the Rebel War Department.

Some unimportant conversation followed, and then, saying we would like to speak with him privately, we led the Judge into the grove of cedars. There we opened our business. He listened with interest, but expressed the opinion that Mr. Davis would refuse to see us, unless we produced credentials from our Government.

"We have none," said the Colonel, in his earnest way; "but we must see him. We only ask a hearing. Then he may hang or shoot us, if he likes."

"Hang, but hear!" answered the Judge, laughing. "That is what you mean?"

"Yes," said the Colonel. "We have that to say which Mr. Davis ought to hear, and we are willing to risk our lives to say it."

"Well," said the Judge, "I will bear your message to the President, and meet you here again—when?"

"To-morrow, at this hour, if you like."

"That may be too early. Suppose we say the next day, Saturday, at twelve o'clock."

"Very well; Saturday let it be." And remounting our horses, we rode back to General Butler's camp.

We remained there the following day, and on the morning of Saturday, the 16th of July, just as the Boston bells were sounding nine, taking him by the hand, we said to him:

"Good by. If you do not see us within ten days, you will know we have 'gone up.'"

"If I do not see you within that time," he replied, "I'll demand you; and if they don't produce you, body and soul, I'll take two for one,—better men than you are,—and hang them higher than Haman. My hand on that. Good by."

At three o'clock that afternoon, mounted on two raw-boned relics of Sheridan's great raid, and armed with a letter to Jeff. Davis, a white cambric handkerchief tied to a short stick, and an honest face,—this last was the Colonel's,—we rode up to the rebel lines. A ragged, yellow-faced boy, with a carbine in one hand, and another white handkerchief tied to another short stick in the other, came out to meet us.

"Can you tell us, my man, where to find Judge Ould, the Exchange Commissioner?"

"Yas. Him and t'other 'Change officers is over ter the plantation beyont Miss Grover's. Ye'll know it by its hevin' nary door nur winder"—the mansion, he meant. "They's all busted in. Foller the bridle-path through the timber, and keep your rag a-flyin', fur our boys is thicker 'n huckelberries in them woods, and they mought pop ye, ef they didn't seed it."

Thanking him, we turned our horses into the "timber," and galloping rapidly on, soon came in sight of the deserted plantation. Lolling on the grass, in the shade of the windowless mansion, we found the Confederate officials. They rose as we approached; and one of us said to the Judge:

"We are late, but it's your fault. Your people fired at us down the river, and we had to turn back and come over-land."

"You don't suppose they saw your flag?"

"No. It was hidden by the trees; but a shot came uncomfortably near us. It struck the water, and ricocheted not three yards off. A little nearer, and it would have shortened me by a head, and the Colonel by two feet."

"That would have been a sad thing for you; but a miss, you know, is as good as a mile," said the Judge, evidently enjoying the "joke."

"We hear Grant was in the boat that followed yours, and was struck while at dinner," remarked Captain Hatch—a gentleman, and about the best-looking man in the Confederacy.

"Indeed! Do you believe it?"

"I don't know, of course;" and his looks asked for an answer. We gave none, for all such information is contraband. We might have told him that Grant, Butler, and Foster examined their position from Mrs. Grover's house—a few hundred yards distant—two hours after the Rebel cannon-ball danced a break-down on the Lieutenant-General's dinner-table.

In addition to the Major Henniken previously spoken of, there were present, on this occasion, several other officials, whose appearance indicated that we were to be welcomed in Richmond.

One of them was a stoutly built man, of medium height, with a short, thick neck, and arms and shoulders denoting great strength. He looked a natural-born jailer, and much such a character as a timid man would not care to encounter, except at long range of a rifle warranted to fire twenty shots a minute, and to hit every time. This was Mr. Charles Javins, of the Richmond Provost-Guard, and he was our shadow in Dixie. Another was a "likely" "cullud gemman," named Jack, who told us he was almost the sole survivor of "Massa Allen's" twelve hundred slaves—"De res' all stole, Massa—stole by you Yankees,"—and the others were two mules hitched to an ambulance, which, over ruts, stumps, and an awful sandy road, bore us safely to the Rebel capital.

To give us a *moonlight view* of the fortifications, Judge Ould proposed to start after sundown; and as it wanted some hours of that time, we seated ourselves on the ground, and entered into conversation. The treatment of our prisoners, the *status* of black troops, and non-combatants, and all the questions which have led to the suspension of exchanges, had been good-naturedly discussed, when the Captain, looking up from one of the Northern papers we had brought him, said—

"Don't you know, it mortifies me that you don't hate us as we hate you? You kill us as Agassiz kills a fly,—because you love us."

"Of course we do. The North is being crucified for love of the South."

"If you love us so, why don't you let us go?" asked the Judge, rather curtly.

"For that very reason,—because we love you. If we let you go, with slavery, and your notions of 'empire,' you'd run straight to barbarism and the Devil."

"We'd take the risk of that. But, let me tell you, if you are going to Mr. Davis with any such ideas, you might as well turn back at once. He can make peace on no other basis than Independence. Recognition must be the beginning, middle, and ending of all negotiations. Our people will accept peace on no other terms."

"I think you are wrong there," said the Colonel. "When I was here a year ago, I met many of your leading men, and they all assured me they wanted peace and reunion, even at the sacrifice of slavery. Within a week, a man you venerate and love has met me at Baltimore, and besought me to come here and offer Mr. Davis peace on such conditions."

"That may be. Some of our old men, who are weak in the knees, may want peace on any terms; but the Southern people will not have it without Independence. Mr. Davis knows them, and you will find he will insist upon that. Concede that, and we'll not quarrel about minor matters."

"We'll not quarrel at all. But it's sundown, and time we were 'on to Richmond.'"

"That 's the 'Tribune' cry," said the Captain, rising; "and I hurrah for the 'Tribune,' for it 's honest, and—I want my supper."

We all laughed, and the Judge ordered the horses. As we were about to start, I said to him:—

"You 've forgotten our parole."

"Oh! never mind that. We 'll attend to that at Richmond."

Stepping into his carriage, and unfurling the flag of truce, he then led the way, by a "short cut," across the cornfield which divided the mansion from the high-road. We followed in the ambulance, our shadow, Mr. Javins, sitting between us and the twilight, and Jack occupying the front seat, and, with a stout whip, "working our passage" to Richmond.

Much that was amusing and interesting occurred during our three-hours' journey, but regard for my word forbids my relating it. Suffice it to say, we saw the "frowning fortifications," we "flanked" the "invincible army," and, at ten o'clock that night, planted our flag (against a lamp-post) in the very heart of the hostile city. As we alighted at the doorway of the Spotswood Hotel, the Judge said to the Colonel,—

"Button your outside coat up closely. Your uniform must not be seen here."

The Colonel did as he was bidden; and, without stopping to register our names at the office, we followed the Judge and the Captain up to No. 60. It was a large, square room, in the fourth story, with an unswept, ragged carpet, and bare white walls, smeared with soot and tobacco-juice. Several chairs, a marble-top table, and a pine wash-stand and clothes-press, straggled about the floor, and in the corners were three beds, garnished with tattered pillow-cases, and covered with white counterpanes, grown gray with longing for soapsuds and a wash-tub. The plainer and humbler of these beds was designed for the burly Mr. Javins; the others had been made ready for the extraordinary envoys (not envoys extraordinary) who, in defiance of all precedent and the "law of nations," had just "taken Richmond."

A single gas-jet was burning over the mantel-piece, and above it I saw a "writing on the wall," which implied that Jane Jackson had run up a washing-score of fifty dollars!

I was congratulating myself on not having to pay that woman's laundry-bills, when the Judge said:

"You want supper. What shall we order?"

"A slice of hot corn-bread would make *me* the happiest man in Richmond."

The Captain thereupon left the room, and, shortly returning, remarked:

"The landlord swears you're from Georgia. He says none but a Georgian would call for corn-bread at this time of night."

On that hint we acted, and when our sooty attendant came in with the supper-things, we discussed Georgia mines, Georgia banks, and Georgia mosquitoes, in a way that showed we had been bitten by all of them. In half an hour it was noised all about the hotel that the two gentlemen the Confederacy was taking such excellent care of were from Georgia.

The meal ended, and a quiet smoke over, our entertainers

rose to go. As the Judge bade us "good-night," he said to us:

"In the morning you had better address a note to Mr. Benjamin, asking the interview with the President. I will call at ten o'clock, and take it to him."

"Very well. But will Mr. Davis see us on Sunday?"

"Oh! that will make no difference."

CHAPTER XXII.

IN RICHMOND.

THE next morning, after breakfast, which we took in our room with Mr. Javins, we indited a note—of which the following is a copy—to the Confederate Secretary of State:

"SPOTSWOOD HOUSE, RICHMOND, VA.,
"*July* 17, 1864.

"Hon. J. P. BENJAMIN, *Secretary of State, etc.*

"DEAR SIR:—The undersigned respectfully solicit an interview with President Davis.

"They visit Richmond only as private citizens, and have no official character or authority; but they are acquainted with the views of the United States Government, and with the sentiments of the Northern people, relative to an adjustment of the differences existing between the North and the South, and earnestly hope that a free interchange of views between President Davis and themselves may open the way to such *official* negotiations as will result in restoring PEACE to the two sections of our distracted country.

"They therefore ask an interview with the President, and, awaiting your reply, are

"Truly and respectfully yours."

This was signed by both of us; and when the Judge called, as he had appointed, we sent it—together with a commendatory letter I had received on setting out, from a near relative of

Mr. Davis—to the Rebel Secretary. In half an hour Judge Ould returned, saying: "Mr. Benjamin sends you his compliments, and will be happy to see you at the State Department."

We found the Secretary—a short, plump, oily little man in black, with a keen black eye, a Jew face, a yellow skin, curly black hair, closely-trimmed black whiskers, and a ponderous gold watch-chain—in the northwest room of the "United States" Custom-House. Over the door of this room were the words, "State Department," and about its walls were hung a few maps and battle-plans. In one corner was a tier of shelves, filled with books,—among which I noticed Headley's "History," Lossing's "Pictorial," Parton's "Butler," Greeley's "American Conflict," a complete set of the "Rebellion Record," and a dozen numbers and several bound volumes of the "Atlantic Monthly,"—and in the centre of the apartment was a black-walnut table, covered with green cloth, and filled with a multitude of "State papers." At this table sat the Secretary. He rose as we entered, and, as Judge Ould introduced us, took our hands, and said:

"I am glad, very glad, to meet you, gentlemen. I have read your note, and"—bowing to me—"the letter you bring from ——. Your errand commands my respect and sympathy. Pray be seated."

As we took the proffered seats, the Colonel, drawing off his "duster," and displaying his uniform, said:

"We thank you for this cordial reception, Mr. Benjamin. We trust you will be as glad to hear us as you are to see us."

"No doubt I shall be, for you come to talk of peace. Peace is what we all want."

"It is, indeed; and for that reason we have come to see Mr. Davis. Can we see him, Sir?"

"Do you bring any overtures to him from your Government?"

"No, Sir. We bring no overtures and have no authority from our Government. We state that in our note. We would be glad, however, to know what terms will be acceptable to Mr. Davis. If they at all harmonize with Mr. Lincoln's views, we will report them to him, and so open the door for official negotiations."

"Are you acquainted with Mr. Lincoln's views?"

"One of us is, fully?"

"Did Mr. Lincoln, *in any way*, authorize you to come here?"

"No, Sir. We came with his pass, but not by his request. We say, distinctly, we have no official, or unofficial, authority. We come as men and Christians, not as diplomatists, hoping, in a frank talk with Mr. Davis, to discover some way by which this war may be stopped."

"Well, gentlemen, I will repeat what you say to the President, and if he follows my advice,—and I think he will,—he will meet you. He will be at church this afternoon; so, suppose you call here at nine this evening. If any thing should occur in the mean time to prevent his seeing you, I will let you know through Judge Ould."

Throughout this interview the manner of the Secretary was cordial; but with this cordiality was a strange constraint and diffidence, almost amounting to timidity, which struck both my companion and myself. Contrasting his manner with the quiet dignity of the Colonel, I almost fancied our positions reversed,

—that, instead of our being in his power, the Secretary was in ours, and momently expected to hear some unwelcome sentence from our lips. There is something, after all, in moral power. Mr. Benjamin does not possess it, nor is he a great man. He has a keen, shrewd, ready intellect, but not the *stamina* to originate, or even to execute, any great good, or great wickedness.

After a day spent in our room, conversing with the Judge, or watching the passers-by in the street,—I would like to tell who they were, and how they looked; but such information is, just now, contraband,—we called again, at nine o'clock, at the State Department.

Mr. Benjamin occupied his previous seat at the table, and at his right sat a spare, thin-featured man, with iron-gray hair and beard, and a clear, gray eye, full of life and vigor. He had a broad, massive forehead, and a mouth and chin denoting great energy and strength of will. His face was emaciated, and much wrinkled, but his features were good, especially his eyes,—though one of them bore a scar, apparently made by some sharp instrument. He wore a suit of grayish-brown, evidently of foreign manufacture, and, as he rose, I saw that he was about five feet ten inches high, with a slight stoop in the shoulders. His manners were simple, easy, and most fascinating; and there was an indescribable charm in his voice, as he extended his hand and said to us:

"I am glad to see you, gentlemen. You are very welcome to Richmond."

And this was the man who was President of the United States, under Franklin Pierce, and who is now the heart, soul, and brains of the Southern Confederacy!

His manner put me entirely at my ease,—the Colonel would be at his, if he stood before Cæsar,—and I replied:

"We thank you, Mr. Davis. It is not often that you meet men of our clothes and our principles in Richmond."

"Not often,—not so often as I could wish; and I trust your coming may lead to a more frequent and a more friendly intercourse between the North and the South."

"We sincerely hope it may."

"Mr. Benjamin tells me that you have asked to see me to—"

And he paused, as if desiring we should finish the sentence. The Colonel replied:

"Yes, Sir. We have asked this interview, in the hope that you may suggest some way by which this war may be stopped. Our people want peace,—your people do, and your Congress has recently said that *you* do. We have come to ask how it can be brought about."

"In a very simple way. Withdraw your armies from our territory, and peace will come of itself. We do not seek to subjugate you. We are not waging an offensive war, except so far as it is offensive-defensive,—that is, so far as we are forced to invade you to prevent your invading us. Let us alone, and peace will come at once.

"But we cannot let you alone so long as you repudiate the Union. That is the one thing the Northern people will not surrender."

"I know. You would deny to us what you exact for yourselves—the right of self-government."

"No, Sir," I remarked. "We would deny you no natural right. But we think Union essential to peace; and, Mr. Davis, *could* two people, with the same language, separated by only an imaginary line, live at peace with each other? Would not disputes constantly arise, and cause almost constant war between them?"

"Undoubtedly, — with this generation. You have sown such bitterness at the South; you have put such an ocean of blood between the two sections, that I despair of seeing any harmony in my time. Our children may forget this war, but *we* cannot."

"I think the bitterness you speak of, Sir," said the Colonel, "does not really exist. *We* meet and talk here as friends; our, soldiers meet and fraternize with each other; and I feel sure that if the Union were restored, a more friendly feeling would arise between us than has ever existed. The war has made us know and respect each other better than before. This is the view of very many Southern men; I have had it from many of them,—your leading citizens."

"They are mistaken," replied Mr. Davis. "They do not understand Southern sentiment. How can we feel any thing but bitterness towards men who deny us our rights? If you enter my house and drive me out of it, am I not your natural enemy?"

"You put the case too strongly. But we cannot fight forever; the war must end at some time; we must finally agree upon something; can we not agree now, and stop this frightful carnage? We are both Christian men, Mr. Davis. Can *you*, as a Christian man, leave untried any means that may lead to peace?"

"No, I cannot. I desire peace as much as you do. I deplore bloodshed as much as you do; but I feel that not one drop of the blood shed in this war is on *my* hands,—I can look up to my God and say this. I tried all in my power to avert this war. I saw it coming, and for twelve years I worked night and day to prevent it, but I could not. The North was mad and blind; it would not let us govern ourselves, and so the war came, and now it must go on till the last man of this generation falls in his tracks, and his children seize his musket and fight our battle, *unless you acknowledge our right to self-government.* We are not fighting for slavery. We are fighting for Independence, and that, or extermination, we *will* have."

"And there are, at least, four and a half millions of us left; so you see you have a work before you," said Mr. Benjamin, with a decided sneer.

"We have no wish to exterminate you," answered the Colonel. "I believe what I have said,—that there is no bitterness between the Northern and Southern people. The North, I know, loves the South. When peace comes, it will pour money and means into your hands to repair the waste caused by the war; and it would now welcome you back, and forgive you all the loss and bloodshed you have caused. But we *must* crush your armies, and exterminate your Government. And is not that already nearly done? You are wholly without money, and at the end of your resources. Grant has shut you up in Richmond. Sherman is before Atlanta. Had you not, then, better accept honorable terms while you can retain your prestige, and save the pride of the Southern people?"

Mr. Davis smiled.

"I respect your earnestness, Colonel, but you do not seem to understand the situation. We are not exactly shut up in Richmond. If your papers tell the truth, it is your capital that is in danger, not ours. Some weeks ago, Grant crossed the Rapidan to whip Lee, and take Richmond. Lee drove him in the first battle, and then Grant executed what your people call a 'brilliant flank movement,' and fought Lee again. Lee drove him a second time, and then Grant made another 'flank movement;' and so they kept on,—Lee whipping, and Grant flanking,—until Grant got where he is now. And what is the net result? Grant has lost seventy-five or eighty thousand men—*more than Lee had at the outset,*—and is no nearer taking Richmond than at first; and Lee, whose front has never been broken, holds him completely in check, and has men enough to spare to invade Maryland and threaten Washington! Sherman, to be sure, *is* before Atlanta; but suppose he is, and suppose he takes it? You know that the farther he goes from his base of supplies, the weaker he grows, and the more disastrous defeat will be to him. And defeat *may* come. So, in a military view, I should certainly say our position was better than yours.

"As to money: we are richer than you are. You smile; but, admit that our paper is worth nothing,—it answers as a circulating medium, and we hold it all ourselves. If every dollar of it were lost, we should, as we have no foreign debt, be none the poorer. But, it *is* worth something; it has the solid basis of a large cotton-crop, while yours rests on nothing, and you owe all the world. As to resources: we do not lack for arms or ammunition, and we have still a wide territory from which to gather supplies. So, you see, we are not in extremities. But, if we were,—if we were without money, without food, without weapons,—if our whole country were desolated, and our armies crushed and disbanded,—could we, without giving up our manhood, give up our right to govern ourselves?

Would *you* not rather die, and feel yourself a man, than live, and be subject to a foreign power?"

"From your stand-point there is force in what you say," replied the Colonel. "But we did not come here to argue with you, Mr. Davis. We came, hoping to find some honorable way to peace, and I am grieved to hear you say what you do. When I have seen your young men dying on the battle-field, and your old men, women, and children starving in their homes, I have felt I could risk my life to save them. For that reason I am here; and I am grieved,—grieved,—that there is no hope."

"I know your motives, Colonel Jaquess, and I honor you for them; but what can I do more than I am doing? I would give my poor life, gladly, if it would bring peace and good-will to the two countries; but it would not. It is with your own people you should labor. It is they who desolate our homes, burn our wheat-fields, break the wheels of wagons carrying away our women and children, and destroy supplies meant for our sick and wounded. At your door lies all the misery and the crime of this war, and it is a fearful,—fearful account."

"Not all of it, Mr. Davis. I admit a fearful account, but it is not *all* at our door. The passions of both sides are aroused. Unarmed men are hanged, prisoners are shot down in cold blood, by yourselves. Elements of barbarism are entering the war from both sides, that should make us—you and me, as Christian men—shudder to think of. In God's name, then, let us stop it. Let us do something, concede something, to bring about peace. You cannot expect, with only four and a half millions, as Mr. Benjamin says you have, to hold out forever against twenty millions."

Again Mr. Davis smiled.

"Do you suppose there are twenty millions at the North determined to crush us?"

"I do,—to crush your *Government*. A small number of our people, a very small number, are your friends,—Secessionists. The rest differ about measures and candidates, but are united in the determination to sustain the Union. Whoever is elected in November, he *must be* committed to a vigorous prosecution of the war."

Mr. Davis still looking incredulous, I remarked—

"It is so, Sir. Whoever tells you otherwise, deceives you. I think I know Northern sentiment, and I assure you it is so. You know we have a system of lyceum-lecturing in our large towns. At the close of these lectures, it is the custom of the people to come upon the platform and talk with the lecturer. This gives him an excellent opportunity of learning public sentiment. Last winter I lectured before nearly a hundred of such associations, all over the North,—from Dubuque to Bangor,—and I took pains to ascertain the feeling of the people. I found a unanimous determination to crush the rebellion and save the Union at every sacrifice. The majority are in favor of Mr. Lincoln, and nearly all of those opposed to him are opposed to him because they think he does not fight you with enough vigor. The radical Republicans, who go for slave-suffrage and thorough confiscation, are those who will defeat him, if he is defeated. But if he is defeated before the people, the House will elect a worse man—worse I mean for you. It is more radical than he is,—you can see that from Mr. Ashley's reconstruction bill,—and the people are more radical than the House. Mr. Lincoln, I know, is about to call out five hundred thousand more men, and I don't see how you *can* resist much longer; but if you do, you will only deepen the radical feeling of the Northern people. They would now give you fair, honorable, *generous* terms; but let them suffer much more, let there be a dead man in every house, as there is now in every village, and they will give you *no* terms,—they will insist on hanging every rebel south of——Pardon my terms. I mean no offence."

"You give no offence," he replied, smiling very pleasantly. "I wouldn't have you pick your words. This is a frank, free talk, and I like you the better for saying what you think. Go on."

"I was merely going to add, that let the Northern people once really feel the war—they do not feel it yet—and they will insist on hanging every one of your leaders."

"Well, admitting all you say, I can't see how it affects our position. There are some things worse than hanging or extermination. We reckon giving up the right of self-government one of those things."

"By self-government you mean disunion—Southern Independence."

"Yes."

"And slavery, you say, is no longer an element in the contest?"

"No, it is not. It never was an essential element. It was only a means of bringing other conflicting elements to an earlier culmination. It fired the musket which was already capped and loaded. There are essential differences between the North and the South, that will, however this war may end, make them two nations."

"You ask me to say what I think. Will you allow me to

say that I know the South pretty well, and never observed those differences?"

"Then you have not used your eyes. My sight is poorer than yours, but I have seen them for years."

The laugh was upon me, and Mr. Benjamin enjoyed it.

"Well, Sir, be that as it may, if I understand you, the dispute between your government and ours is now narrowed down to this: Union or Disunion."

"Yes; or, to put it in other words, Independence or Subjugation."

"Then the two governments are irreconcilably apart. They have no alternative but to fight it out. But, it is not so with the people. They are tired of fighting and want peace; and, as they bear all the burden and suffering of the war, is it not right they should have peace, and have it on such terms as they like?"

"I don't understand you; be a little more explicit."

"Well. Suppose the two governments should agree to something like this: To go to the people with two propositions; say: Peace, with Disunion and Southern Independence, as your proposition; and: Peace, with Union, Emancipation, No Confiscation, and Universal Amnesty as ours. Let the citizens of all the United States (as they existed before the war) vote 'Yes,' or 'No,' on these two propositions, at a special election within sixty days. If a majority vote Disunion, our government to be bound by it, and to let you go in peace. If a majority vote Union, yours to be bound by it, and to stay in peace. The two governments can contract in this way, and the people, though constitutionally unable to decide on peace or war, can elect which of any two propositions shall govern their rulers. Let Lee and Grant, meanwhile, agree to an armistice.

This would sheathe the sword; and, if once sheathed, it would never again be drawn by this generation."

"The plan is altogether impracticable. If the South were only one State, it might work; but, as it is, if one Southern State objected to emancipation, it would nullify the whole thing, for you are aware the people of Virginia cannot vote slavery out of South Carolina, or the people of South Carolina vote it out of Virginia."

"But three-fourths of the States can amend the Constitution. Let it be done in that way—in *any* way, so that it be done by the people. I am not a statesman or a politician, and I do not know just how such a plan could be carried out; but you get the idea—that the PEOPLE shall decide the question."

"That the *majority* shall decide it, you mean. We seceded to rid ourselves of the rule of the majority, and this would subject us to it again."

"But the majority must rule finally, either with bullets or ballots."

"I am not so sure of that. Neither current events nor history shows that the majority rules, or ever did rule. The contrary, I think, is true. Why, Sir, the man who shall go before the Southern people with such a proposition—with *any* proposition which implied that the North was to have a voice in determining the domestic relations of the South—could not live here a day! He would be hanged to the first tree, without judge or jury."

"Allow me to doubt that. I think it more likely he would be hanged if he let the Southern people know the majority could not rule," I replied, smiling.

"I have no fear of that," rejoined Mr. Davis, also smiling

most good-humoredly. "I give you leave to proclaim it from every house-top in the South."

"But, seriously, Sir, you let the majority rule in a single State; why not let it rule in the whole country?"

"Because the States are independent and sovereign. The country is not. It is only a confederation of States; or rather it *was*: it is now *two* confederations."

"Then we are not a *people*—we are only a political partnership?"

"That is all."

"Your very name, Sir, '*United* States,' implies that," said Mr. Benjamin. "But, tell me, are the terms you have named—Emancipation, No Confiscation, and Universal Amnesty—the terms which Mr. Lincoln authorized you to offer us?"

"No, Sir. Mr. Lincoln did not authorize me to offer you any terms. But I *think* both he and the Northern people, for the sake of peace, would assent to some such conditions."

"They are *very* generous," replied Mr. Davis, for the first time during the interview showing some angry feeling. "But Amnesty, Sir, applies to criminals. We have committed no crime. Confiscation is of no account unless you can enforce it; and Emancipation! You have already emancipated nearly two millions of our slaves, and if you will take care of them, you may emancipate the rest. I had a few when the war began. I was of some use to them; they never were of any to me. Against their will you 'emancipated' them; and you may 'emancipate' every negro in the Confederacy, but we will be free! We will govern ourselves! We *will* do it, if we have to see every Southern plantation sacked, and every Southern city in flames!"

"I see, Mr. Davis, it is useless to continue this conversation," I replied; "and you will pardon us if we have seemed to press our views with too much pertinacity. We love the old flag, and that must be our apology for intruding upon you at all."

"You have not intruded upon me," he replied, resuming his usual manner. "I am glad to have met you, both. I once loved the old flag as well as you do. I would have died for it; but now it is to me only the emblem of oppression."

"I hope the day may never come, Mr. Davis, when *I* say that," said the Colonel.

A half-hour's conversation on other topics—not of public interest—ensued, and then we rose to go. As we did so the Rebel President gave me his hand, and, bidding me a kindly "good-by," expressed the hope of seeing me again in Richmond in happier times—when peace should have returned—but with the Colonel his parting was particularly cordial. Taking his hand in both of his, he said to him:

"Colonel, I respect your character and your motives, and I wish you well—I wish you every good I can wish you consistently with the interests of the Confederacy."

The quiet, straightforward bearing, and magnificent moral courage of our "fighting parson" had evidently impressed Mr. Davis very favorably.

As we were leaving the room, he added:

"Say to Mr. Lincoln from me, that I shall at any time be pleased to receive proposals for peace on the basis of our Independence. It will be useless to approach me with any other."

When we went out, Mr. Benjamin called Judge Ould, who had been waiting during the whole interview—two hours—at the other end of the hall, and we passed down the stairway together. As I put my arm within that of the Judge, he said to me:

"Well, what is the result?"

"Nothing but war—war to the knife."

"Ephraim is joined to his idols—let him alone," added the Colonel, solemnly.

The next day we visited Castle Thunder, Libby Prison, and the hospitals occupied by our wounded, and at sundown passed out of the Rebel lines, thankful, devoutly thankful, that we were once again under the folds of the old flag.

Thus ended our visit to Richmond. I have endeavored to sketch it faithfully. The conversation with Mr. Davis I took down shortly after returning to the Union lines, and I have tried to report his exact language, extenuating nothing and coloring nothing that he said. Some of his sentences, as I read them over, appear stilted and high-flown, but they did not sound so when uttered. As listened to, they seemed the simple, natural language of his thought. He spoke deliberately, apparently weighing every word, and well knowing that all he said would be given to the public.

He is a man of great ability. Our interview explained to me why with no money and no commerce, with nearly every one of their important cities in our hands, and with an army greatly inferior in numbers and equipment to ours, the Rebels have held out so long. It is because of the energy, sagacity, and indomitable will of Jefferson Davis. Without him the Rebellion would crumble to pieces in a day; with him it may continue to be, even in disaster, a power that will tax the whole energy and resources of the nation.

The Southern people want peace. Many of the Southern leaders want it—both my companion and I, by correspondence and intercourse with them, know this—but there can be no peace so long as Mr. Davis controls the South. Ignoring Slavery, he himself states the issue—the only issue with him—Union or Disunion. That is it. We must conquer or be conquered. We can negotiate only with the bayonet. We can have peace only by putting forth all our strength, crushing the Southern armies, and overthrowing the Southern Government.

THE END.

Mrs. Mary J. Holmes' Works.

MARIAN GREY.—A Novel. . . . . 12mo. cloth bound,
'LENA RIVERS.— . . . . do.
MEADOW BROOK.— . . . . . . do.
OMESTEAD ON THE HILLSIDE.— . do.
DORA DEANE.— . . . . do.
COUSIN MAUDE.— . . . . do.
DARKNESS AND DAYLIGHT.—(In press.) do.

Artemus Ward.

HIS BOOK.—An irresistibly funny volume of writings by the immortal American humorist and showman; with plenty of comic illustrations to match. . 12mo. cl. bound, $1.25

Miss Augusta J. Evans.

BEULAH.—A novel of great power and interest. Cl. bd., $1.50

Richard B. Kimball.

WAS HE SUCCESSFUL?— A novel. 12mo. cl. bound, $1.50
UNDERCURRENTS.— . . . do. do. $1.50
SAINT LEGER.— . . . . do. do. $1.50
ROMANCE OF STUDENT LIFE.— do. do.
IN THE TROPICS.—Edited by R. B. Kimball. do.

Cuthbert Bede.

THE ADVENTURES OF VERDANT GREEN.—A rollicking, humorous novel of student life in an English University; with more than 200 comic illustrations. . 12mo. cl. bd., $1.25

Edmund Kirke.

AMONG THE PINES.—A thrilling picture of life at the South. 12mo., paper covers, 75 cts., . . or cloth bound,
MY SOUTHERN FRIENDS; OR, LIFE IN DIXIE.—12mo., paper covers, 75 cts., ... or cloth bound,
WHAT I SAW IN TENNESSEE.—Paper, 75 cts., or cl. bd.,

The Central Park.

THE ORIGIN, PROGRESS, AND DESCRIPTION, OF THE MAGNIFICENT CENTRAL PARK AT NEW YORK.—Beautifully illustrated with more than 50 exquisite photographs of the principal views and objects of interest. One large quarto, sumptuously bound in . . . . Turkey morocco, $25.00

Ernest Renan.

THE LIFE OF JESUS.—Translated from the original French by C. E. Wilbour. . . . . 12mo. cloth bound, $1.50

A. S. Roe's Works.

A LONG LOOK AHEAD.— . A novel. . 12mo. cloth,
I'VE BEEN THINKING.— . . do. . . do.
TRUE TO THE LAST.— . . do. . . . do.
THE STAR AND THE CLOUD.— do. . . . do.
HOW COULD HE HELP IT.— . do. . . . do.
LIKE AND UNLIKE.— . . . do. . . . do.
TO LOVE AND TO BE LOVED.— do. . . . do.
TIME AND TIDE.— . . . . do. . . . do.

Walter Barrett, Clerk.

THE OLD MERCHANTS OF NEW YORK CITY.—Being personal incidents, interesting sketches, and bits of biography concerning nearly every leading merchant in New York. Two series, ... 12mo. cloth bound, each, $1.50

Rev. John Cumming, D.D., of London.

THE GREAT TRIBULATION; OR, THINGS COMING ON THE EARTH.— Two series, ... 12mo. cloth bound, each,
THE GREAT PREPARATION; REDEMPTION DRAWETH NIGH.— Two series. . . . . 12mo. cloth bound, each,
THE GREAT CONSUMMATION; OR, THE WORLD AS IT WILL BE.— Two series. . . . . 12mo. cloth bound, each,
TEACH US TO PRAY.—A volume of devotional sermons on the Lord's Prayer. . . . . . 12mo. cloth bound,

M. Michelet's Works.

LOVE (L'AMOUR).—Translated from the French. 12m. cl., $1.25
WOMAN (LA FEMME.)—Translated from the French. . . $1.25
THE MORAL HISTORY OF WOMEN.— do. . . $1.25
WOMAN MADE FREE.—From the French of D'Hericourt, $1.25

Novels by Ruffini.

DR. ANTONIO.—A love story of Italy. . 12mo. cloth, $1.50
LAVINIA; OR, THE ITALIAN ARTIST.— . do. $1.50
DEAR EXPERIENCE.—With humorous illustrations. do. $1.25
VINCENZO; OR, SUNKEN ROCKS.—Paper covers. . .

F. D. Guerrazzi.

BEATRICE CENCI.—A historical novel. Translated from the Italian; with a portrait of the Cenci, from Guido's famous picture in Rome. . . . . 12mo. cloth bound, $1.50

Fred. S. Cozzens.

HE SPARROWGRASS PAPERS.—A laughable picture cf Sparrowgrass's trials in living in the country; with humorous illustrations by Darley. 12mo. cl. bound, ... $1.25

Epes Sargent.

PECULIAR.—A very clever new novel. . 12mo. cloth, $1.50

Charles Reade.

THE CLOISTER AND THE HEARTH; OR, MAID, WIFE, AND WIDOW.—A magnificent historical novel. By the Author of "Peg Woffington," etc. Reade's best work. Octavo, cl. bd., $1.50

The Orpheus C. Kerr Papers.

A collection of exquisitely satirical and humorous military criticisms. Two series. . 12mo. cloth bound, each, $1.25

T. S. Arthur's New Works.

LIGHT ON SHADOWED PATHS.— 12m. cl., $1.25

OUT IN THE WORLD.—(In press.) . . . . do.

Stephen Massett.

DRIFTING ABOUT.—By "Jeems Pipes," of Pipesville; with many comic illustrations. . . . . . 12mo. cloth, $1.25

Joseph Rodman Drake.

THE CULPRIT FAY.—A faery poem; tinted paper, cloth,

Mother Goose for Grown Folks.

Humorous rhymes for grown people; based upon the famous "Mother Goose Melodies." Tinted paper, cl. bd.,

Hearton Drille.

TACTICS; OR, CUPID IN SHOULDER STRAPS.—A vivacious and witty West Point love story. . . . 12mo. cloth, $1.00

J. C. Jeaffreson.

A BOOK ABOUT DOCTORS.—A humorous and entertaining volume of sketches about famous physicians and surgeons. . . . . 12mo. cloth, $1.50

Jas. H. Hackett.

NOTES AND COMMENTS ON SHAKSPEARE.—By the great American Falstaff; with portrait of the Author. 12mo. cl., $.

New Sporting Work.

THE GAME FISH OF THE NORTH.—An entertaining as well as instructive volume. Illustrated. . . 12mo. cloth, $1.50

Doesticks' Humorous Works.

DOESTICKS; WHAT HE SAYS.—With comic illusts. 12m. cl., $1.50
PLURIBUSTAH.— . . . . . . do. do. $1.50
THE ELEPHANT CLUB.— . . do. do. $1.50

H. De Balzac's Novels.

CESAR BIROTTEAU.—Translated from the French, 12m. cl.,
PETTY ANNOYANCES OF MARRIED LIFE.— do. do.
THE ALCHEMIST.— . . . . do. do.
EUGENIE GRANDET.— . . . . do. do.

D. D. Home (or Hume).

INCIDENTS IN MY LIFE.—By the celebrated spirit medium; with an introduction by Judge Edmonds. 12mo. cl., $1.25

Thomas Bailey Aldrich.

BABIE BELL, AND OTHER POEMS.—Blue and gold binding, $1.00
OUT OF HIS HEAD.—An eccentric romance. 12mo. cl., $1.00

Adam Gurowski.

DIARY.—During the years 1861 to '63, in Washington. Two volumes, each, ... $1.25

Edmund C. Stedman.

ALICE OF MONMOUTH.— . 12mo., tinted paper, cloth, $1.00
LYRICS AND IDYLS.— . . . . 75 cts.
THE PRINCE'S BALL.—With humorous illustrations. . 50 cts.

Alexander Von Humboldt.

LIFE AND TRAVELS.—With an introduction by Bayard Taylor. A book for every library. . . 12mo. cloth, $1.50

Richard H. Stoddard.

THE KING'S BELL.— 12mo. cloth bound, tinted paper, 75 cts.
THE MORGESONS.—A novel. By Mrs. R. H. Stoddard. $1.00

M. T. Walworth.

LULU.—A novel of life in Washington. . 12mo. cloth, $1.25

Hugh Miller.

A LIFE of the great Geologist and Author. 12mo clo., $1.50

Miss Dinah Muloch.

A WOMAN'S THOUGHTS ABOUT WOMEN.—A new work by th Author of "John Halifax," etc. . . 12mo. cloth, $1.25

Isaac Taylor.

THE SPIRIT OF HEBREW POETRY.—With a biographical intro duction by Wm. Adams, D.D., of N. Y. 8vo. cl., $2.50

Miscellaneous Works.

*HUSBAND & WIFE; OR, HUMAN DEVELOPMENT.—12mo. cl., $1.25
ROCKFORD.—A novel. By Mrs. L. D. Umsted. do. $1.00
OUTHWOLD.— do. do. do. $1.00
WANDERINGS OF A BEAUTY.—By Mrs. Edwin James. $1.00
THE YACHTMAN'S PRIMER.—By T. R. Warren. do. 50 cts.
SPREES AND SPLASHES.—By Henry Morford. . do. $1.00
THE U. S. TAX LAW.—"Government Edition." . do. 75 cts
THE PRISONER OF STATE.—By D. A. Mahony. . do. $1.25
THE PARTISAN LEADER.—By Beverly Tucker. . do. $1.25
CHINA AND THE CHINESE.—By W. L. G. Smith. do. $1.00
AROUND THE PYRAMIDS.—By Gen. Aaron Ward. do.
TREATISE ON DEAFNESS.—By E. B. Lighthill, M.D. do. $1.00
THE FLYING DUTCHMAN.—By John G. Saxe. . . do. 50 cts.
NATIONAL CHESS BOOK.—By D. W. Fiske. . . do. $1.50
GARRET VAN HORN.—By J. S. Sauzade. . . . do. $1.25
TWENTY YEARS AROUND THE WORLD. J. G. Vassar. 8vo. $3.50
NATIONAL HYMNS.—By Richard Grant White. 8vo. $1.00
FORT LAFAYETTE.—By Benjamin Wood. 12mo. cloth, $1.00
ALFIO BALZANI.—By Domenico Minnelli. . . do. $1.25
THE NATIONAL SCHOOL FOR THE SOLDIER.— . do. 50 cts.
ORIENTAL HAREMS.—Translated from the French. do. $1.25
LOLA MONTEZ.—Her life and lectures. . . . do. $1.50
ESSAYS.—By George Brimley. . . . . do. $1.25
GEN. NATHANIEL LYON.—A life. . . . . . do. $1.00
PHILIP THAXTER.—A novel. . . . . . . do. $1.00
FROM HAYING TIME TO HOPPING.—A novel. . do. $1.00
JOHN DOE AND RICHARD ROE.—By E. S. Gould. do. $1.00
MARRIED OFF.—An illustrated poem. . . . . do. 50 cts.
ROUMANIA.—By Dr. Jas. O. Noyes. . . . . do. $1.50
HUSBAND *vs.* WIFE.—A poem illustrated. . . . do. 50 cts
BROWN'S CARPENTER'S ASSISTANT.— 4to. $5.00
TRANSITION.—Edited by Rev. H. S. Carpenter. 12mo. cl., $1.00
DEBT AND GRACE.—By Rev. C. F. Hudson. . . do. $1.25
THE VAGABOND.—By Adam Badeau. . . . . do. $1.00
COSMOGONY.—By Thos. A. Davies. 8vo. $1.50
ANSWER TO HUGH MILLER.—By T. A. Davies. 12mo., $1.25
EDGAR POE AND HIS CRITICS.—By Mrs. Whitman. do. 75 cts
HARTLEY NORMAN.—A novel. . . . . do. $1.25

www.ingramcontent.com/pod-product-compliance
Lightning Source LLC
LaVergne TN
LVHW010218110826
845151LV00004B/1133
9781425526993